FAIRY T
AND THE ART OF
SUBVERSION

FAIRY AND TALES THE ART OF

Subversion

THE CLASSICAL GENRE FOR CHILDREN AND THE PROCESS OF CIVILIZATION

JACK ZIPES

Routledge
New York

Published in 1988 by Methuen, Inc.
Reprinted in 1991 by Routledge
An imprint of Routledge, Chapman & Hall, Inc.
29 West 35th Street
New York, NY 10001

© Jack Zipes 1983
First published in 1983 by Heinemann Educational Books Ltd.

Library of Congress Cataloging-in-Publication Data

Zipes, Jack David.
  Fairy tales and the art of subversion.

  Bibliography: p.
  Includes index.
  1. Fairy tales—History and criticism.   2. Children—
Books and reading.   3. Socialization.   4. Moral
development.   I. Title.
[PN3437.Z56   1988]   398.2'1   87-31344
ISBN 0-415-90513-3

Printed in the United States of America

For Toby, Simon, Anna and Adam

Contents

Acknowledgements

This book was made possible by a Fulbright Grant from the International Exchange of Scholars which allowed me to spend a year at the Johann Wolfgang Goethe-Universität in Frankfurt am Main, where I taught and conducted research. In particular, I am indebted to Klaus Doderer, Director of the Institut für Jugendbuchforschung, for the encouragement and assistance he provided me. During the course of my work I profited from various discussions with Thomas Elsaesser and from the suggestions of Roni Natov and Ralph Cohen, who published different and abbreviated drafts of Chapters 3 and 7 in *The Lion and the Unicorn* and *New Literary History*. Finally, I should like to thank David Hill for his kind support and Caroline Lane and Betty Low for their fine editorial work in preparing this book.

1 Fairy-Tale Discourse: Towards a Social History of the Genre

Language and style are blind forces. Writing is an act of historical solidarity. Language and style are objects. Writing is a function. It is the relation between creation and society. It is literary language transformed by its social destination. It is the form grasped in its human intention and thus tied to the great crises of history.

Roland Barthes
Le degré zéro de l'écriture (1953)

Even though the fairy tale may be the most important cultural and social event in most children's lives, critics and scholars have failed to study its historical development as genre. There are chapters on the fairy tale in histories of children's literature, essays and even books on the fairy tale for adults, in-depth psychological explorations of the fairy tale's effect on children, and structuralist and formalist studies of individual tales galore. But no history of the fairy tale for children, in particular, no social history. Just a gap.

Non-history is history. Or, the acceptance of the gap means that brief descriptive outlines and chronologies of the fairy tale pass for history. Perhaps the most remarkable outcome of the so-called historical studies of literary fairy tales for children is the sense one gains that they are ageless. The best fairy tales are supposedly universal. It does not matter when or why they were written. What matters is their enchantment as though their bedtime manner can always be put to use to soothe the anxieties of children or help them therapeutically to realize who they are. Nor should one dissect or study fairy tales in a socio-political context, for that might ruin their magic power.

Fairy tales for children as universal, ageless, therapeutic, miraculous, and beautiful. This is the way they have come down to us in history. Inscribed on our minds, as children and then later as adults, is the impression that it is not important to know about the mysterious past of fairy tales just as long as they are there and continue to be written. The past is mysterious. The history of the fairy tale for children is mystery.

Fredric Jameson claims that 'history is *not* a text, not a narrative, master or otherwise, but that, as an absent cause, it is inaccessible to us except in textual form, and that our approach to it and to the Real itself necessarily passes through prior textualization, its narrativization in the political unconscious'.[1] It follows, then, out of necessity that we write our own texts to gain a sense not simply of what has happened in reality but what also has happened on psychological, economic, cultural and other levels, to free ourselves of the dictates of other socio-historical texts which have prescribed and ordered our thinking and need to be dis-ordered if we are to perceive for ourselves the processes that produce social structures, modes of production, and cultural artefacts. To write an historical text (or any text for that matter) implies that one has a world-view, an overall perspective of history, an ideology, whether conscious or unconscious, and the writing of such a text will tend either to test this view or legitimate it. Textual form depends on the method one chooses. We place a value on how and what we write.

Jameson talks about the necessity of developing a method of mediations which will enable us to grasp and evaluate history in the most comprehensive manner possible:

> This operation is understood as a process of *transcoding*: as the invention of a set of terms, the strategic choice of a particular code or language, such that the same terminology can be used to analyze and articulate two quite different structural levels of reality. Mediations are thus a device of the analyst, whereby the fragmentation and automization of the various regions of social life (the separation, in other words, of the ideological from the political, the religious from the economic, the gap between daily life and the practice of academic disciplines) is at least locally overcome, on the occasion of a particular analysis.[2]

Jameson's method could be called interdisciplinary but that would be too simplistic, for he does not want to bring disciplines together in a traditional positivist way to study literature from different statistical and strategic angles. Rather he wants to invent an ideological code and method which will subsume different approaches so he can grasp the underlying forces which have caused gaps in history and prevented our understanding the essence of literary creation. He seeks to explore the political unconscious, and it is obvious that he wants to develop many of the notions first elaborated by Roland Barthes in *Le degré zéro de l'écriture* (1953) and *Mythologies* (1957). For Jameson the individual literary work is a *symbolic act*, 'which is grasped as the imaginary resolution of real contradiction'.[3] Such a definition is helpful in understanding the origins of the literary fairy tale for children because it immediately perceives the process of writing as part of a social process, as a kind of intervention in a continuous discourse, debate, and conflict about power and social relations. Jameson sees ideology not as something 'which informs or invests symbolic production; rather the aesthetic act itself is ideological, and the production of aesthetic or narrative form is to be seen as an ideological act in its own right, with the function of inventing imaginary or formal "solutions" to unresolvable contradictions'.[4]

Certainly one can speak about the single literary fairy tale for children as a *symbolic act* infused by the ideological viewpoint of the individual author. Almost all critics who have studied the emergence of the literary fairy tale in Europe[5] agree that educated writers purposely appropriated the oral folk tale and converted it into a type of literary discourse about mores, values, and manners so that children would become civilized according to the social code of that time. The writers of fairy tales for children *acted* ideologically by presenting their notions regarding social conditions and conflicts, and they *interacted* with each other and with past writers and storytellers of folklore in a public sphere.

This interaction led to an institutionalized symbolic discourse on the civilizing process which served as the basis for the fairy-tale genre. For example, writing literary tales for children in France was predicated on their acceptance at Louis XIV's court and in prominent Parisian salons. The oral tale had flourished for a long time in villages and nurseries, part of a popular discourse, part of a discourse between governesses and children of the upper class. It had even seen literary light in the mass-marketed 'blue books' distributed by peddlers for consummation by peasants and the lower classes.[6] However, it was disdained as a literary form by the aristocratic and bourgeois classes until it received courtly approval through Madame de Maintenon and Fénelon; that is, until it could be codified and used to reinforce an accepted discursive mode of social conventions advantageous to the interests of the intelligentsia and *ancien régime*,[7] which made a fashion out of exploiting the ideas and productivity of the bourgeoisie. There is an interesting parallel which one could draw with the institution of *conversation* at this time. A non-compulsive elegant mode of conversing was developed at the court and salons which paradoxically emanated from a compulsion to respect strict rules of decorum.[8] The speaker was compelled to be non-compulsive and the audience, spontaneous in its reception of stories and exchange of remarks. The more folk tales could be subjected to the rules of conversation, the more they were ornamented and accepted within the dominant discourse. This was the historical sociogenetic origination of the literary fairy tale for children. Writing fairy tales was a choice, an option exercised within an institution, a manner of imposing one's conversation on the prescribed fairy-tale discourse.

Jameson is again instructive in his definition of genre.

> Genres are essentially literary *institutions*, or social contracts between writer and a specific public whose function is to specify the proper use of a particular cultural artefact. The speech acts of daily life are themselves marked with indications and signals (intonation, gesturality, contextual deitics and pragmatics) which ensure their appropriate reception. In the mediated situations of a more complicated social life – and the emergence of writing has often been taken as paradigmatic of such situations – perceptual signals must be replaced by conventions if the text in question is not to be abandoned to a drifting multiplicity of uses (as *meanings* must, according to Wittgenstein, be described). Still, as texts free themselves more and more from an immediate performance situation, it becomes ever more difficult to enforce a given generic rule on their readers. No small part of the art of writing, indeed, is absorbed by this (impossible) attempt to devise a foolproof mechanism for the automatic exclusion of undesirable response to a given literary utterance.[9]

In the case of the literary fairy tale for children as genre, it appears fruitless to me to begin a definition based on the morphological study of Vladimir Propp[10] or the semiotic practice of Algirdas-Julien Greimas[11] as many critics have done. To be sure, Propp and Greimas are useful for comprehending textual structures and signs of the tales, but they provide no overall methodological framework for locating and grasping the essence of the genre, the substance of the symbolic act as it took form to intervene in the institutionalized literary discourse of society.

This becomes apparent when one reads the remarkably informative essay *Du Conte merveilleux comme genre* (On the Magic Folk Tale as Genre) by Marie-Louise Tenèze, who uses the works of Propp and Max Lüthi in order to grasp the kernel (*un noyau irréductible*) of what constitutes the magic of the folk tale.[12] She begins with Propp's thesis that there are a limited number of functions in the magic folk tale with an identical succession of events. The hero lacks something and goes in search for aid (intermediaries) to achieve happiness, most often marriage. The structure of every magic folk tale conforms to this quest. Then she combines Propp's ideas with those of Lüthi, who sees the hero of a magic folk tale as a wanderer charged with carrying out a task.

Since the answer or solution to this task is known in advance, there is no such thing as chance or coincidence in a folk tale. This accounts for the precise, concrete style of all the tales, and their composition is a detailing of the ways in which the hero takes steps to survive and complete his mission. According to Tenèze, the rich variety of folk tales stems from the freedom given to each narrator to alter the functions and tasks within the fixed schema. Her synthesis of Propp and Lüthi leads her to the following formulation:

> The magic folk tale reveals itself in its very core to be like the narrativization of the situation of the hero between the 'response' and the 'question', that is between the means obtained and the means employed. In other words, it is the relation between the hero – who is explicitly or implicitly but always assured of *aid in advance*, guaranteed – and the difficult situation in which he finds himself during the course of action that I propose as the constitutive criterion of the genre.[13]

By combining Propp's thesis with Lüthi's, Tenèze endeavors to elaborate a structural approach which stresses the dynamics and changeability of the tale, avoiding the pitfalls of the static models of Propp and Lüthi. She draws an interesting parallel to the primitive North American Indian ritual of puberty described by Claude Lévi-Strauss in *Tristes Tropiques*,[14] where adolescents were placed in the wilderness and left alone to survive and develop a sense of power while they were also expected to become aware of the absurdity and desperation one would experience by leaving the social order. Tenèze believes that

> like the real hero of this custom, the hero of the magic folk tale ventures, alone and far from his familar surroundings, to the perilous fringe of an exceptional experience capable of supplying him with a 'personal provision of power', his insertion into the world – and thus, there is a magic solution to the absurd and desperate endeavor to leave the social order which is played out in the universe of fiction. Isn't the folk tale a response to the oppressive interrogation of reality?[15]

Like Propp and Lüthi, Tenèze favors the structural approach to explain the essence of the magic folk tale. In other words, it is through the structure or composition of the tale that we can gain an understanding of its meaning or enunciation, what it is trying to communicate. The difficulty with this approach, as Tenèze realizes, is that, if all folk tales have essentially the same 'morphology' (even though the functions may be varied), they all express the same thing, some kind of universal statement about the plight of humanity. The form itself is its meaning, and the historicity of the individual creator (or creators) and society disappears. Such formalist approaches to folk and fairy tales account in great part for the reason why we see the tales as universal, ageless, and eternal. The tendency here is to homogenize creative efforts so that the differences of human and social acts become blurred.

Tenèze is much too aware of the failing of the structural approach to be satisfied with it, for the second half of her essay on the genre explores other aspects which may help us define its essence such as its relation to myth and legend and to the narrator and community. In her survey of criticism dealing with reception aesthetics, she stresses the significance of specific narrators and their audiences, their norms and values, all which must be taken into account if we are to grasp the core of the genre, especially the significance of its development. This leads Tenèze to conclude that

> when we envisage it in its concrete cultural formations, in spite of the character of the world which we recognize in it, the magic folk tale needs to be inscribed in the functional totality of the system of expression of the community in question. Even more than this, it needs to be situated in the life of this community itself. This is the research which must now be carried out in studies of the European folk tale.[16]

Whereas it is extremely difficult to study the historical origins and social significance of a folk tale (the relationship between narrator and audience) because we lack much information about primitive tribes and societies, it is not so difficult to define the historical rise of the literary fairy tale for children. It seems to me that any definition of this genre must begin with the premise that the individual tale was indeed a *symbolic act* intended to transform a specific oral folk tale (and sometimes a well-known literary tale) and designed to rearrange the motifs, characters, themes, functions and configurations in such a way that they would address the concerns of the educated and ruling classes of late feudal and early capitalist societies. What Tenèze amply discusses as the dynamic structure of the folk tale is what August Nitschke[17] has evaluated in terms of autodynamics, heterodynamics, and metamorphosis of primitive tribes and modern societies. Nitschke holds that every community and society in history can be characterized by the way human beings arrange themselves and perceive time, and this gives rise to a dominant activity (also called a line of motion). The perspectives and positions assumed by members of society toward the dominant activity amount to a configuration. The configuration designates the character of a social order since the temporal–corporeal arrangement is designed around a dominant activity that shapes the attitudes of people toward work, education, social development and death. Hence, the configuration of society is the pattern of arrangement and rearrangement of social behavior related to a socialized mode of perception. In the folk tale the temporal–corporeal arrangement reflects whether there are perceived to be new possibilities for participation in the social order or whether there must be a confrontation when possibilities for change do not exist. This is why, in each new stage of civilization, in each new historical epoch, the symbols and configurations of the tales were endowed with new meaning, transformed, or eliminated in reaction to the needs and conflicts of the people within the social order. The aesthetic arrangement and structure of the tales were derived from the way the narrator or narrators perceived the possibility for resolution of social conflicts and contradictions or felt change was necessary.

If we examine the vast group of European folk tales of the feudal and early capitalist periods, those tales with which we are most familiar and which were recorded very early, that which is our legacy, we must bear in mind that their configurations and symbols were already marked by a sociopolitical perception and had entered into a specific institutionalized discourse before they were transformed into literary tales for children of the European upper classes. For instance, Heide Göttner-Abendroth has demonstrated convincingly in *Die Göttin und ihr Heros*[18] that the matriarchal world view and motifs of the original folk tales underwent successive stages of 'patriarchalization'. That is, by the time the oral folk tales, originally stamped by matriarchal mythology, circulated in the Middle Ages, they had been transformed in different ways: the goddess became a witch, evil fairy, or stepmother; the active, young princess was changed into an active hero; matrilineal marriage and family ties became patrilineal; the essence of the symbols, based on matriarchal rites, was depleted and made benign; the pattern of action which concerned maturation and integration was gradually recast to stress domination and wealth.

As a pagan or non-Christian art form, one that was variable depending on the natural condition or social situation which was its reference, the folk tale developed a partiality for everything metallic and mineral and conceived of a world which was solid and imperishable. Such a set and highly structured world can be linked to notions of medieval patriarchalism, monarchy, and absolutism in the fifteenth, sixteenth and seventeenth centuries. The world of the folk tale is inhabited largely by kings, queens, princes, princesses, soldiers, peasants, animals, and supernatural creatures (witches, fairies, elves, dwarves, goblins, giants) – rarely by members of the bourgeoisie or the church. Nor are there machines, signs of industrialization, elaborate descriptions of commerce and town life. In other words, the main characters and concerns of a monarchistic, patriarchal, and feudal society are presented, and the focus is on class struggle and competition for power among the aristocrats themselves and between the peasantry and aristocracy. Hence, the central theme of all the folk tales of this particular pre-capitalist period: 'might makes right'.[19] *He* who has power can exercise *his* will, right wrongs, become ennobled, amass money and land, win women as prizes and social prestige. Tenèze was correct when she placed her finger on power and oppression as the key concerns of the folk tales, and this is why the people, largely peasants, were predominantly attracted to the tale and became its prime carriers: the oral folk tales were those symbolic acts in which they enunciated their aspirations and projected the magic possibility in an assortment of imaginative ways so that anyone could become a knight in shining armor or a lovely princess. They also presented the stark realities of power politics without disguising the violence and brutality of everyday life. Starvation of children, rape, corporeal punishment, ruthless exploitation – these are some of the conditions which are at the root of the folk tale, conditions which were so overwhelming that they demanded symbolic abstraction.[20]

As Lüthi has shown,[21] the folk tale's manner of portrayal is direct, clear, paratactical, and one-dimensional in its narrative perspective, and this narrative position reflects the limitations of feudal life where alternatives to one's situation were extremely limited. So it is in the folk tale. Despite magical transformation, there is no mention of another world. Only one side of the characters and living conditions is described. *Everything is confined to a realm without morals*, where class and power determine power relations. Hence, the magic and miraculous serve to rupture the feudal confines and represent metaphorically the conscious and unconscious desires of the lower classes to seize power. In the process, power takes on a moral quality. The fact that the people as carriers of the tales do not *explicitly* seek a total revolution of social relations does not minimize the utopian aspect in the *imaginative* portrayal of class conflict. Whatever the outcomes of the tales are – and for the most part, they are happy ends and 'exemplary' in that they affirm a more just feudal order with democratizing elements – the impulse and critique of the 'magic' are rooted in an historically explicable desire to overcome oppression and change society.

In the seventeenth century children of all classes listened to these tales. The peasants did not exclude children when stories were told around the hearth, and lower-class wet-nurses and governesses related the same tales to children of the upper classes. The folk tale was the staple of what was to become the literary fairy tale for children. Before this could occur, however, it was necessary to prescribe the form and manner in which the tales would be adapted and used to entertain and instruct children. The adaptation of folk material, an act of symbolic appropriation, was a re-codification of the material to make it suitable for the discursive requirements of French court society and bourgeois salons. The first writers of fairy tales had to demonstrate the social value of the genre before literary fairy tales could be printed – for adults and children alike. The morality and ethics of a male-dominated Christian civil order had to become part and parcel of the literary fairy tale. This was a given, and it was with this rule in mind, whether one agreed with it or not, that the early French writers of fairy tales began writing – acted symbolically.

Children were now being taken seriously as a separate age group with a special set of characteristics, and it was considered most important to advance the cause of *civilité* with explicit and implicit rules of peda-gogization so that the manners and mores of the young would reflect the social power, prestige, and hierarchy of the ruling classes. Socialization through fairy tales. Internalization of values. We must remember that the fairy tale for children originated in a period of absolutism when French culture was setting standards of *civilité* for the rest of Europe. Exquisite care was thus taken to cultivate a discourse on the civilization process through the fairy tale for the benefit of well-raised children. In this regard fairy tales for children were no different than the rest of the literature (fables, primers, picture books, sermons, didactic stories, etc.) which conveyed a model of the exemplary child that was to be borne in mind while reading. Fairy tales and children's literature were written with the purpose of socializing children to meet definite normative expectations at home and in the public sphere. The behavioral standards were expressly codified in books on manners and civility. This means that the individual symbolic act of writing the literary fairy tale expressed a certain level of social consciousness and conscience which were related to the standard mode of socialization at that time.

In her discussion of the origins of the literary fairy tale for children in Europe, Denise Escarpit has made it clear that the purpose of the tale from the beginning was to instruct and amuse, that is, to make moral lessons and social strictures palatable.

> It was a utilitarian moralism which taught how to 'act in a proper way', that is, to insert oneself into society docilely, but astutely without disrupt-ing society and also without creating trouble for oneself. One thing is quite clear: there was a threefold manipulation by the author – a mani-

pulation which served a cultural and personal politics; a manipulation of a social kind which presented a certain image of society; a moralistic manipulation which adhered to the code of bourgeois moralism at the end of the seventeenth century. It was this possibility of multiple manipulation which constituted the power of the tale. According to how the tale was cloaked, it could assume very diverse forms which were functions of social and cultural imperatives at the time. And, in the same way, according to social and cultural imperatives, the tale experienced periods of favor and disfavor. This is the reason why it was transformed into an erotic tale, a philosophical one, or a pedagogical moral tale. It was the latter which directed itself to children.[22]

There is obviously a danger in seeing the fairy tale written for children too much in terms of manipulation. If this were its central role or function, one would have to speak about the genre as a conspiracy. As I have endeavored to demonstrate, however, the literary fairy tale for children, as it began to constitute itself as genre, became more an institutionalized discourse with manipulation as one of its components. This *discourse* had and continues to have many levels to it: the writers of fairy tales for children entered into a dialogue on values and manners with the folk tale, with contemporary writers of fairy tales, with the prevailing social code, with implicit adult and young readers, and with unimplied audiences. The shape of the fairy-tale discourse, of the configurations within the tales, was molded and bound by the European civilizing process which was undergoing profound changes in the sixteenth, seventeenth and eighteenth centuries. The profundity of the literary fairy tale for children, its magic, its appeal, is marked by these changes, for it is one of the cornerstones of our bourgeois heritage. As such, it both revolutionized the institution of literature at that time while abiding by its rules. Perrault saw it as modern, making history, history in the making through innovative symbolic acts.

To write a social history of the literary fairy tale for children in relation to the bourgeois civilizing process is an immense task – and it is not the project of this book. However, I do want to try to provide a framework for such a social history by investigating the contours of the fairy-tale discourse on civilization. My focus in the first four chapters is on the major *classical* writers in Europe and America from the seventeenth to the twentieth centuries, mainly on Charles Perrault, Jacob and Wilhelm Grimm, Hans Christian Andersen, George MacDonald, Oscar Wilde, and L. Frank Baum. These writers are significant because they helped evolve, expand, and reform the discourse and have thus been rewarded with 'classical' status in our cultural heritage. The reasons for their 'classicity' vary, for their symbolic acts were made either to legitimize or criticize the course of the western civilizing process. Some even converted the fairy-tale discourse to subvert it. The subversion through symbolical innovation and involution is amply demonstrated in the last two chapters which deal with the struggle for domination over the fairy-tale discourse during the Weimar and Nazi periods in Germany and the post-war attempts in the West at large to create liberating tales for children.

My concern is largely with the fairy-tale discourse as dynamic part of the historical civilizing process, with each symbolic act viewed as an intervention in socialization in the public sphere. To have a fairy tale published is like a symbolic public announcement, an intercession on behalf of oneself, of children, of civilization. It is an historical statement. History is not conceived of here as chronology but rather absence and rupture – in need of a text. The symbolic act of writing a fairy tale is problematized by the asking of questions which link the fairy tale to society and our political unconscious. How and why did certain authors try to influence children or adult images of children through the fairy tale? How did these authors react to the prescribed fairy-tale discourse and intervene to alter it according to their needs and social tendencies? My own critical text is obviously an endeavor to make tl. *absent cause* of history speak for itself, and I avowedly seek a political understanding of our notion of classicism and classical fairy tales, the process of selection, elimination, and reward. The fairy tales we have come to revere as classical are not ageless, universal, and beautiful in and of themselves, and they are not the best therapy in the world for children. They are historical prescriptions, internalized, potent, explosive, and we acknowledge the power they hold over our lives by mystifying them.

Notes

1 *The Political Unconscious: Narrative as a Socially Symbolic Act* (Ithaca: Cornell University Press, 1981), p. 35.
2 *Ibid.*, p. 40.
3 *Ibid.*, p. 77.
4 *Ibid.*, p. 79.
5 Cf. Marc Soriano, 'From tales of warning to formulettes: the oral tradition in French children's literature,' *Yale French Studies*, **43** (1969), pp. 24–43, and *Guide de littérature pour la jeunesse* (Paris: Flammarion, 1975); Isabelle Jan, *Essai sur la littérature enfantine* (Paris: Éditions Ouvrières, 1969); Dieter Richter and Johannes Merkel, *Märchen, Phantasie und soziales Lernen* (Berlin: Basis, 1974); F.J. Harvey Darton, *Children's Books in England*, 2nd edn. (Cambridge: Cambridge University Press, 1960). There are numerous other studies which touch upon this point.
6 See Robert Mandrou, *De la culture populaire aux XVIIe et XVIIIe siècles* (Paris: Stock, 1964).

7   See Teresa DiScanno, *Les Contes de Fées à l'époque classique (1680–1715)* (Naples: Liguori, 1975), pp. 20–30.
8   Cf. Claudia Schmölders (ed.), *Die Kunst des Gesprächs* (Munich: Deutscher Taschenbuch Verlag, 1979), pp. 9–67.
9   *The Political Unconscious*, pp. 106–7.
10   *Morphology of the Folktale*, ed. by Louis Wagner and Alan Dundes (Austin: University of Texas Press, 1968).
11   *Sémantique structurale* (Paris: Larousse, 1964).
12   In *Approches de nos traditions orales*, ed. by Marie-Louise Tenèze (Paris: G.-P. Maisonneuve et Larose, 1970), pp. 11–65.
13   *Ibid.*, pp. 23–4.
14   (Paris: Plon, 1955), pp. 29–30.
15   'Du Conte Merveilleux comme genre,' pp. 28–9.
16   *Ibid.*, p. 65.
17   *Soziale Ordnungen im Spiegel der Märchen*, 2 vols. (Stuttgart: Frommann-Holboog, 1977).
18   Munich: Frauenoffensive, 1980.
19   Cf. the chapter 'Might makes right – the politics of folk and fairy tales' in my book *Breaking the Magic Spell: Radical Theories of Folk and Fairy Tales* (London: Heinemann, 1979), pp. 20–40.
20   Cf. Eugen Weber, 'Fairies and hard facts: the reality of folktales,' *Journal of the History of Ideas*, **XLII** (1981), pp. 93–113.
21   See *Das europäische Volksmärchen*, 2nd rev. edn. (Bern: Francke, 1960) and *Die Gabe im Märchen und in der Sage* (Bern: Francke, 1943).
22   *La littérature d'enfance et de jeunesse en Europe* (Paris: Presses Universitaires de France, 1981), pp. 39–40.

2 Setting Standards for Civilization through Fairy Tales: Charles Perrault and his Associates

In the case of those cultures which I have named 'archaic', there is, in contrast to our own culture, a much clearer awareness extant that we can only always *be* that what we are when, at the same time, we are what we are *not*, that we can only know who we are when we have experienced our limits and thus have surpassed them, as Hegel might say.

This does not mean, however, that we are to drive the stakes of our limits further and further into the wilderness, that we are perpetually to root out, cultivate, and categorize that which is 'outside' us. Rather this means that we ourselves are to become wild in order not to *place ourselves at the mercy* of our own wildness, in order to gain thereby an awareness of ourselves as tame, as cultural creatures.

Hans Peter Duerr
Traumzeit (1978)

I

Published in 1697, Charles Perrault's *Histoires ou contes du temps passé* appeared at a time when there was a major shift in social norms and manners. As Philippe Ariès has noted,

although demographic conditions did not greatly change between the thirteenth and seventeenth centuries, and although child mortality remained at a very high level, a new sensibility granted these fragile, threatened creatures a characteristic which the world had hitherto failed to recognize in them: as if it were only then that the common conscience had discovered that the child's soul too was immortal. There can be no doubt that the importance accorded to the child's personality was linked to the growing influence of Christianity on life and manners.[1]

Thus, it is not by chance that Perrault directed his energies in writing his fairy tales for the most part to civilize children and to prepare them for roles which he idealistically believed they should play in society.

Since Perrault's fairy tales were created at the point in history when more and more European writers began composing explicitly for children as separate entities and when standards were first being set for the development of modern children's literature, his works must be viewed as part of a larger social phenomenon. In fact, he and numerous friends and associates were responsible for a vertible deluge of literary fairy tales in the eighteenth century. To be sure, the majority of the tales still courted favor primarily with adults, but there was an overwhelming tendency in these fairy stories to provide models of behavior for the rearing and schooling of upper-class children. In fact, the literary fairy tales differed remarkably from their precursors, the oral folk tales, by the manner in which they portrayed children and appealed to them as a possibly distinct audience. The fairy tales were cultivated to assure that young people would be properly groomed for their social functions. At first the fairy tales were adapted from the oral tales of nurses, governesses and servants of the lower classes and then refined to be told in courtly circles. Some were even published randomly in the latter part of the seventeenth century. But, by the 1690s a tremendous vogue of writing and circulating literary fairy tales for children and adults had been set in motion.[2] In 1696, the year in which Perrault issued a separate edition of his prose *Sleeping Beauty*, his niece Marie-Jeanne Lhéritier published *L'Adroite Princesse ou les Aventures de Finette*, which was later to be celebrated as the work of Perrault due to its similar tone and style. About this time Mlle Catherine Bernard incorporated two fairy tales in her novel *Inès de Cordue*, and then in 1697 Perrault's prose tales appeared along with two volumes of fairy stories by Madame Marie-Catherine D'Aulnoy, and a smaller collection by Mlle Charlotte-Rose Caumont de la Force. In addition, fairy-tale plays were now produced. In 1698 Paul-François Nodot published his *Histoire de Melusine* followed by Jean de Prechac's *Contes moins Contes que les autres*, Madame Henriette-Julie de Murat's *Contes des Fées*, Madame D Aulnoy's four volumes *Contes Nouveaux ou les Fées à la Mode*, and other anonymous collections of fairy tales. In the ensuing one hundred years French high society was literally inundated with fairy tales. Not only did bourgeois and aristocratic writers explore and exploit the treasures of French folklore, but they also borrowed from the Italian literary tradition, especially the works by Giovanni Francesco Straporola (*Le piacevoli notti*, 1550) and Giambattista Basile (*Pentamerone*, 1634–6), and they began to translate oriental fairy tales which had a tremendous influence. In 1704 Galland published part of the *Arabian Nights*, and in 1707 Petit de Lacroix edited a collection of Persian fairy tales under the title *A Thousand and One Days*.

There were innumerable polished writers in the eighteenth century who either experimented ingeniously with the fairy-tale genre or simply imitated the examples set by Perrault, D'Aulnoy, Murat, and Prechac at the end of the seventeenth century. Among the more unique and interesting writers were Gabrielle-Suzanne de Villeneuve (*Contes marins ou la Jeune Amériquaine*, 1740–3), Jacques Cazotte (*Mille et une fadaise, contes à dormir debout*, 1742), Claude-Philippe de Caylus (*Le Prince Courtebotte et la Princesse Zibeline*, 1741–3), Jeanne-Marie Leprince de Beaumont (*Magasin des enfants*, 1757), and Charles Duclos (*Acajou et Ziphile*, 1762). Even Jean-Jacques Rousseau wrote a tale entitled *La Reine Fantastique* in 1758. The fairy-tale vogue eventually culminated in Charles-Joseph de Mayer's remarkable collection of the major literary fairy tales published in the seventeenth and eighteenth centuries. He printed them in forty-one volumes as *Le Cabinet des fées ou Collection choisie des contes des fées et autres contes merveilleux* (1785–9).

Significantly the fairy-tale boom subsided with the outbreak of the French Revolution, when the interests of the lower classes were made more manifest, and the result was a shift in socio-cultural perspective. However, the French literary fairy tales did continue to exercise a powerful influence in Germany.[3] Certainly Mozart's *The Magic Flute* (1791) emanated from this tradition, and such writers as Wieland, Musäus, Goethe, Tieck, Novalis, Brentano, Eichendorff, Fouqué, Chamisso, Hoffmann and the Brothers Grimm were all beneficiaries of the French vogue in one form or another. In general the rise of the French literary fairy tale at the end of the seventeenth century can be regarded as the source of the flowering of fairy tales in Europe and America in the nineteenth century. More specifically, I am talking about a literary heritage which was first intended for the upper classes and gradually spread to lower social echelons, and I am concerned here more with the fairy tales as they became directed toward children to set exemplary standards of behavior in the civilizing process.

In France the development of those fairy tales which were to form the genre for children of breeding was initiated for the most part by Perrault, who had taken a special and active interest in the education of his own children. He was followed by such writers as Marie-Jeanne Lhéritier, Marie-Catherine D'Aulnoy, Gabrielle-Suzanne de Villeneuve and Jeanne-Marie Leprince de Beaumont, who cultivated the tales largely in a moral vein. That is, there were two major tendencies among French fairy-tale writers: either they took the genre seriously and endeavored to incorporate ideas, norms, and values in the narrative structure that they considered worthy of emulation for both the child and adult reader; or they parodied the genre because they considered it trivial and associated magic and the miraculous with the superstitions of the lower classes who were not to be taken seriously anyway. Both sets of writers demonstrated remarkable finesse and literally transformed the common folk tale into 'high' art. To be sure, one could speak of authors who did in fact trivialize the fairy-tale genre by grossly imitating the more skilled writers just to become a social or what we would call today a commercial success. Yet, whatever their purpose of writing a fairy tale was, all the authors employed the tale to engage in an ongoing institutionalized discourse about mores and manners in the seventeenth and eighteenth centuries.

Perrault's own contribution to the development of the literary fairy tale for children is a contradictory one. He is responsible for shaping folklore into an exquisite literary form and endowing it with an earnest and moral purpose to influence the behavior of children in a tasteful way. However, at the same time he is also 'guilty' of setting stringent standards of comportment which were intended to regulate and limit the nature of children's development. This contradictory position is also evident in the works of Lhéritier, D'Aulnoy, Prechac, Leprince de Beaumont, and others: they sought to civilize children to inhibit them, and perhaps pervert their natural growth. This is not to argue that Perrault and his associates had nefarious plans and conspired to fill children's heads with false illusions. On the contrary, despite his ironic attitude toward folklore and his double intention of writing for children and adults with moral fervor and charm, Perrault was most sincere in his intentions to improve the minds and manners of young people. In the *Preface* to the *Contes en Vers* (1695), he argued that people of good taste have recognized the substantial value of the tales. 'They have noticed that these trifles [the tales] were not mere trifles, that they contained a useful moral, and that the playful narrative surrounding them had been chosen only to allow the stories to penetrate the mind more pleasantly and in such a manner to instruct and amuse at the same time.'[4] Perrault compared his tales with those of his forebears

> who always took care that their tales contained a praiseworthy and instructive moral. Virtue is rewarded everywhere, and vice is always punished. They all tend to reveal the advantage in being honest, patient, prudent, industrious, obedient and the evil which can befall them if they are not that way. Sometimes the fairies give a gift to a young girl who answers them with civility, and with each word that she speaks, a diamond or a pearl falls from her mouth. And another girl who answers

them brutally has a frog or a toad fall from her mouth. Sometimes there are children who become great lords for having obeyed their father or mother, or others who experience terrible misfortune for having been vicious and disobedient. No matter how frivolous and bizarre all these fables are in their adventures, it is certain that they arouse a desire in children to resemble those whom they see become happy and at the same time a fear of the misfortunes which befall wicked characters because of their wickedness. Is it not praiseworthy of fathers and mothers when their children are still not capable of appreciating solid truths stripped of all ornaments to make them love these truths, and, as it were, to make them swallow them by enveloping them in charming narratives which correspond to the weakness of their age? It is incredible how avaraciously innocent souls whose natural rectitude has not yet been corrupted receive these hidden instructions.[5]

This argument was repeated in the 1697 dedication in the *Histoires ou contes du temps passé*,[6] and later, in the *Dedication* to the 1729 English translation of Perrault's tales, Robert Samber continued the didactic tradition by stressing their educational and moral value:

It was however objected, that some of them were very low and childish, especially the first. It is very true, and therein consists their Excellency. They therefore who made this as an Objection, did not seem very well to understand what they said; they should have reflected they are designed for children: And yet the Author hath so ingeniously and masterly contrived them, that they insensibly grow up, gradually one after another, in Strength and Beauty, both as to their Narration and Moral, and are told with such a Naiveté, and natural innocent Simplicity, that not only children, but those of Maturity, will also find in them uncommon Pleasure and Delight.[7]

During the course of history, Perrault's tales and those of his associates succeeded admirably in their cultural mission: contemporary fairy tales have been greatly informed by the aesthetics and ideology of seventeenth and eighteenth century French fairy tales which have become part and parcel of a general civilizing process in the West. There is a direct line from the Perrault fairy tale of court society to the Walt Disney cinematic fairy tale of the culture industry. Obviously, many samples of the French fairy-tale vogue have not survived the test of time and have been replaced by more adequate modern-day equivalents. But, for the most part, Perrault and his associates stamped the very unreflective and uncritical manner in which we read and receive fairy tales to the present. What we praise as our classical fairy-tale heritage, however, has a dark side to it which I should like to discuss in terms of the modern western civilizing process. To penetrate this dark side of fairy tales in relation to their socializing function for children, I want to elaborate upon the notions of civilization developed by Norbert Elias in his two-volume study *The Civilizing Process*[8] as they pertain to Perrault. Then I want to examine Perrault's major tales and some by his associates in light of their contradictory contribution to the education of children through literature.

My foremost concern is how fairy tales operate ideologically to indoctrinate children so that they will conform to dominant social standards which are not necessarily established in their behalf. Here I should like to make it clear that the ideology carried by the 'classical' literary fairy tales since the seventeenth century and their ideological impact on children are difficult to pinpoint in a specific scientific way. Given the constant changes in the classical tales, the socio-literary variables in different countries, and the relative nature of reception since the seventeenth century, one must pay close attention to the socio-psychological mechanisms through which ideology exercises an influence on readers of fairy tales. Therefore, it is advisable to uncover paradigmatic patterns, which may correspond to social configurations, to shed light on the way ideology works. As Christian Zimmer has said,

> to grapple with ideology is to grapple with a phantom since ideology has neither a body nor a face. It has neither origin nor base which one could recast to provide the battle against it with a precise and well-defined object. Ideology only manifests itself under the form of fluid, of the diffuse, of permanent polymorphism and acts through infiltration, insinuation and impregnation. . . Ideology does not have a real language and especially not one of violence. Its total lack of aggression, its capacity to transform itself into everything, its infinite malleability, permits it to assume the mask of innocence and neutrality. And above all, as I have said, to blend itself with reality itself. Finally, its most supreme ruse is to delimit a kind of preserved *secteur* which it has called amusement (*divertissement*) and which it has cut off from reality by decree – always *menaced* as such by subversion. . . (moreover it acts on two levels: that of daily life and that of the lapse of the daily, the dream, the imaginary). Amusement is thus a direct creation of ideology. It is always alienation in power. To amuse oneself is to disarm oneself.[9]

At its point of origin for children the literary fairy tale was designed both to divert as amusement and instruct ideologically as a means to mold the inner nature of young people. Like the ideology of amusement which it embraces, the classical fairy tale of Perrault and his associates was, and still is, considered harmless and entertaining. Yet, considered as one of the vital socializing elements in western civilization, the literary fairy tale has always been more a subject of concern and debate than we tend to realize, for, as childhood assumed a more precious and distinct state of experience, the social forces dominating education constantly checked and investigated to see whether the 'standard' fairy tale maintained an 'ideology of harmlessness', that is, discreet inquiry and censorship have always been employed to guarantee that fairy tales were more or less constructed to follow the classical pattern and to reinforce the dominant social codes within the home and school. It is impossible and foolish to speak about a one-dimensional literary plot formed by the classical fairy tale and conservative guardians of culture. Yet, it is important to examine the complex patterns which have historically emerged in the civilizing process to trace how harmful or contradictory the literary fairy tale has been even though it has enjoyed a celebrated place in our hearts.

II

Norbert Elias' remarkable socio-historical study of the civilizing process is most useful for illuminating the dark socializing side of the classical fairy tales because he stresses the interrelationship between the sociogenetic evolution of society and the psychogenetic make-up of human beings:

> Even in civilized society no human being comes into the world civilized, and . . . the individual civilizing process that he compulsorily undergoes is a function of the social civilizing process. Therefore, the structure of the child's effects and consciousness no doubt bears a certain resemblance to that of 'uncivilized' peoples, and the same applies to the psychological stratum in grown-ups which, with the advance of civilization, is subjected to more or less heavy censorship and consequently finds an outlet in dreams, for example. But since in our society each human being is exposed from the first moment of life to the influence and the molding of civilized grown-ups, he must indeed pass through a civilizing process in order to reach the standard attained by his society in the course of its history, but not through the individual historical phases of the social civilizing process.[10]

Elias demonstrates that the major socio-political shift in favor of absolutism and religious orthodoxy in the latter part of the seventeenth century determined modern western attitudes toward civilization. The decentralized societies of the Middle Ages ceded to more centralized and regulated nation-states and principalities which abandoned lax notions of *courteoisie* (soon to be called barbaric) for more stringent notions of *civilité*, partly introduced and reinforced by the bourgeoisie, at least in France and England.

It is important to understand the cultural and political input of large *secteurs* of the bourgeoisie in France if we are to grasp Perrault's role in 'civilizing' the folk tale and transforming it into the literary fairy tale for upper-class children. The French aristocracy of the sixteenth and seventeenth centuries displayed a unique capacity to adopt and use the best elements from other classes. The nobility provided access for a select group of reliable people of the third estate to its circles, which were expanded as the need arose to secure aristocratic rule throughout the nation. Perrault was among the fortunate members of the *haute bourgeoisie* to be honored by the court.[11] He was a high, royal civil servant, one of the first members of the Académie Française, a respected polemicist, and a significant figure in literary salons. Moreover, he endorsed the expansive political wars of Louis XIV and believed in the exalted mission of the French absolutist regime to 'civilize' Europe and the rest of the world. Perrault supported the 'manifest destiny' of seventeenth-century France not only as a public representative of the court but privately in his family and was also one of the first writers of children's books who explicitly sought to 'colonize' the internal and external development of children in the mutual interests of a bourgeois–aristocratic elite.

The interaction between the French nobility and bourgeoisie must be carefully studied to grasp the sociogenetic import of literary fairy tales for children in western culture. Elias makes this connection clear:

> Both the courtly bourgeoisie and the courtly aristocracy spoke the same language, read the same books, and had, with particular gradations, the same manners. And when the social and economical disproportionalities burst the institutional framework of the ancien regime, when the bourgeoisie became a nation, much of what had originally been the specific and distinctive social character of the courtly aristocracy and then also of the courtly-bourgeois groups, became, in an ever widening movement and doubtless with some modification, the national character. Stylistic conventions, the forms of social intercourse, effect-molding, esteem for courtesy, the importance of good speech and conversation, articulateness of language and much else – all this is first formed in France within courtly society, then slowly changes, in a continuous diffusion, from a social into a national character.[12]

By the time Perrault had begun writing his fairy tales, the major crises of the Reformation period which had been manifested drastically in the massive witchhunts between 1490 and 1650 had been temporarily resolved, and they resulted in greater rationalization and regulation of social and spiritual life. This civilizing process coincided with an increase in socioeconomic power by the bourgeoisie, particularly in

France and England, so that the transformed social, religious, and political views represented a blend of bourgeois–aristocratic interests. The *homme civilisé* was the former *homme courteois*, whose polite manners and style of speech were altered to include bourgeois qualities of honesty, diligence, responsibility, and asceticism. To increase its influence and assume more political control the French bourgeoisie was confronted with a twofold task: to adapt courtly models in a manner which would allow greater *laissez-faire* for the expansion and consolidation of bourgeois interests; to appropriate folk customs and the most industrious, virtuous, and profitable components of the lower classes to strengthen the economic and cultural power of the bourgeoisie. In this regard the French bourgeoisie was indeed a middle or mediating class, although its ultimate goal was to become self-sufficient and to make the national interests identical with its own.

One way of disseminating its values and interests and of subliminally strengthening its hold on the civilizing process was through literary socialization. Since childhood had become more distinguished as a separate phase of growth and was considered as the crucial base for the future development of the individual character, special attention was now paid to children's manners, clothes, books, toys, and general education. Numerous books, pamphlets, and brochures appeared in the sixteenth and seventeenth centuries which dealt with table manners, natural functions, bedroom etiquette, sexual relations, and correct speech.[13] The most classic example was Erasmus of Rotterdam's *De Civiltate morum puerilum* (*On Civility in Children*, 1530). Also important were the works of Giovanni della Casa (Galateo, 1558), C. Calviac (*Civilité*, 1560), Antoine de Courtin, (*Nouveau traité de civilité*, 1672), François de Callières (*De la science du monde des connoissances utiles à la conduite de la vie*, 1717) and LaSalle (*Les Règles de la bienséance et de la civilité chrétienne*, 1729). It was impossible for a member of the aristocratic or bourgeois class to escape the influence of such manuals which became part of the informal and formal schooling of all upper-class children. These same views were disseminated to the peasantry through the cheap pamphlets of *la bibliothèque bleue*. Coercion exerted by members of high society to act according to *new* precepts of good behavior increased so that the codes of dress and manner became extremely stringent and hierarchical by the end of the seventeenth century. Though not conspired, the rational purpose of such social pressure was to bring about an internalization of social norms and mores so that they would appear as second nature or habit. Yet, self-control was actual social control, and it was a mark of social distinction not to 'let go of oneself' or to 'lose one's senses' in public. As Elias has noted, the system of standardization and social conditioning had assumed fairly concrete contours with multi-level controls by the mid-seventeenth century.

> There is a more or less limited courtly circle which first stamps the models only for the needs of its own social situation and in conformity with the psychological condition corresponding to it. But clearly the structure and development of French society as a whole gradually makes ever broader strata willing and anxious to adopt the models developed above them: they spread, also very gradually, throughout the whole of society, certainly not without undergoing some modification in the process.[14]

As French society became more regulated and as efforts were made to bring about a homogeneous state, the pressures placed on children to conform to role models became more severe. In keeping with rigid social standards which denounced open forms of sexual behavior, table manners, dress, and natural functioning as 'barbaric' and 'uncivilized' – that is, ways which had been commonly accepted by the upper classes prior to the sixteenth century – it became important to cultivate feelings of shame and to arouse anxiety in children when they did not conform to a more inhibiting way of social conduct. Restraint and renunciation of instinctual gratification were part of a socio-religious code which illuminated the proper way to shape human drives and ideas so that children would learn docilely to serve church and state. Perhaps one of the main reasons for the rise of a 'state of childhood' by the end of the seventeenth century was the rise of a greater discrepancy between adult and child as the civilizing process became geared more instrumentally to dominate nature. The entire period from 1480 to 1650 can be seen as a historical transition in which the Catholic Church and the reform movement of Protestantism combined efforts with the support of the rising mercantile and industrial classes to rationalize society and literally to exterminate social deviates who were associated with the devil such as female witches, male werewolves, Jews, and gipsies. In particular, women were linked to the potentially uncontrollable natural instincts,[15] and, as the image of the innocent, naive child susceptible to wild natural forces arose, the necessity to control and shelter children became more pronounced. Social non-conformism and deviation had to be punished brutally in the name of civility and Christianity. Hundreds of thousands if not millions of people, according to H. R. Trevor-Roper,[16] were executed to arouse fear and anxiety while new models of male and female behavior were created to exalt a more ascetic way of life. The standards of conduct, discipline, and punishment,[17] formed in the name of absolutist Christian rulers, helped create divisions which were to operate in favor of the rising bourgeois industrial and mercantile classes. In order to make the overwhelming number of subjects in a given nation-state or principality pliable and serviceable, tests to control human instincts were first made among the members of the upper classes themselves and then spread to the lower classes. Thus, the introduction of the knife and fork as instrumental and dignified tools for eating, sitting straight at the table, hierarchical forms of serving, maintaining a certain posture while speaking or moving in a prescribed way,[18] repressing one's bodily functions, wearing special dress signifying one's social class – all these measures taken in the fifteenth and sixteenth centuries were meant to transform positive pleasure components which had been formerly accepted and regarded as harmless into negative manners which caused displeasure, revulsion, and distaste in the seventeenth century.

Elias notes that 'precisely by this increased social proscription of many impulses, by their "repression" from the surface of social life and of consciousness, the distance between the personality structure and behavior of adults and children is necessarily increased'.[19] In other words, childhood became identified as a state of 'natural innocence' and potentially corruptible by the end of the seventeenth century, and the civilizing of children – social indoctrination through anxiety provoking effects and positive reinforcement – operated on all levels in manners, speech, sex, literature, and play. Instincts were to be trained and controlled for their socio-political use value. The supervised rearing of children was to lead to the *homme civilisé*.

Civilité is the codeword which can provide the key to understanding how Perrault's tales and those of his associates assumed a unique and powerful role within the French socialization process. Moreover, they incorporated standards of comportment for children and adults which have been adopted in our own time and are still of actual interest and concern. Let us, therefore, turn to Perrault's prose tales now to grasp what he meant by *civilité* and to question the underlying moral assumption of civilization in the classical fairy tales.

III

If we regard the seven prose fairy tales in *Histoires ou contes du temps passé* as providing behavioral patterns and models for children, then they can be divided into two distinct groups based on gender. *Sleeping Beauty, Little Red Riding Hood, Blue Beard, The Fairies,* and *Cinderella* are aimed directly at females; *Puss in Boots, Ricky of the Tuft* and *Little Tom Thumb* address males. By focusing on the examplary qualities, which distinguish the heroines from the heroes, we shall see how carefully Perrault wove notions of *civilité* into the fabric of his tales.

In *Sleeping Beauty*, the princess is actually endowed with the following 'gifts' by the fairies: beauty, the temper of an angel, grace, the ability to dance perfectly, the voice of a nightingale, and musicality. In other words, she is bred to become the ideal aristocratic lady. Further, she is expected to be passive and patient for a hundred years until a prince rescues and resuscitates her. Her *manner* of speech is such that she charms the prince, and he marries her. Then she must demonstrate even more patience when her children are taken from her by the ogress. Such docility and self-abandonment are rewarded in the end when the prince returns to set things right. Perrault then added a verse moral which sings a hymn of praise to patience.

Little Red Riding Hood, the only warning tale of the volume, which ends on an unhappy note, still provides a model of behavior for girls. By giving expression to her fancy, she brings about both her grandmother's downfall and her own. Thus, by negative example, the reader learns what a good girl should be like. In fact, the moral tells us that young girls, who are pretty, well-bred, and courteous, should never talk to strangers or let themselves go. Otherwise, they will be swallowed by wolves. In other words, they must exercise control over their sexual and natural drives or else they will be devoured by their own sexuality in the form of a dangerous wolf.

In *Blue Beard* the message is almost the same except that the wife of Blue Beard is saved because she realizes her error and says her prayers. Here the heroine is beautiful, well-bred, but too curious. Again the moral explains that it is a sin to be curious and imaginative for a woman and that she must exercise self-control. This message is softened by a second moral which ironically implies that the relationship between men and women have changed: men are no longer the monsters they used to be and women have more power. Nevertheless, the female role is dictated by conditions that demand humility and self-discipline.

In *The Fairies* one daughter is played off against the other. The youngest is beautiful, gentle, sweet, and hard-working in the household. She never utters a complaint. The other is disagreeable, arrogant, and lazy. Since the younger exhibits the proper polite manners in helping a poor village dame, she is given a gift: with every word she utters, a flower or precious stone falls from her lips. She is eventually rewarded with a prince while her sister is banished from the house and dies. The moral celebrates kindness.

Just as the daughter in *The Fairies* is an industrious, self-effacing housekeeper, so, too, Cinderella, who also has her negative counterparts. In the fairy tale named after her, Cinderella is described as sweet, gentle, and diligent. Later, when she is properly dressed as a type of fashion queen, she is also the most beautiful woman in the world. Her 'excellent' qualities are recognized by the prince who marries her, and the moral praises the *bonne grace* of Cinderella, which accounts for her winning ways.

Perrault's fairy tales which 'elevate' heroines reveal that he had a distinctly limited view of women. His ideal *'femme civilisée'* of upper-class society, the composite female, is beautiful, polite, graceful, industrious, properly groomed, and knows how to control herself at all times. If she fails the obedience test, she is punished, as in Red Riding Hood's case, but this girl's fate is exceptional and belongs to a particular genre of warning tales which will be discussed later in more detail. The task confronted by Perrault's model female is to show reserve and patience, that is, she must be passive until the right man comes along to recognize her virtues and marry her. She lives only through the male and for marriage. The male acts, the female waits. She must cloak her instinctual drives in polite speech, correct manners, and elegant clothes. If she is allowed to reveal anything, it is to demonstrate how submissive she can be.

In commenting on how Perrault portrays women in his tales, Lilyane Mourey has explained that 'the concept of "morality" assumes here a very particular value mixed with irony and satire. Perrault argues for the total submission of the woman to her husband. Feminine coquetry (which is only the privilege of the dominant class) disturbs and upsets him: it could be the sign of female independence. It opens the way for the amorous conquest which endangers one of the fundamental values of society – the couple, the family. As we have seen, the heroines of the tales are very pretty, loyal, dedicated to their household chores, modest and docile and sometimes a little stupid insofar as it is true that stupidity is almost a quality in women for Perrault. Intelligence could be dangerous. In his mind as in that of many men (and women) beauty is an attribute of woman, just as intelligence is the attribute of man.'[20]

Of course, Perrault's disposition was totally different in his fairy tales which focused on male protagonists. In *Puss in Boots* the actual hero of the story is Puss, who needs the proper implements (a pair of boots and a pouch) to serve his master. The cat is the epitome of the educated bourgeois secretary who serves his master with complete devotion and diligence. He has such correct manners and wit that he can impress the king, and he uses his intelligence to dispose of an ogre and arrange a royal marriage for his low-born master. Thus, he can end his career by becoming a *grand seigneur*. Perrault provides us with a double moral here: one stresses the importance of possessing *industrie et savoir faire*, while the other extols the virtues of dress, countenance, and youth to win the heart of a princess.

In *Ricky of the Tuft* we learn again that it is not so much beauty and modesty which counts for men but brains and ambition. Prince Ricky is ugly and misshapen, but he has an abundance of intelligence and the power to bestow the same degree of intelligence on the person he loves best. As the tale would have it, Ricky meets a stupid beautiful princess who promises to marry him in a year if he endows her with brains. After she enjoys her new brains for a year, she wants to break her engagement, but Ricky's polite manners and ability lead her to believe that she now has the power to make him appear handsome. Mind wins over matter, and both short morals underline the virtue of good sense.

Certainly good sense and wit play a major role in *Little Tom Thumb*, too. Here the tiny hero, the youngest of seven sons, is described as kind and smart. Of all the brothers, he is the most prudent and most shrewd. Consequently he assumes leadership when the brothers are abandoned in the woods without food and money. He tricks the ogre and ogress, saves his brothers, and gains a fortune because he can outsmart everyone. Despite his size – and the moral emphasizes this – Tom Thumb demonstrates that brains are better to have than brawn.

The composite male hero of Perrault's tale is strikingly different from the composite female. None of the heroes is particularly good looking, but they all have remarkable minds, courage, and deft manners. Moreover, they are all ambitious and work their way up the social ladder: the cat becomes a *grand seigneur*; the prince acquires a beautiful princess to increase his social prestige; Tom Thumb becomes a rich and respected courtier. Unlike the fairy tales dealing with women where the primary goal is marriage, these tales demonstrate that social success and achievement are more important than winning a wife. In other words, women are incidental to the fates of the male characters whereas males endow the lives of females with purpose. The heroes are active, pursue their goals by using their minds, and exhibit a high degree of civility. If anything, their virtues reflect upon the courtly bourgeoisie during King Louis XIV's reign, if not upon Perrault's very own character.

By examining the major features and behavior of Perrault's male and female protagonists, it becomes crystal clear that he sought to portray ideal types to reinforce the standards of the civilizing process set by upper-class French society. Not only did Perrault inform his plots with normative patterns of behavior to describe an exemplary social constellation, but he also employed a distinct bourgeois–aristocratic manner of speech which was purposely contrived to demonstrate the proper way to converse with eloquence and civility. Polite conventions, eloquent phrases, and rationalities were employed to distinguish the characters as having high social rank and proper breeding. In addition Perrault used formal description to show the exemplary nature of his protagonists. For instance, Cinderella's transformation from 'slutty/maid' to 'virtuous/princess', accomplished by the fairy godmother, was in part an exercise in fashion design. Perrault wanted to display what superior people should wear and how they should carry themselves. 'All the ladies paid close attention to her hairdo and clothes with the intention of resembling her on the morrow provided that they could find materials just as beautiful and tailors just as talented.'[21] Cinderella displays all the graces expected from a refined, aristocratic young lady. Moreover, she has perfect control over her feelings and movements. She does not disgrace her sisters but treats them with dignity. Her composure is most admirable, and, when it comes time to depart, she demonstrates great self-discipline tempered with politeness.

Perrault's narrative style matches the décor, characters, and virtues which he describes. Each fairy tale exudes a polished baroque air. As stylist, Perrault cultivated a simple, frank and graceful style which incorporated the eloquent turns of high French practiced in court society and bourgeois circles. His ironic sense of humor allowed him to distance himself from the magical world, to poke fun at certain incidents, especially in the verse morals, and yet, he could still plead a case for civilized behavior: he took these stories seriously as examples of modern literature in his debate about *les Anciens et les Modernes* with Boileau. In this respect he also took care to provide a blend of bourgeois–aristocratic standards to demonstrate how modern fairy tales could be used for morally and ideologically acceptable purposes.

More than he realized, Perrault was responsible for the literary 'bourgeoisification' of the oral folk tale,[22] and he paved the way for founding a children's literature which would be useful for introducing manners to children of breeding. If we examine the origins of the eight prose tales in *Histoires ou contes du temps passé*, we can trace most of the motifs to oral folk tales which circulated in Perrault's time and to literary works by Straporola, Basile, and French writers, who had already adapted folk material. In other words, Perrault amalgamated folk and literary motifs and shaped them in a unique way to present his particular bourgeois view of social manners. In doing this Perrault shifted the narrative perspective of the popular folk-tale genre from that of the peasantry to that of the bourgeois–aristocratic elite. This may not seem so significant at first, but, viewed in terms of the socialization of children, it had dire consequences on the way children came to perceive their own status, sexuality, social roles, manners and politics. As we have already seen in the case of the heroes and heroines, the shifting of the narrative perspective was not a mere stylistic refining of uncouth expression and social views, but it meant a substantial transformation of the manner in which society or reality was to be depicted. In terms of the literary fairy-tale genre for children, Perrault radically changed familiar folk-tale characters, settings, and plots to correspond to a civilizing process aimed at regulating the inner and outer nature of children. As already demonstrated in the works of Ariès and Elias, the rearing of children was designed more and more to convey prescriptions and prohibitions, and Perrault shaped the tales to deprive the 'folk' of its say in the matter and at the same time to establish a social codex or manual by which young people were expected to abide. Just how crucial Perrault's shifting of the narrative perspective was for the socialization of children can be traced in each individual tale. Let us look at two which are most revealing: *Little Red Riding Hood* and *Cinderella.*

Until recently it was generally believed that Perrault did not use an oral folk tale as the basis for his literary rendition of *Little Red Riding Hood.* However, the research efforts of Paul Delarue, Marianne Rumpf, and Marc Soriano[23] have proven conclusively that Perrault was acquainted with an oral tale widely known in France which runs more or less as follows.

A little peasant girl goes to visit her grandmother carrying freshly baked bread and butter. On her way she meets a werewolf who asks her where she is going and which path she is taking, the one of needles or the one of pins. He takes the shorter path, arrives at the grandmother's house, eats her, and puts part of her flesh in a bin and her blood in a bottle. Then the little girl arrives. The werewolf disguised as the grandmother gives her the flesh to eat and the blood to drink. A crow scolds her for doing this. The werewolf tells her to throw each article of clothing into the fire since she will not be needing her clothes anymore. She gets into bed and asks ritual questions, the first one concerned with how hairy the werewolf's body is. When the werewolf finally reveals that he intends to eat her, she alertly replies that she has to relieve herself outside. He tells her to do it in the bed. She insists that she must do it outside. So the werewolf ties a piece of rope around her leg and allows her to go outside to take care of her natural functions. However, she ties the rope around a tree and runs home. The deceived werewolf follows in hot pursuit but fails to catch her.

This tale which has a long French tradition was told from the late Middle Ages up to the present. It became so prominent between the fifteenth and seventeenth centuries because of the great superstitious belief in werewolves[24] and the great witchhunt. There were numerous notorious cases of werewolf trials, and thousands of men and women were persecuted and exterminated because they were charged with being werewolves.[25] The tale about the girl *without* a red cap and name and with a werewolf was also popular in the region where Perrault's family had lived, and it is more than likely that he was influenced by some version of the folk tale when he wrote his unique literary story. Of course, he felt impelled to make many drastic changes, and Paul Delarue maintains

> the common elements that are lacking in the literary story are precisely those which would have shocked the society of his period by their cruelness (the flesh and blood of the grandmother tasted by the child), their puerility (Road of Pins, Road of Needles), and their impropriety (question of the girl on the hairy body of the grandmother). And it seems plausible that Perrault eliminated them while he kept in the tale a folk flavor and freshness which make it an imperishable masterpiece.[26]

While there is no doubt that Perrault took care not to offend the tastes of upper-class society, it is debatable whether he really retained the *folk* qualities, for he totally corrupted the perspective and import of the warning tale.

Instead of really warning girls against the dangers of predators in forests, the tale warns girls against their own natural desires which they must tame. The brave little peasant girl, who can fend for herself and shows qualities of courage and cleverness, is transformed into a delicate bourgeois type, who is helpless, naive and culpable, if not stupid. In the folk tale the little girl displays a natural, relaxed attitude toward her body and sex and meets the challenge of a would-be seducer. In Perrault's literary fairy tale Little Red Riding Hood is chastised because she is innocently disposed toward nature in the form of the wolf and woods, and she is *raped* or punished because she is guilty of not controlling her natural inclinations.

Guilt was never a question in the original folk tale. The little girl, who meets a werewolf and drinks the blood and eats the flesh of her grandmother, acts out an initiation ritual which has two aspects to it: the pattern of the ritual reflected a specific French peasant tradition and a general 'archaic' belief. In those regions of France, where the tale was popular, the tale was related to the needlework apprenticeship, which young peasant girls underwent, and designated the arrival of puberty and initiation into society.[27] The girl proves that she is mature and strong enough to *replace* the grandmother. This specific tradition is connected to the general archaic belief about witches and wolves as crucial for self-understanding. Hans Peter Duerr has demonstrated that

> in the archaic mentality, the fence, the hedge, which separated the realm of wilderness from that of civilization did not represent limits which were insurpassable. On the contrary, this fence was even torn down at certain times. People who wanted to live within the fence *with awareness* had to leave this enclosure at least once in their lifetime. They had to have roamed the woods as wolves or 'wild persons'. That is, to put it in more modern terms: they had to have experienced the wildness in themselves, their *animal nature*. For their 'cultural nature' was only one side of their being, bound by fate to the animallike *fylgja*, which became visible to those people who went beyond the fence and abandoned themselves to their 'second face'.[28]

In facing the werewolf and temporarily abandoning herself to him, the little girl sees the animal side of her self. She crosses the border between civilization and wilderness, goes beyond the dividing line to face death in order to live. Her return home is a move forward as a whole person. She is a wo/man, self-aware, ready to integrate herself in society *with awareness*.

Such a symbolical ritual expressed in the original folk tale about a strong young woman confused and irritated Perrault. His hostility toward the pagan folk tradition and fear of women were exhibited in all his tales. In *Cinderella* it is important to recall that the different oral folk versions emanated from a matriarchal tradition which depicted the struggles of a young woman (aided by her dead mother as the conserver of society) to regain her stature and rights within society.[29] After Cinderella is humiliated, forced to put on rags, and compelled to perform hard labor, she does not turn her cheek but rebels and struggles to offset her disadvantages. In doing so she *actively* seeks help and uses her wits to attain her goal which is not marriage but recognition. She is not clothed in baroque manner, nor does she wear a glass slipper which could easily break. Rather, she is dressed in a way which will reveal her true identity. The recovering of the lost leather slipper and marriage with the prince is symbolically an affirmation of her strong independent character. In Perrault's literary fairy tale, Cinderella is changed to demonstrate how submissive and industrious she is. Only because she minds her manners is she rescued by a fairy godmother and a prince. Perrault ridicules the folk version while projecting another model of passive femininity which was to be taken seriously by the audience for which he was writing.

Lilyane Mourey has aptly remarked that 'Perrault's suppressions, omissions or additions to the folk tales allow us to conclude that he did not see his task as restoring them in their authenticity. Those stories which he found interesting and amusing became above all the privileged places where the man, the politician and the academician could put his ideas and his fantasies to work in a leisurely way and sometimes to make caricatures. For it is this tone which the moralities assume at times and which emerges from one moment to the next in the tales. This explains why Perrault selected only a small number from the ensemble of the folktale repertory. He retained the tales which "pleased" him, which "attracted" him for infinite and complex reasons because they offered him the possibility to develop (or to indicate at the very least) some of his preoccupations and some of his feelings on a literary, political, and social level. Since women were at the center of his reflections, Perrault spontaneously chose the tales which show the situation of women. The ideal "virtues" of a woman such as Perrault conceived them – beauty, sweetness, kindness, obedience to the husband, dedication to the main- tenance of the home, lack of coquetry, and loyalty – are indissolubly linked with one another and reinforce one another in contrast to the behavior of women whom Perrault denounces, women of the aristocracy and *haute bourgeoisie* with whom he came in contact as reputable civil servant, academician, and *homme de cour.'*[30]

IV

Perrault's social views on manners and morality were not always shared by the other French writers of fairy tales. Yet, despite differences in intention and style, it is significant for the development of the fairy tale for children that there was general agreement in the ideological and aesthetical tendency among them. Here the crucial factor to consider is the social standard to which all French writers subscribed: the literary fairy tale was to be used as a vehicle to discuss proper breeding and behavior exemplified by models drawn from the practice in court society and bourgeois circles and the theoretical writings on manners. Each author distinguished himself or herself by the refined and original contribution he or she made to this discussion. The center of concern was civility, and the fairy-tale discourse reflected variations on this theme and became increasingly moralistic as children were regarded as the major audience.

It is almost impossible to examine the manifold ways in which Perrault's associates employed the literary fairy tale to set standards for civilization. Yet, it is possible to compare different works as representative of the general manner in which traditional motifs were cultivated to express upper-class notions of behavior. Therefore, I want to take one major theme which has received almost uniform treatment up through the present in order to discuss the underlying reasons why it assumed what one could call a 'classical' fairy-tale form. The theme centers on 'beauty and the beast', and the specific tales that I shall discuss will enable us to see the close connections between psychogenetic and sociogenetic civilizing factors as they became embodied by symbolic configurations within the development of the fairy-tale discourse and gave rise to the most widely known version of *Beauty and the Beast*. Only the most prominent tales will be discussed: Perrault's *Ricky of the Tuft* (1696), Mlle Bernard's *Ricky of the Tuft* as related in her novel *Inès de Cordoue* (1696), Madame D'Aulnoy's *Le Mouton* (*The Ram*, 1697), *La Grenouille bienfaisante* (*The Beneficent Frog*, 1697), and *Serpentin Vert* (*The Green Serpent*, 1697), Madame de Villeneuve's *Beauty and the Beast* (1740), and Madame Leprince de Beaumont's *Beauty and the Beast* (1756).

Most discussions of the 'beauty and the beast' cycle have emphasized its positive aspects, particularly those that have studied the psychological implications. For instance, Bruno Bettelheim has asserted that *Beauty and the Beast*

> foreshadows by centuries the Freudian view that sex must be experienced by the child as disgusting as long as his sexual longings are attached to his parent, because only through such a negative attitude toward sex can the incest taboo, and with it the stability of the human family remain secure. But once detached from the parent and directed to a partner of more suitable age, in normal development, sexual longings no longer seem beastly – to the contrary, they are experienced as beautiful.[31]

And Jacques Barchilon seconds this thesis in his comprehensive essay on this subject:

> Not to be afraid of the beast is to make it disappear. This means abandoning infantile fantasies, becoming a woman and accepting a reality which is much more tangible and satisfying than dreams. Beauty matures. She accepts the sexual reality of the beast with lucidity. Thereby, she gets rid of her taboos and infantile fears.[32]

All this sounds very convincing from a contemporary pseudo-Freudian perspective. The analyses, however, are unhistorical and too glib. The pseudo-Freudian approach to literature suggests that children are born with basic fears, anxieties, and wishes. But, if we examine the development of the individual and family in different societies in relation to the civilizing process, we can see that instinctual drives are conditioned and largely determined through interaction and interplay with the social environment. Human sexuality has not been static, and, as Michel Foucault, Norbert Elias, and Jos Van Ussel have demonstrated about the historical development of sexuality,[33] there was an important shift in European attitudes in the sixteenth and seventeenth centuries so that the open display of sex and bodily functions gradually became curtailed. Restriction and revulsion toward frank sexual behavior replaced open acceptance of sexual and bodily functions. The roles of males and females became more rigidly defined: men became more closely associated with reason, temperance, activism, and sovereign order; females became more identified with irrationality, whimsy, passivity, and subversive deviance.

From an historical psychological point of view, one which endeavors to trace the connections between the psychogenetic and sociogenetic factors, the fairy tale assumes great importance because it reveals how social mores and values were induced in part through literature and constituted determinants in the rearing of an individual child. The 'beauty and the beast' tales were not and are not important in the civilizing process because they enabled and enable children and adults to overcome 'natural' psychic conflicts and to accept their innate sexuality. On the contrary, they were and are important because they set standards for sexual and social conduct which complied with inhibiting forms of socialization and were to be internalized by the readers and auditors of the tales. Though the narrative perspective may vary, the starting point for the discourse on manners through fairy tales affirms the dominant Christian absolutist view regarding the regulation of inner and outer nature in favor of male hegemony and rationalized industry.

If we compare those oral folk tales about the animal bridegroom, which stem from matriarchal societies, with those literary fairy tales about 'beauty and the beast' at the end of the seventeenth century, it becomes evident that the transformations in the portrayal of sexual configurations and cultural patterns were connected to significant changes within the civilization process itself. As Heide Göttner-Abendroth has shown, the man is

> a wild, roving beast (wolf, bear, horse, raven, swan) in most of the animal bridegroom tales, and this condition represents his homelessness and undomesticity. That is, in the eyes of the matriarchal woman, who created a cultivated environment for herself, he has never developed beyond the condition of a predatory animal that roams the woods. He is still covered by fur or feathers, while she wears human clothes which she herself has made. The male condition as human is not yet extant, or it is one of 'death', which is the meaning of the state of 'enchantment' as

beast. The transformation into an animal is likened to death and is the male condition, and it is worse than that of the female because it does not mean initiation into a higher form of life. Rather the male has not yet reached the cultural level of the human (= woman). It is up to the woman to bring him salvation by making human clothes for him and accepting him into her house as a domesticated inhabitant.[34]

The symbolical cultural pattern of matriarchy, which designated the female as initiator of human action and integration, experienced constant changes over the course of centuries in both the oral and literary tradition. The result was that, by the end of the seventeenth century, the original female bringer of salvation could only find her own 'true' salvation by sacrificing herself to a man in his house or castle, symbolical of submission to patriarchal rule.

As the most famous and perhaps the most talented fairy-tale writer at the end of the seventeenth century, Perrault continued the patriarchal cycling of 'beauty and the beast' in a form that was to be emulated by many other writers of his time. Although he did not employ an animal bridegroom in his tale *Ricky of the Tuft*, we do know that he based his story partly on Apuleius' *Cupid and Psyche* of the second century and Straporola's tale *Re Porco* of the sixteenth century, to demonstrate the superiority of male intelligence over feminine beauty.[35] What needs to be stressed about Perrault's tale is his insistence that the female cannot behave civilly or live happily without the male to temper her. Even when given the power of reason, or rather, particularly when given the power of reason, the female is dangerous. Perrault's princess wants to break her promise to the hideous Ricky because she realizes that she can win the favors of a more handsome man and perhaps be more satisfied. Thus, Ricky must exercise all the powers of his superior reason to convince her rationally that she now has it within her 'discretion and good qualities of her soul and mind'[36] to regard him in a more pleasing light: the beast is really true nobility. In sum, Perrault's tale presents a 'civilized' version of the taming of the shrew whereby the female must learn to deny her sexual urges and subordinate her wishes and drives to please the reasonable male who knows what is best for her. Though ugly and misshapen, he endows her life with the spiritual discipline and dignity it would otherwise lack.

If we examine this fairy tale in its historical context, then it becomes evident why it fits sociologically and psychologically into the civilizing process. First, younger women of bourgeois and aristocratic circles were constantly being forced into marriages of convenience with elderly men, who were not always physically appealing or likeable. Secondly, women had become equated with potential witchlike figures by the end of the seventeenth century so that control of their alleged sexual powers of seduction was linked by church and state to control of diabolical forces.[37] Thirdly, open sexuality had become a clandestine affair, that is, it was to be hidden and privatized because the church had ordained sex without marriage a sin and repulsive. As we know, a properly groomed child was to learn to fear and find sex disgusting. Finally, instead of projecting the female's fear of sexuality, the tale depicts Perrault's own fear of women and perhaps of his own sexual drives which he disguised so that he could accept them in a more 'civilized' form. From his fears and desires he shaped the configurations of the fairy tale to engender an aesthetic–ideological constellation of dependable and temperant male governance over whimsical female naiveté.

Perrault's projection of the beauty and beast constellation must be linked to the peculiar and dubious views he held on sexuality and manners. However, he was not idiosyncratic. In fact, his opinions were shared by many of his peers, and furthermore, they were fervently endorsed by many a literary lady. The very year before Perrault published his tale, Mlle Bernard included a different version of *Riquet à la Houppe* in her novel *Inès de Cordoue*. A relative of Corneille and Fontenelle, and a respected writer in her own right, Mlle Bernard was well-known and associated in the same circles as Perrault, and there is some speculation as to whether she influenced him. That is, however, somewhat irrelevant since the topic had already become a subject of social and cultural discourse. La Fontaine published his version of the classical story of *Psyche and Cupid* in 1669. In 1670 Molière and Corneille used the story as the basis for a tragic ballet in five acts first performed at court in 1670 and subsequently in public in 1671. What is significant is that both Mlle Bernard and Perrault employed the same literary constellation to engage in a discourse on manners which was to become part of the fairy-tale heritage for children. Moreover, Mlle Bernard appears to have identified with the oppressed heroine and to have had male assistance in writing her tale.[38]

Her plot differs in a unique and fascinating way from Perrault's. The story begins as follows:

> A great nobleman of Grenada, who possessed all the riches worthy of his birth, was grieved by a domestic tragedy which poisoned everything constituting his fortune. His only daughter, born with all the traits which make for beauty, was so stupid that her beauty itself only rendered her more disagreeable. Her actions were without grace. Her figure, though slender, was heavy because it lacked a soul in its body.[39]

The task set by the narrative concerns the acquisition of a 'soul' or 'reason' for Mama, which is the name given to the princess. One day she encounters a hideous creature, Ricky of the Tuft, who is king of the gnomes. Since he is aware of her difficulties, he offers her intelligence if she will marry him after a year. Obviously she accepts, not realizing that she will fall in love with a young man named Arada. After a year has elapsed, her relationship with Arada makes her unwilling to marry Ricky, who, despite his beastly appearence, is a gentleman and gives her a choice: either she can return to her father's kingdom where she will resume being stupid, or she can retain her acquired intelligence and live with him in his splendid underground kingdom as queen of the gnomes. She decides to marry him, and her intelligence increases to the point that she can easily continue her clandestine affair with Arada. When Ricky discovers this, he punishes her by making her stupid during the day and intelligent during the night. She responds by continuing her affair in the evening. Finally, Ricky takes his vengeance by transforming Arada into his twin, and the queen must spend the rest of her life unable to make a distinction between husband and lover. In fact, she must learn to accept the reasonable rule of ugliness.

In many respects Mlle Bernard is more harsh in her treatment of the female figure and more severe in insisting on proper forms of civilizing young people than Perrault. The princess becomes wily, deceitful, and sexual once she has the brains to match her beauty. She can hardly be tamed. Ricky's superiority resides in the power of his mind to transform things. He is fair in his treatment of her, and he acts vengefully after it becomes apparent to him that his wife can only be domesticated when deprived of free will. The message delivered by this tale states unequivocally that women must be placed under constant surveillance even when they are endowed with reason to temper their appetites: they are potentially destructive and may be harmful to civil order.

Madame D'Aulnoy elaborates on this topic in one of her beauty and the beast tales entitled *The Ram*. Here Merveilleuse, the youngest daughter of a king, must flee the court under threat of death because the king wrongly thinks that she is insolent. Lost in a forest she encounters a talking ram, a prince, who had been transformed into an animal by the evil fairy Ragotte. He provides asylum for Merveilleuse in grand and civil fashion. Gradually she learns to love the beast and intends to wait five years when his sentence of enchantment will end and he can resume human form. However, she learns that her sister is to be married and desires to attend the wedding celebration. The ram gives her permission to visit her home providing that she promises to return. Otherwise, he will perish. She gives him her word and returns. Yet, when her second sister marries, she goes home again, and the joyous reconciliation with her father makes her forget the ram who dies as a result of her neglect, and his death causes her the 'greatest misery'[40] at her happiest moment.

D'Aulnoy depicts both the negative and positive power of beauty. When docile and obedient, it can benefit male nobility. On the other hand, when it loses control over itself, beauty can destroy domestic tranquility and masculine dignity. The well-groomed lady must never forget her self-sacrificing and submissive function in her relationship with a lord, no matter how ugly he may be. It is a mark of social distinction when a beautiful lady is willing to abandon herself to a monster to save other people. This is evident in D'Aulnoy's fairy tale *The Beneficent Frog*, in which Princess Moufette reveals her constancy through her readiness to be eaten by a dragon. Of course, she is saved by her fiancé Prince Moufy, and the dragon, too, turns out to be a noble lord, who exhibits fine manners when his bestial shell disappears.

D'Aulnoy's most classic statement on the beauty and beast theme is in *The Green Serpent*. Not only does she have her heroine Laidronette read the story about *Psyche and Cupid* to learn a lesson, but she also masterly weaves motifs from such other tales as *Sleeping Beauty* into the plot to create a marvelous model of prudence for young women. Laidronette has many adventures and learns to deal with her ugliness and overcome her imprudent curiosity. For her good sense and behavior she is rewarded by the good fairy Protectrice in a double manner: first, she is transformed into a beautiful woman and given the name Queen Discrete; then she is allowed to sacrifice herself for the Green Serpent, who is transformed into a noble prince, the saved as savior.

All D'Aulnoy's fairy tales provide moral lessons, and the ones which involve 'beauty and the beast' reiterate the message of Perrault's tales. The woman must be constantly chastised for her curiosity, unreliability, and whimsy. True beauty depends on prudence and discretion which is figuratively depicted by the heroine either sacrificing herself to a male beast or submitting to his commands and wishes because he has a noble soul and civil manners. The hidden message in all these tales is a dictum which the women of D'Aulnoy's time including D'Aulnoy herself[41] had to obey or else face degradation and ostracism: control your natural inclinations and submit to the fate which male social standards decree. Civility meant enduring the anguish of self-denial because men sought to rationalize their fear of women, sexuality, and equality by establishing regulations that deprived women and other oppressed groups of self-expression and independence. There are some signs in D'Aulnoy's works that she sought to criticize artibrary male behavior, but, for the most part, she compromised herself under great social pressure. Indeed, the sad state of the dark side of the classical fairy tales is that women writers themselves gave more expression to male needs and hegemony than their own.

The two most classic examples of this self-abnegation are the fairy tales entitled *La Belle et la Bête* by Mme de Villeneuve and Mme Leprince de Beaumont published respectively in 1740 and 1756. The basic plot is the same in both versions which are didactic discourses on manners, morals, and social class. The general narrative line depicts the fortunes of a very rich merchant whose children (six boys and six girls in Villeneuve's story and three boys and three girls in Beaumont's) become spoiled and arrogant because of the family's accumulation of wealth. Indeed, with the exception of Beauty, all the children aspire beyond their class. Hence, this eminently *'nouveau riche'*, bourgeois family must be taught a lesson. The merchant loses his money and social prestige, and the children are compelled to adjust to hard work on a country estate which is the only property left to the family's name. The boys are diligent, but the daughters resent the fact that they must perform menial chores, cannot wear fancy clothes, and attend balls. They remain haughty, arrogant, and vain. Only Beauty, the youngest, exhibits modesty and self-sacrificial tendencies. In addition, she displays how industrious and good tempered she can be during these trying times. When her father takes a trip to recoup the family fortune and finds himself in danger of losing his life because he transgresses against the beast (i.e. nobility), Beauty as model of humility and obedience saves her father by agreeing to live with the monster. Later, impressed by the civilty and noble nature of the beast (appearances are obviously deceiving, i.e. male aristocrats may look like beasts, but they have gentle hearts and kind manners), she develops a great affection for him. Yet, it is only after she visits her family and almost causes the beast's death by her long departure that she realizes she loves him and is willing to marry him. Suddenly he is transformed into a handsome prince and explains that he had been condemned to remain a beast until a beautiful, virtuous virgin should consent to wed him. As usual, marriage is the ultimate reward for a good girl's behavior, whereas the man not only acquires a bride but has his rights and property restored to him as a sovereign. In other words, his virility is confirmed and no longer placed in jeopardy.

Generally speaking the longer version of *Beauty and the Beast* by Mme de Villeneuve is either ignored or considered irrelevant when compared with the more concise rendition by Mme Leprince de

Beaumont which is more popular and often considered superior. Both tales are, however, fascinating in their own right, and a comparison between the two will demonstrate how consciously both authors cultivated their tales to participate in the discourse about the civilizing process. At the outset it is important to stress that Mme Leprince de Beaumont wrote her fairy tale sixteen years after the appearance of Mme de Villeneuve's version and that it was purposely shortened and made moralistic so that it could better serve to improve the manners of upper-class youngsters when it was published in her *Magasin des enfants, ou dialogues entre une sage gouvernante et plusieurs de ses élèves de la première distinction.* In 1758 a German translation appeared entitled *Der Frau Maria le Prince de Beaumont Lehren der Tugend und Weisheit für die Jugend,* and three years later an English version was printed in *The Young Misses Magazine.* Since then it has served as the primary model for most modern 'beauty and the beast' adaptations in the western world.

Whereas Mme Leprince de Beaumont represented a social perspective on breeding which was very much open to the alliance of the bourgeoisie and aristocracy (thus guaranteeing its future success), Mme de Villeneuve was more rigid in delineating class behavior and propriety. Her tale, which exceeded three hundred pages in its original publication in *La Jeune Amériquaine et les contes marins,* was directed largely at adults and contained elaborate descriptions of the beast's court and remarkable psychological digressions in the form of dreams. There are also several points in the plot and contents which diverge from Mme Leprince de Beaumont's tale. Beauty's sisters are described in a negative way as indolent, petty, and jealous, but they are not punished, nor are they used as exact counterparts since it turns out they do not come from the same social class. The beast does not simply ask Beauty to marry him. Rather, he asks her to sleep with him. She refuses, and his discreet manner of respecting her wishes makes a great impression on her. Moreover, he appears to her in dreams and wins her spiritual love. When she finally does consent to sleep with him, they do not have sexual intercourse, for that would be contrary to decorum which called for the consecration of marriage. Besides, there is an important anti-climax here. The beast's queen mother arrives with the good fairy. The beast is transformed into a handsome prince, but then his mother protests against the *mésalliance,* even though Beauty is most virtuous. There is a long discussion between the good fairy, the mother, Beauty and the prince as to whether the daughter of a merchant, no matter how chaste, prudent, modest, and obedient, is worthy enough to become the wife of a prince of royal blood. The problem is eventually solved when the fairy reveals that Beauty is in actuality of noble blood and was given to the merchant to be raised for her own safekeeping. Revealed in all her majesty, Beauty now bestows her blessings on the members of her adopted bourgeois family (including her nasty stepsisters) and rewards them with money, position, and proper mates.

The constellation is altered somewhat in Mme Leprince de Beaumont's tale. She is actually more rigorous and demanding on a moral and ethical scale. She approves of the alliance between the bourgeoisie and aristocracy, but then demands even stricter adherence to the dominant social code. She makes her views known through stark contrasts and pithy descriptions of proper behavior.[42] Beauty is designed to conform in the perfect bourgeois, virtuous fashion, and the Beast embodies all the genteel and dignified characteristics of the nobility. Here he does not ask to sleep with Beauty but politely requests that she become his wife. When she finally accepts, the beautiful fairy presents the handsome prince to her in this manner: 'Come and receive the reward of your judicious choice; you have preferred virtue before either wit or beauty, and deserve to find a person in whom all these qualifications are united: you are going to be a great queen, I hope the throne will not lessen your virtue or make you forget yourself.'[43] In contrast, her sisters are transformed into statues and placed by the gates to the royal couple's estate to warn against the evils of maliciousness and envy.

Social deviates, such as the sisters, are brutally punished, and it is even possible to interpret the fortunes of the merchant's clan as a test of a bourgeois family in danger of overstepping the bounds of propriety. The rational expectations of the narrative perspective call for an internalization of the Christian–rationalistic normative pattern to foster social notions of aesthetics and virtues which all children were to accept, especially young girls. Mme Leprince de Beaumont spent approximately twenty years as a governess in London where she taught young girls and wrote prolifically on the subject of manners. In addition to *Beauty and the Beast*, she wrote other fairy tales such as *Prince Spirituel*, similar to *Ricky of the Tuft*, and numerous stories which preached feminine submissiveness. As Barchilon has remarked: 'This feminine submissiveness undoubtedly demands an explanation. Mme Leprince de Beaumont addressed an audience of young girls in pre-puberty and always took care to insist on this note of submissiveness. She wanted to prepare them for ''life'' that is for marriage ordained according to the normally accepted bourgeois conventions.'[44]

There is a distinct cultural pattern which emerges when we examine the treatment of the beauty and beast theme from Charles Perrault and

Mlle Catherine Bernard to Mme Leprince de Beaumont or from 1696 to 1756. What began as a fairy-tale discourse on manners with examples set for adults and children developed into a fairy-tale sermon primarily for children. There is no more room for critical discourse after Mme de Villeneuve's version of *Beauty and the Beast*: a distinct constellation becomes fixed as a classical set of rules and behavior for proper boys and girls in Mme Leprince Beaumont's tale. Temperance and rationality reign in the end. The mark of beauty for a female is to be found in her submission, obedience, humility, industry, and patience; the mark of manliness is to be found in his self-control, politeness, reason, and perseverance. Moreover, as the configurations were developed individually in each 'beauty and the beast' tale in relation to the civilizing process, it became clear that the female character could only assume her 'civil' form if she were willing to sacrifice herself for a beastlike male. By denying herself, she could obtain what all women supposedly wanted and want – namely marriage in the form of male domination. The male character could only assume his 'civil' form when socially deviant forces were tamed and when the female was not a threat but was actually charmed or tranquilized by his rationality. Interestingly, the woman has the power to save or destroy the man who always represents civility and rationality. The male protagonist is *never* responsible for the world being out of joint. Each tale depicts him as a victim (generally transfigured by a wicked female fairy) and a model of bourgeois *raisonnement*.

Yet, as we have seen, there is a dark side to this bourgeois *raisonnement* as it manifests itself in the civilizing process and in the origins of the literary fairy-tale tradition for children in western culture. In the case of *Beauty and the Beast* the classical constellation was carried in different forms by Charles Lamb's poetical version in 1811 and by the Brothers Grimm in their 1812 and 1815 editions of *Household Tales: The Frog Prince, King of the Golden Mountain, Bearskin,* and *Snow White* and *Rosebud*. The nineteenth century saw a proliferation of *Beauty and the Beast* narratives as broadsheet, abridged moralistic tale for the masses, and drama. It reached its 'classical' highpoint in Sir Arthur Quiller-Couch's adaptation. In the twentieth century there have been countless *Beauty and the Beast* stories, plays, operas, musicals, and films, the most famous of which is Jean Cocteau's *La Belle et la Bête* (1946). We continue to celebrate the charm and grace of this tale and others similar to it which have come down to us in our literary heritage. We continue to enjoy this harmless pastime of telling classical fairy tales to our children not realizing the possible harm of harmlessness.

Notes

1   *Centuries of Childhood: A Social History of Family Life* (New York: Knopf, 1962), p. 43.

2   The two most significant studies of this vogue are Mary Elizabeth Storer, *La Mode des contes des fées (1685-1700)* (Paris: Champion, 1928) and Jacques Barchilon, *Le Conte merveilleux français de 1690 à 1790* (Paris: Champion, 1975). Both include extensive bibliographies on the subject.

3   Cf. Gonthier-Louis Fink, *Naissance et apogée du conte merveilleux en Allemagne 1740-1800* (Paris: Annales Littéraires de l'université de Besançon, 1966) and Jack Zipes, *Breaking the Magic Spell: Radical Theories of Folk and Fairy Tales* (London: Heinemann, 1979). See esp. Chapters II and III.

4   *Contes de Perrault*, ed. by Gilbert Rouger (Paris: Garnier, 1967), p. 3. All translations in this chapter are my own unless otherwise indicated.

5   *Ibid.*, pp. 5-6.

6   *Ibid.*, p. 89.

7   *The Authentic Mother Goose Fairy Tales and Nursery Rhymes*, ed. by Jacques Barchilon and Henry Petit (Denver: Swallow, 1960), pp. iv-v.

8   *The History of Manners*, trans. by Edmund Jephcott, Vol. I (New York: Urizen, 1978). The second volume has yet to appear. This fascinating study was first published as *Über den Prozess der Zivilisation* (Basel: Haus zum Falken, 1939) and received scant attention because of World War II and the author's difficulties during emigration. It was rediscovered and reissued in 1969 by Francke Verlag in Bern. Since then it has had a profound influence on major European sociologists and historians. See the essays by Wolf Lepenies, 'Norbert Elias: an outsider of unprejudiced insight,' pp. 57-64 and Andreas Wehowsky, 'Making ourselves more flexible than we are - reflections on Norbert Elias,' pp. 65-82, and the review by George Mosse, pp. 178-83, all in *New German Critique*, **15** (fall, 1978).

9   *Cinéma et politique* (Paris: Seghers, 1974), p. 138.

10 *The Civilizing Process* (New York: Urizen, 1978), p. xiii.

11 The most thorough and stimulating account of Perrault's life and works is Marc Soriano's *Les Contes de Perrault, Culture savante et traditions populaires* (Paris: Gallimard, 1968). See also his other book *Le Dossier Perrault* (Paris: Hachette, 1972).

12 *The Civilizing Process*, p. 36. See also Donata Elschenbroich, *Kinder werden nicht geboren* (Bensheim: päd. extra, 1980).

13 *Ibid.*, pp. 59-143.

14 *Ibid.*, p. 108.

15 Cf. Andrea Dworkin, *Woman Hating* (New York: Dutton, 1974); Claudia Honnegger, *Die Hexen der Neuzeit. Studien zur Sozialgeschichte eines kulturellen Deutungsmusters* (Frankfurt am Main: Suhrkamp, 1978); Sylvia Bovenschen, 'The contemporary witch, the historical witch, and the witch myth,' *New German Critique*, **15** (fall, 1978), pp. 83-120; Hans Peter Duerr, *Traumzeit. Über die Grenze Zwischen Wildnis und Zivilisation* (Frankfurt am Main: Syndikat, 1978), pp. 13-90.

16 'The European witch-craze of the sixteenth and seventeenth centuries,' in *Religion, the Reformation and Social Change* (London: Macmillan, 1967), pp. 90-192.

17 Cf. Michel Foucault, *Discipline and Punish* (New York: Pantheon, 1979).

18 Cf. Rudolf Zur Lippe, *Naturbeherrschung am Menschen*, 2 vols. (Frankfurt am Main: Suhrkamp, 1974).

19 *The Civilizing Process*, p. 143.

20 *Introduction aux Contes de Grimm et de Perrault* (Paris: Minard, 1978), p. 40.

21 *Contes de Perrault*, p. 102.

22 I have endeavored to develop this concept more thoroughly in my book *Breaking the Magic Spell: Radical Theories of Folk and Fairy Tales*.

23   Cf. Paul Delarue, 'Le petit chaperon rouge,' in *Le Conte Populaire Français*, Vol. I (Paris: Editions Erasme, 1957), pp. 337–8; Marianne Rumpf, 'Rotkäppchen. Eine vergleichende Märchenuntersuchung' (Diss. Universität Göttingen, 1951) and 'Ursprung und Entstehung von Warn-und Schreckmärchen,' *FF Communications*, **160** (1955), pp. 3–16; Marc Soriano, 'From tales of warning to formulettes: the oral tradition in French children's literature,' *Yale French Studies*, **43** (1969), pp. 24–43; Jack Zipes, *The Trials and Tribulations of Little Red Riding Hood* (London: Heinemann, 1982).

24   See Elliott O'Donell, *Werewolves* (London: Methuen, 1912); Konrad Müller, *Die Werwolfsage* (Karlsruhe: Macklotsche, 1937); and Montague Summers, *The Werewolf* (Hyde Park: University Books, 1966).

25   *Ibid.*

26   *The Borzoi Book of French Folk Tales* (New York: Knopf, 1956), p. 383.

27   Yvonne Verdier, 'Grands-mères, sie vous saviez: le Petit Chaperon Rouge dans la tradition orale,' *Cahiers de Littérature Orale*, 4 (1978), pp. 17–55.

28   *Traumzeit*, p. 82 (op. cit., note 15).

29   For an exhaustive study of the countless *Cinderella* versions, see Marian Roalfe Cox, *Cinderella. Three Hundred and Forty-five Variants* (London: Publications of the Folklore Society, 1892). Most important is Jane Yolen's article, 'America's Cinderella,' *Children's Literature in Education*, **8** (1977), pp. 21–9. Yolen emphasizes that the positive depiction of Cinderella as an active heroine in the folk tradition becomes warped by Perrault's time. The matriarchal basis of the tale is confirmed in August Nitschke's *Soziale Ordnungen im Spiegel der Märchen*, 2 vols. (Stuttgart: Fromann-Holzboog, 1977) and in Heide Göttner-Abendroth's *Die Göttin und ihr Heros* (Munich: Frauenoffensive, 1980).

30   *Introduction aux contes de Grimm et de Perrault*, p. 36.

31   *The Uses of Enchantment* (New York: Knopf, 1976), pp. 307–08.

32   *Le Conte merveilleux francais de 1690 à 1790*, p. 10.

33   Cf. Foucault's *The History of Sexuality* (New York: Pantheon, 1979); Elias' *The Civilizing Process*; and van Ussel's *Sexualunterdrückung: Geschichte der Sexualfeindschaft* (Giessen: Focus, 1977).

34   'Matriarchale mythologie', in *Weiblich-Männlich*, ed. by Brigitte Wartmann (Berlin: Ästhetik & Kommunikation, 1980), p. 224. See also her book, *Die Göttin und ihr Heros*, pp. 134–71.

35   Cf. Detlev Fehling, *Armor und Psyche: Die Schöpfung des Apuleius und ihre Einwirkung auf das Märchen* (Wiesbaden: Steiner, 1977).

36   *Contes de Perrault*, p. 180.

37   See Claudia Honegger, *Die Hexen der Neuzeit* and Sylvia Bovenschen, 'The contemporary witch, the historical witch, and the witch myth' (op. cit., note 15).

38   See Jeanne Roche-Mazon, *Autor des contes de fées* (Paris: Didier, 1968), pp. 61–91.

39   'Riquet à la houppe', in *Contes de fées du grand siècle*, ed. by Mary Elizabeth Storer (New York: Publications of the Institute of French Studies, Columbia University, 1934), p. 78.

40   *D'Aulnoy's Fairy Tales* (Philadelphia: McKay, 1923), pp. 238–9.

41   Madame D'Aulnoy had great difficulties with her own husband, whom she found extremely disagreeable. She accused him of a crime and brought him to trial. The case turned against her, however, and she was banished from Paris. Two of her accomplices in the conspiracy against her husband were beheaded. Another one of her friends, Madame Ticquet, was executed for killing her own husband. Somehow Mme D'Aulnoy was involved in this murder and barely escaped with her life. See Storer, *La Mode des contes de fées*, pp. 18–41 and Jeanne Roche-Mazon, *En marge de 'l'Oiseau bleu'* (Paris: L'Artisan du Livre, 1930) and the chapter, 'Le voyage d'Espagne de Madame D'Aulnoy,' in *Autor des contes de fées*, pp. 7–20.

42 For instance, when the merchant and his family move to the country, Mme Leprince de Beaumont remarks:
In the beginning she [Beauty] found it very difficult, for she had not been used to work as a servant, but in less than two months she grew stronger and healthier than ever. After she had done her work, she read, played on the harpsichord, or else sung whilst she spun. On the contrary, her two sisters did not know how to spend their time; they got up at ten, and did nothing but saunter about the whole day, lamenting the loss of their fine clothes and acquaintances. Do but see our youngest sister, said they, one to the other, what a poor, stupid mean-spirited creature she is, to be contented with such an unhappy dismal situation. The good merchant was of a quite different opinion, he knew very well that Beauty outshone her sisters, in her person as well as her mind, and admired her humility and industry, but above all her humility and patience; for her sisters not only left her all the work of the house to do, but insulted her every moment.
See Iona and Peter Opie, *The Classic Fairy Tales* (New York: Oxford University Press, 1974), p. 183.

43 *Ibid.*, p. 195.

44 *Le Conte merveilleux francais de 1690 à 1790*, p. 92.

3 Who's Afraid of the Brothers Grimm? Socialization and Politicization through Fairy Tales

The wolf, now piously old and good,
When again he met Red Riding Hood
Spoke: 'Incredible, my dear child,
What kinds of stories are spread – they're wild.

As though there were, so the lie is told,
A dark murder affair of old.
The Brothers Grimm are the ones to blame.
Confess! It wasn't half as bad as they claim.'

Little Red Riding Hood saw the wolf's bite
And stammered: 'You're right, quite right.'
Whereupon the wolf, heaving many a sigh,
Gave kind regards to Granny and waved good-bye.

Rudolf Otto Wiemer
The Old Wolf (1976)

Over 170 years ago the Brothers Grimm began collecting original folk tales in Germany and stylized them into potent literary fairy tales. Since then these tales have exercised a profound influence on children and adults alike throughout the western world. Indeed, whatever form fairy tales in general have taken since the original publication of the Grimms' narratives in 1812, the Brothers Grimm have been continually looking over our shoulders and making their presence felt. For most people this has not been so disturbing. However, during the last fifteen years there has been a growing radical trend to overthrow the Grimms' benevolent rule in fairy-tale land by writers who believe that the Grimms' stories contribute to the creation of a false consciousness and reinforce an authoritarian socialization process. This trend has appropriately been set by writers in the very homeland of the Grimms, where literary revolutions have always been more common than real political ones.[1]

West German writers[2] and critics have come to regard the Grimms' fairy tales and those of Andersen, Bechstein, and their imitators as 'secret agents' of an education establishment which indoctrinates children to learn fixed roles and functions within bourgeois society, thus curtailing their free development.[3] This attack on the conservatism of the 'classical' fairy tales was mounted in the 1960s, when numerous writers began using them as models to write innovative, emancipatory tales, more critical of changing conditions in advanced technological societies based on capitalist production and social relations. What became apparent to these writers and critics was that the Grimms' tales, though ingenious and perhaps socially relevant in their own times, contained sexist and racist attitudes and served a socialization process which placed great emphasis on passivity, industry, and self-sacrifice for girls and on activity, competition, and accumulation of wealth for boys. Therefore, contemporary West German writers moved in a different, more progressive direction by parodying and revising the fairy tales of the eighteenth and nineteenth centuries, especially those of the Grimms.

For the most part, the 'classical' fairy tales have been reutilized or what the Germans call *umfunktioniert*: the *function* of the tales has been literally turned around so that the perspective, style, and motifs of the narratives expose contradictions in capitalist society and awaken children to other alternatives for pursuing their goals and developing autonomy. The reutilized tales *function against* conformation to the standard socialization process and are meant to *function for* a different, more emancipatory society which can be gleaned from the redirected socialization process symbolized in the new tales. The quality and radicalism of these new tales vary from author to author.[4] And it may even be that many of the writers are misguided, despite their good intentions. Nevertheless, they have raised questions about the sociopolitical function of fairy tales, and just this question-raising alone is significant. Essentially they reflect upon and seek to understand how the messages in fairy tales tend to repress and constrain children rather than set them free to make their own choices. They assume that the Grimms' fairy tales have been fully accepted in all western societies and have ostensibly been used or misused in furthering the development of human beings – to make them more functional within the capitalist system and to prescribe choice. If one shares a critique of capitalist society, what then should be changed in the Grimms' tales to suggest other possibilities? What sociogenetic structural process forms the fairy tales and informs the mode by which the human character is socialized in capitalist society?

Before looking at the literary endeavors made by West German writers to answer these questions, it is important to discuss the nature of the Grimms' fairy tales and the notion of socialization through fairy tales. Not only have creative writers been at work to reutilize the fairy tales, but there have been a host of progressive critics who have uncovered important historical data about the Grimms' tales and have explored the role that these stories have played in the socialization process.

I

Until recently it was generally assumed that the Grimm Brothers collected their oral folk tales mainly from peasants and day laborers, that they merely altered and refined the tales while remaining true to their perspective and meaning. Both assumptions have been proven false.[5] The Grimms gathered their tales primarily from petit bourgeois or educated middle-class people, who had already introduced bourgeois notions into their versions. In all cases the Grimms did more than simply change and improve the style of the tales: they expanded them and made substantial changes in characters and meaning. Moreover, they excluded many other well-known tales from their collection, and their entire process of selection reflected the bias of their philosophical and political point of view. Essentially, the Grimm Brothers contributed to the literary 'bourgeoisification' of oral tales which had belonged to the peasantry and lower classes and had been informed by the interests and aspirations of these groups. This is not to say that they purposely sought to betray the heritage of the common people in Germany. On the contrary, their intentions were honorable: they wanted the rich cultural tradition of the common people to be used and accepted by the rising middle classes. It is for this reason that they spent their lives conducting research on myths, customs, and the language of the German people. They wanted to foster the development of a strong national bourgeoisie by unravelling the ties to Germanic traditions and social rites and by drawing on related lore from France and central and northern Europe. Wherever possible, they sought to link the beliefs and behavior of characters in the folk tales to the cultivation of bourgeois norms.

> It was into this nineteenth century where a bourgeois sense for family had been developed that the Grimms' fairy tales made their entrance: as the book read to children by mothers and grandmothers and as reading for the children themselves. The Grimms countered the pedagogical doubts from the beginning with the argument that the fairy-tale book was written both for children and for adults, but not for the badly educated

. . . The enormous amount of editions and international circulation of the Grimms' fairy tales as literary fairy tales can also be explained by their bourgeois circle of consumers. Here is where the circle closes. Aside from the questionable nature of the 'ancient Germanic' or even 'pure Hessian' character of the collection, we must consider and admire the genial talents of the Brothers, who were able to fuse random and hetero-geneous material transmitted over many years into the harmonious totality of the *Children and Household Tales*. They were thus able to bring about a work which was both 'bourgeois' and 'German' and fully corresponded to the scientific temper and emotional taste of their times. The general room for identification provided for the bourgeoisie com-pletely encompassed the virtues of a national way of thinking and German folk spirit, and the Grimms' *Children and Household Tales* contained all this in the most superb way. Its success as a book cannot be explained without knowledge of the social history of the nineteenth century.[6]

The sources of the tales were European, old Germanic, and bourgeois. The audience was a growing middle-class one. The Grimms saw a mission in the tales and were bourgeois missionaries. And, although they never preached or sought to convert in a crass manner, they did modify the tales much more than we have been led to believe. Their collection went through seven editions during their own lifetime and was constantly enlarged and revised. Wilhelm Grimm, the more conservative of the two brothers, did most of the revisions, and it is commonly known that he endeavored to clean up the tales and make them more respectable for bourgeois children – even though the original publication was not expressly intended for children. The Grimms collected the tales not only to 'do a service to the history of poetry and mythology,' but their intention was to write a book that could provide pleasure and learning.[7] They called their edition of 1819 an '*Erziehungsbuch*' (an educational book) and discussed the manner in which they made the stories more pure, truthful and just. In the process they carefully eliminated those passages which they thought would be harmful for children's eyes.[8] This became a consistent pattern in the revisions after 1819. Once the tales had seen the light of print, and, once they were deemed appropriate for middle-class audiences, Wilhelm consistently tried to meet audience expectations. And the reading audience of Germany was becoming more *Biedermeier* or Victorian in its morals and ethics. As moral sanitation man, Wilhelm set high standards, and his example has been followed by numerous 'educators,' who have watered down and cleaned up the tales from the nineteenth century up to the present.

Thanks to the 1975 re-publication of the neglected 1810 handwritten manuscript side by side with the published edition of the tales of 1812 by

Heinz Rölleke, we can grasp the full import of the sanitation process in relation to socialization. We can see how each and every oral tale was conscientiously and, at times, drastically changed by the Grimms. For our purposes I want to comment on three tales to show how different types of changes relate to gradual shifts in the norms and socialization process reflecting the interests of the bourgeoisie. Let us begin with the opening of *The Frog Prince* and compare the 1810 manuscript with the editions of 1812 and 1857.

1810 Manuscript
The king's daughter went into the woods and sat down next to a cool well. Then she took a golden ball and began playing with it until it suddenly rolled down into the well. She watched it fall to the bottom from the edge of the well and was very sad. Suddenly a frog stuck his head out of the water and said: 'Why are you complaining so?' 'Oh, you nasty frog, you can't help me at all. My golden ball has fallen into the well.' Then the frog said: 'If you take me home with you, I'll fetch your golden ball for you.'[9]

1812 Edition
Once upon a time there was a king's daughter who went into the woods and sat down next to a cool well. She had a golden ball with her that was her most cherished toy. She threw it high into the air and caught it and enjoyed this very much. One time the ball went high into the air. She had already stretched out her hand and curled her fingers to catch the ball when it fell by her side onto the ground and rolled and rolled right into the water.

The king's daughter looked at it in horror. The well was so deep that it was impossible to see the bottom. She began to cry miserably and complain: 'Oh! I would give anything if only I could have my ball again! My clothes, my jewels, my pearls and whatever I could find in the world.' While she was complaining, a frog stuck his head out of the water and said: 'Princess, why are you lamenting so pitifully?' 'Oh,' she said, 'you nasty frog, you can't help me! My golden ball has fallen into the well.' The frog said: 'I won't demand your pearls, your jewels, and your clothes, but if you accept me as your companion, and if you let me sit next to you at your table and eat from your golden plate and sleep in your bed, and if you cherish and love me, then I'll fetch your ball for you.'[10]

1857 Edition
In olden times when making wishes still helped, there lived a king whose

daughters were all beautiful, but the youngest was so beautiful that the sun itself, who has seen so much, was astonished by her beauty each time it lit upon her face. Near the royal castle there was a great dark wood, and in the wood under an old linden tree there was a well. And when the day was quite hot, the king's daughter would go into the woods and sit by the edge of the cool well. And if she was bored, she would take a golden ball and throw it up and catch it again, and this was the game she liked to play most.

Now it happened one day that the golden ball, instead of falling back into the little hand of the princess when she had tossed it up high, fell to the ground by her side and rolled into the water. The king's daughter followed it with her eyes, but it disappeared. The well was deep, so deep that the bottom could not be seen. Then she began to cry, and she cried louder and louder and could not console herself at all. And as she was lamenting, someone called to her. 'What is disturbing you, princess? Your tears would melt a heart of stone.' And when she looked to see where the voice came from there was nothing but a frog stretching his thick ugly head out of the water. 'Oh, is it you, old waddler?' she said. 'I'm crying because my golden ball has fallen into the well.' 'Be quiet and stop crying,' the frog answered. 'I can help you, but what will you give me if I fetch your ball again?' 'Whatever you like, dear frog,' she said. 'My clothes, my pearls and jewels, and even the golden crown that I'm wearing.' 'I don't like your clothes, your pearls and jewels and your golden crown, but if you love me and let me be your companion and playmate, let me sit at your table next to you, eat from your golden plate and drink from your cup, and sleep in your bed, if you promise me this, then I shall dive down and fetch your golden ball for you again.'[11]

By comparing these three versions we can see how *The Frog Prince* became more and more embroidered in a short course of time – and this did not occur merely for stylistic reasons. In the original folk tale of 1810 the setting is simple and totally lacking in frills. There is no castle. The incident appears to take place on a large estate. The king's daughter could well be a peasant's daughter or any girl who goes to a well, finds a ball, loses it, and agrees to take the frog home if he finds the ball for her. He has no other desire but to sleep with her. There is no beating around the bush in the rest of the narrative. It is explicitly sexual and alludes to a universal initiation and marital ritual (derived from primitive matriarchal societies), and in one other version, the princess does not throw the frog against the wall, but kisses it as in the *Beauty and Beast* tales. Mutual sexual recognition and acceptance bring about the prince's salvation. In both the 1812 and 1857 versions the princess provides more of an identification basis for a bourgeois child, for she is unique, somewhat spoiled, and very wealthy. She thinks in terms of monetary payment and basically treats the frog as though he were a member of a lower caste – an attitude not apparent in the original version. The ornate description serves to cover or eliminate the sexual frankness of the original tale. Here the frog wants to be a companion and playmate. Sex must first be sweetened up and made to appear harmless since its true form is repulsive. The girl obeys the father, but like all good bourgeois children she rejects the sexual advances of the frog, and for this she is rewarded. In fact, all three versions suggest a type of patriarchal socialization for young girls that has been severely criticized and questioned by progressive educators today, but the final version is most consistent in its *capacity* to combine feudal folk notions of sexuality, obedience, and sexual roles with bourgeois norms and attirement. The changes in the versions reveal social transitions and class differences which attest to their dependency on the gradual ascendancy of bourgeois codes and tastes.

Even the earlier French '*haute bourgeois*' values had to be altered by the Grimms to fit their more upright, nineteenth-century middle-class perspective and sense of decency. Let us compare the beginning of Perrault's *Le Petit Chaperon Rouge* with the Grimms' 1812 *Rotkäppchen* since the French version was their actual source.

Le Petit Chaperon Rouge (1697)

Once upon a time there was a little village girl, the prettiest that was ever seen. Her mother doted on her, and her grandmother doted even more. This good woman made a little red hood for her, and it became the girl so well that everyone called her Little Red Riding Hood.

One day her mother, having baked some biscuits, said to Little Red Riding Hood: 'Go and see how your grandmother is feeling; someone told me that she was ill. Take her some biscuits and this little pot of butter.' Little Red Riding Hood departed immediately for the house of her grandmother, who lived in another village.[12]

Rotkäppchen (1812)

Once upon a time there was a small sweet maid. Whoever laid eyes on her loved her. But it was her grandmother who loved her most. She never had enough to give the child. One time she gave her a present, a small hood made out of velvet, and since it became her so well, and since she did not want to wear anything but this, she was simply called Little Red Riding Hood. One day her mother said to her: 'Come, Red Riding Hood, take this piece of cake and bottle of wine and bring it to grandmother. She is sick and weak. This will nourish her. Be nice and good and give her my regards. Be orderly on your way and don't veer from the path, otherwise you'll fall and break the glass. Then your sick grandmother will have nothing.'[13]

In a recent article on Perrault's *Little Red Riding Hood*, Carole and D. T. Hanks Jr. have commented on the 'sanitization' process of the Grimms and later editors of this tale. 'Perrault's tale provides a classic example of the bowlderizing which all too often afflicts children's literature. Derived from the German version, 'Rotkäppchen' (Grimm No. 26), American versions of the tale have been sanitized to the point where the erotic element disappears and the tragic ending becomes comic. This approach emasculates a powerful story, one which unrevised is a metaphor for the maturing process.'[14] The word 'emasculates' is an unfortunate choice to describe what happened to Perrault's tale (and the original folk tales) since it was the rise of authoritarian patriarchal societies that was responsible for fear of sexuality and stringent sexual codes. Secondly, Perrault's tale was not written only for children but also for an educated upperclass audience which included children.[15] The development of children's literature, as we know, was late, and it only gradually assumed a vital role in the general socialization process of the eighteenth and nineteenth centuries. Therefore, Perrault's early tale had to be made more suitable for children by the Grimms and had to reinforce a more conservative bourgeois sense of morality. This moralistic impulse is most apparent in the changes the Grimms made at the very beginning of the tale. Little Red Riding Hood is no longer a simple village maid but the epitome of innocence. It is not enough, however, to be innocent. The girl must learn to fear her own curiosity and sensuality. So the narrative purpose corresponds to the socialization for young girls at that time: if you do not walk the straight path through the sensual temptations of the dark forest, if you are not orderly and moral (*sittsam*),[16] then you will be swallowed by the wolf, i.e, the devil or sexually starved males. Typically the savior and rebirth motif is represented by a male hunter, a father figure devoid of sexuality. Here again the revisions in word choice, tone, and content cannot be understood unless one grasps the substance of education and socialization in the first half of the nineteenth century.

Let us take one more example, a short section from the Grimms' 1810 and 1812 versions of *Snow White*.

1810 Manuscript

When Snow White awoke the next morning, they asked her how she happened to get there. And she told them everything, how her mother the queen had left her alone in the woods and went away. The dwarfs took pity on her and persuaded her to remain with them and do the cooking for them when they went to the mines. However, she was to beware of the queen and not let anyone in the house.[17]

1812 Edition
When Snow White awoke, they asked her who she was and how she happened to get in the house. Then she told them how her mother wanted to have her put to death, but that the hunter spared her life, and how she had run the entire day and finally arrived at their house. So the dwarfs took pity on her and said: 'If you keep our house for us, and cook, sew, make the beds, wash and knit, and keep everything tidy and clean, you may stay with us, and you will have everything you want. In the evening, when we come home, dinner must be ready. During the day we are in the mines and dig for gold, so you will be alone. Beware of the queen and let no one in the house.'[18]

These passages again reveal how the Grimms had an entirely different socialization process in mind when they altered the folk tales. Snow White is given instructions which are more commensurate with the duties of a bourgeois girl, and the tasks which she performs are implicitly part of her moral obligation. Morals are used to justify a division of labor and the separation of the sexes. Here, too, the growing notion that the woman's role was in the home and that the home was a shelter for innocence and children belonged to a conception of women, work, and child-rearing in bourgeois circles more so than to the ideas of the peasantry and aristocracy. Certainly, the growing proletarian class in the nineteenth century could not think of keeping wives and children at home, for they had to work long hours in the factories. Snow White was indeed a new kind of princess in the making and was constantly remade. In the 1810 version the father comes with doctors to save his daughter. Then he arranges a marriage for her daughter and punishes the wicked queen. In the margin of their manuscript, the Grimms remarked: 'This ending is not quite right and is lacking something.'[19] Their own finishing touches could only be topped by the prudish changes made by that twentieth-century sanitation man, Walt Disney.

Aside from situating the compilation of folk tales and grasping the literary transformations within a socio-historical framework, it is even more important to investigate the pervasive influence which the Grimms have had in the socialization process of respective countries. We know that the Grimms' collection (especially the 1857 final edition) has been the second most popular and widely circulated book in

Germany for over a century, second only to the Bible. We also know that the tales and similar stories are the cultural bread and basket of most children from infancy until 10 years of age. Studies in Germany show that there is a fairy-tale reading age between 6 and 10.[20] Otherwise the tales have already been read or told to the children by adults before they are 6. Incidentally, this process of transmission means that certain groups of adults are constantly re-reading and re-telling the tales throughout their lives. Ever since the rise of the mass media, the Grimms' tales (generally in their most prudish and prudent version) have been broadcast by radio, filmed, recorded for records, tapes, and video, used as motifs for advertisements, and commercialized in every manner and form imaginable. Depending on the country and relative reception, these particular tales have exercised a grip on our minds and imagination from infancy into adulthood, and, though they cannot be held accountable for negative features in advanced technological societies, it is time – as many West German writers believe – to evaluate how they impart values and norms to children which may actually hinder their growth, rather than help them to come to terms with their existential condition and mature autonomously as Bruno Bettelheim and others maintain.[21]

Here we must consider the socialization of reading fairy tales with the primary focus on those developed by the Brothers Grimm. In discussing socialization I shall be relying on a general notion of culture which is defined by the mode through which human beings objectify themselves, come together, and relate to one another in history and materialize their ideas, intentions, and solutions, in the sense of making them more concrete. By concrete I also mean to imply that there are forms people create and use to make their ideas, intentions and solutions take root in a visible, audible, and generally perceptible manner so that they become an actual part of people's daily lives. Thus, culture is viewed as an his-torical *process* of human objectification, and the level and quality of a national culture depends on the socialization developed by human beings to integrate young members into the society and to reinforce the norms and values which legitimize the sociopolitical systems and which guarantee some sort of continuity in society.[22]

Reading as internalization, or technically speaking as resubjectifi-cation, has always functioned in socialization processes, whether it be the conscious or unconscious 'understanding' of signs, symbols, and letters. In modern times, that is, since the Enlightenment and rise of the bourgeoisie, reading has been the passport into certain brackets of society and the measure by which one functions and maintains a certain place in the hierarchy.[23] The reading of printed fairy tales in the nineteenth century was a socially exclusive process: it was conducted mainly in bourgeois circles and nurseries, and members of the lower classes who learned how to read were not only acquiring a skill, they were acquiring a value system and social status depending on their conformity to norms controlled by bourgeois interests. The social function of reading is not to be understood in a mechanistic or reductive way, i.e., that reading was solely a safeguard for bourgeois hegemony and only allowed for singular interpretations. Certainly the introduction of reading to the lower classes opened up new horizons for them and gave them more power. Also the production of books allowed for a variety of viewpoints often contrary to the ruling forces in society. In some respects reading can function explosively like a dream and serve to challenge socialization and constraints. But, unlike the dream, it is practically impossible to determine what direct effect a fairy tale will have upon an *individual* reader in terms of validating his or her own existence. Still, the tale does provide and reflect upon the cultural boundaries within which the reader measures and validates his or her own identity. We tend to forget the socio-historical frameworks of control when we talk about reading and especially the reading of fairy tales. Both socialization and reading reflect and are informed by power struggles and ideology in a given society or culture. The Grimms' fairy tales were products not only of the struggles of the common people to make themselves heard in oral folk tales – symbolically representing their needs and wishes – but they also became *literary* products of the German bourgeois quest for identity and power. To this extent, the norms and value system which the Grimms cultivated within the tales point to an objectified, standard way of living which was intended and came to legitimate the general bourgeois standard of living and work, not only in Germany but throughout the western world.

In all there were fifty-one tales in the original manuscript of 1810. Some were omitted in the 1812 book publication, and those which were included were all extensively changed and stylized to meet middle-class taste. This process of conscious alteration for social and aesthetic reasons was continued until 1857. The recent findings which have stressed and documented this are not merely significant for what they tell us about the Grimms' method of work or the relation of the tales to late feudal and early bourgeois society in Germany. They have greater ramifications for the development of the literary fairy tales in general, especially in view of socialization through reading.

II

First of all, through understanding the subjective selection process and adaptation methods of the Grimms, we can begin to study other collections of folk tales, which have been published in the nineteenth and twentieth centuries, and analyze similar transcription methods in light of education and socialization. Recent attention has been paid to the role of the narrator of the tales in folklore research, but the role of the collector and transcriber is also significant, for we have seen how consciously and unconsciously the Grimms integrated their world views into the tales and those of their intended audience as well. The relationship of the collector to audience is additionally significant since printed and transcribed folk tales were not meant to be reinserted into circulation as books for the original audience. As Rudolf Schenda has demonstrated in *Volk ohne Buch*,[24] the lower classes did not and could not use books because of their lack of money and training. Their tradition was an oral one. The nineteenth-century and early twentieth-century transcription of folk tales was primarily for the educated classes, young and old. The reception of the tales influenced the purpose and style of the collectors. This remains true up through the present.

As I have noted, psychologists have explored the relationship between dream and fairy-tale production, and moreover they have endeavored to explore the special role which fairy tales have played in socialization. One of the most succinct and sober analyses of why the fairy tale in particular attracts children and functions so well in the socialization process has been made by Emanuel K. Schwartz. He argues that

> the struggle between what is perceived as the 'good parent' and the 'bad parent' is one of the big problems of childhood. In the fairy tale the bad mother is commonly seen as the witch (phallic mother). The great man, the father figure (Oedipus), represents the hero, or the hero-to-be, the prototype, for the young protagonist of the fairy tale. The process of social and psychological change, characteristic of the fairy tale, is childishly pursued, and magic is used to effect changes. On the other hand, experience with having to struggle for the gratification and the fulfillment of wishes results in a social adherence to and the development of an understanding of social norms and social conformities. This does not mean, however, that the reinforcement of an awareness of socialization results in submissiveness; but a certain amount of common sense, which goes into conforming with the social *mores*, is a realistic necessity for children and adults alike.[25]

To a certain extent, Schwartz minimizes the inherent dangers in such narratives as the Grimms' fairy tales which function to legitimize certain repressive standards of action and make them acceptable for children. Reading as a physical and mental process involves identification before an internalization of norms and values can commence, and identification for a child comes easily in a Grimms' fairy tale. There is hardly one that does not announce who the protagonist is, and he or she commands our identification almost immediately by being the youngest, most oppressed, the wronged, the smallest, the most naive, the weakest, the most innocent, etc. Thus, direct identification of a child with the major protagonist begins the process of socialization through reading.

Although it is extremely difficult to determine exactly what a child will absorb on an unconscious level, the patterns of most Grimms' fairy tales draw conscious attention to prescribed values and models. As children read or are read to, they follow a social path, learn role orientation, and acquire norms and values. The pattern of most Grimms' fairy tales involves a struggle for power and autonomy. Though there are marked differences among the tales, it is possible to suggest an overall pattern which will make it clear why and how they become functional in the bourgeois socialization process.

Initially the young protagonist must leave home or the family because power relations have been disturbed. Either the protagonist is wronged, or a change in social relations forces the protagonist to depart from home. A task is imposed, and a hidden command of the tale must be fulfilled. The question which most of the Grimms' tales ask is: how can one learn – what must one do to use one's powers rightly in order to be accepted in society or recreate society in keeping with the norms of the *status quo*? The wandering protagonist always leaves home to reconstitute home. Along the way the male hero learns to be active, competitive, handsome, industrious, cunning, acquisitive. His goal is money, power, and a woman (also associated with chattel). His jurisdiction is the open world. His happiness depends on the just use of power. The female hero learns to be passive, obedient, self-sacrificing, hard-working, patient, and straight-laced. Her goal is wealth, jewels, and a man to protect her property rights. Her jurisdiction is the home or castle. Her happiness depends on conformity to patriarchal rule. Sexual activity is generally postponed until after marriage. Often the tales imply a postponement of gratification until the necessary skills, power, and wealth are acquired.

For a child growing up in a capitalist society in the nineteenth and twentieth centuries, the socialization process carried by the pattern and norms in a Grimms' fairy tale functioned and still functions to make such a society more acceptable to the child. Friction and points of conflict are minimized, for the fairy tale legitimates bourgeois society by seemingly granting upward mobility and the possibility for autonomy. All the Grimms' tales contain an elaborate set of signs and codes. If there is a wrong signaled in a Grimms' fairy tale – and there is always somebody being wronged, or a relation disturbed – then it involves breaking an inviolate code which is the basis of benevolent patriarchal rule. Acceptable norms are constituted by the behavior of a protagonist whose happy end indicates the possibility for resolution of the conflicts according to the code. Even in such tales as *How Six Travelled through the World, Bremen Town Musicians, Clever Gretel,* and *The Blue Light,* in which the downtrodden protagonists overthrow oppressors, the social relations and work ethos are not fundamentally altered but reconstituted in a manner which allows for more latitude in the hierarchical social system – something which was desired incidentally by a German bourgeoisie incapable of making revolutions but most capable of making compromises at the expense of the peasantry. Lower-class members become members of the ruling elite, but this occurs because the ruling classes need such values which were being cultivated by the bourgeoisie – thrift, industry, patience, obedience, etc. Basically, the narrative patterns imply that skills and qualities are to be developed and used so that one can compete for a high place in the hierarchy based on private property, wealth, and power. Both command and report[26] of the Grimms' fairy tales emphasize a *process* of socialization through reading that leads to internalizing the basic nineteenth-century bourgeois norms, values, and power relationships, which take their departure from feudal society.

For example, let us consider *The Table, the Ass and the Stick* to see how functional it is in terms of male socialization. It was first incorporated into the expanded edition of the Grimms' tales in 1819, deals mainly with lower middle-class characters, focuses on males, and will be the basis for a discussion about a reutilized tale by F. K. Waechter. All the incidents concern master/slave relationships. Three sons are in charge of a goat, who rebels against them by lying and causing all three to be banished by their father, a tailor. After the banishment of the sons, the tailor discovers that the goat has lied. So he shaves her, and she runs away. In the meantime, each one of the sons works diligently in a petit bourgeois trade as joiner, miller, and turner. They are rewarded with gifts by their masters, but the two eldest have their gifts stolen from them by the landlord of a tavern. They embarrass the father and bring shame on the family when they try to show off their gifts which the landlord had replaced with false ones. It is up to the third son to outsmart the landlord, bring about a family reunion, and restore the good name of the family in the community through exhibiting its wealth and power. The father retires as a wealthy man, and we also learn that the goat has been duly punished by a busy bee.

Though the father 'wrongs' the boys, his authority to rule remains unquestioned throughout the narrative; nor are we to question it. The blame for disturbing the seemingly 'natural' relationship between father and sons is placed on liars and deceivers, the goat and the landlord. They seek power and wealth through devious means. The elaborated code of the tale holds that the only way to acquire wealth and power is through diligence, perseverance, and honesty. The goal of the sons is submission to the father and maintenance of the family's good name. The story enjoins the reader to accept the norms and values of a patriarchal slave/master relationship and private property relations. In general, there is nothing wrong with emphasizing the qualities of 'diligence, perseverance, and honesty' in a socialization process, but we are talking about socialization through a story that upholds patriarchal domination and the accumulation of wealth and power for private benefit as positive goals.

In almost all the Grimms' fairy tales, male domination and master/slave relationships are rationalized so long as the rulers are benevolent and use their power justly. If 'tyrants' and parents are challenged, they relent or are replaced, but the property relationships and patriarchy are not transformed. In *The Table, the Ass and the Stick* there is a series of master/slave relationships: father/son, patriarchal family/goat, master/apprentice, landlord/son. The sons and other characters are socialized to please the masters. They work to produce wealth and power for the father, who retires in the end because the sons have accumulated wealth in the proper, diligent fashion according to the Protestant Ethic. The goat and landlord are punished for different reasons: the goat because she resented the master/slave relationship; the landlord because, as false father, he violated the rules of private property. Although this remarkable fairy tale allows for many other interpretations, viewed in light of its function in the bourgeois socialization process, we can begin to understand why numerous West German writers began looking askance at the Brothers Grimm during the rise of the anti-authoritarian movement of the late 1960s.

III

Actually the reutilization and transformation of the Grimms' tales were not the inventions of West German writers, nor were they so new.[27]

There was a strong radical tradition of rewriting folk and fairy tales for children which began in the late nineteenth century and blossomed during the Weimar period until the Nazis put an end to such experimentation. This tradition was revived during the 1960s, when such writers as Hermynia Zur Mühlen, Lisa Tetzner, Edwin Hoernle, and Walter Benjamin[28] were rediscovered and when the anti-authoritarian movement and the Left began to focus on children and socialization. One of the results of the general radical critique of capitalism and education in West Germany has been an attempt to build a genuine, non-commercial children's public sphere which might counter the exploitative and legitimizing mechanisms of the dominant bourgeois public sphere. In order to provide cultural tools and means to reutilize the present public sphere for children, groups of people with a progressive bent have tried to offset the racism, sexism, and authoritarian messages in children's books, games, theaters, tv, and schools by creating different kinds of emancipatory messages and cultural objects with and for children.

In children's literature, and specifically in the area of fairy tales, there have been several publishing houses which have played an active role in introducing reutilized fairy tales created to politicize the children's public sphere, where children and adults are to cooperate and conceive more concrete, democratic forms of play and work in keeping with the needs and wishes of a participating community.[29] Obviously the rise of a broad left-oriented audience toward the end of the 1960s encouraged many big publishers to direct their efforts to this market for profit, but not all the books were published by giant companies or solely for profit. And, in 1982, when the so-called New Left is no longer so new nor so vocal as it was during the late 1960s, there are still numerous publishing houses, large and small, which are directing their efforts toward the publication of counter-cultural or reutilized fairy-tale books and children's literature. My discussion will limit itself and focus on the reutilized Grimms' tales published by Rowohlt, Basis, Schlot, and Beltz & Gelberg. In particular I shall endeavor to demonstrate how these fairy tales reflect possibilities for a different socialization process from standard children's books.

In 1972 the large Rowohlt Verlag established a book series for children entitled 'rororo rotfuchs' under the general editorship of Uwe Wandrey. An impressive series was developed and now contains a wide range of progressive children's stories, histories, autobiographies, handbooks, and fairy tales for young people between the ages of 4 and 18. Here I want to concentrate on two of the earlier and best efforts to reutilize old fairy tales.

Friedrich Karl Waechter, illustrator and writer,[30] has written and drawn numerous politicized fairy tales and fairy-tale plays for children. One of his first products, *Tishlein deck dich und Knüppel aus dem Sack* (*Table Be Covered and Stick Out of the Sack*, 1972) is a radical rendition of the Grimms' *The Table, the Ass, and the Stick*. His story takes place in a small town named Breitenrode a long time ago. (From the pictures the time can be estimated to be the early twentieth century.) Fat Jakob Bock, who owns a large lumber mill and most of the town, exploits his workers as much as he can. When a young carpenter named Philip invents a magic table that continually spreads as much food as one can eat upon command, Bock (the name means ram in German) takes over the invention and incorporates it since it was done on company time. He promises Philip his daughter Caroline if he now invents a 'stick out of the sack' – the power Bock needs to guard his property. Philip is given the title of inventor and put to work as a white-collar worker separating him from his friends, the other carpenters, who had helped him build the magic table. At first Philip and his friends are not sure why Bock wants the stick, but an elf named Xram (an anagram for Marx spelled backwards) enlightens them. They decide to work together on this invention and to keep control over it. But, when it is finished, Bock obtains it and plants the magic table as stolen property in the house of Sebastien, a 'trouble-maker', who always wants to organize the workers around their own needs. Bock accuses Sebastien of stealing the table and asserts that he needs the stick to punish thieves like Sebastien and to protect his property. However, Philip exposes Bock as the real thief, and the greedy man is chased from the town. Then the workers celebrate as Philip announces that the magic table will be owned by everyone in the town while Xram hides the stick. The final picture shows men, women, children, dogs, cats, and other animals at a huge picnic sharing the fruits of the magic table while Bock departs.

Like the narrative itself, Waechter's drawings are intended to invert the present socialization process in West Germany. The story-line is primarily concerned with private property relations, and it begins traditionally with the master/slave relationship. The ostensible command of the tale – 'obey the boss and you'll cash in on the profits' – is gradually turned into another command – 'freedom and happiness can only be attained through collective action and sharing.' The narrative flow of the tale confirms this reversed command, and the reading process becomes a learning process about socialization in capitalist society. Philip experiences how the fruits of collective labor expended by himself and his friends are expropriated by Bock. With the magical help of Xram (i.e., the insights of Marx) the workers learn to take control over their own labor and to share the fruits equally among themselves. Here the master/slave relationship is concretely banished, and the new work and social relationships are based on cooperation and collective ownership of the means of production. The virtues of Philip and the workers – diligence, perseverence, imagination, honesty – are used in a struggle to overcome male domination rooted in private property relations. Socialization is seen as a struggle for self-autonomy against exploitative market and labor conditions.

In Andreas and Angela Hopf's *Der Feuerdrache Minimax* (*The Fire Dragon Minimax*, 1973), also an illustrated political fairy tale,[31] the authors use a unique process to depict the outsider position of children and strange-looking creatures and also the need for the outsider to be incorporated within the community if the community is to develop. The Hopfs superimpose red drawings of Minimax and the little girl Hilde onto etchings of medieval settings and characters.[32] The imposition and juxtaposition of red figures on black and white prints keep the reader's focus on contrast and differences. The narrative is a simple reutilization of numerous motifs which commonly appear in the Grimms' tales and associate dragons, wolves, and other animals with forces of destruction endangering the *status quo*. *The Fire Dragon Minimax* demonstrates how the *status quo* itself must be questioned and challenged.

The story takes place during the Middle Ages in the walled town of Gimpelfingen. While sharpening his sword, the knight causes sparks to fly, and the town catches fire. There is massive destruction, and the dragon is immediately blamed for the fire, but Hilde, who had fled the flames, encounters Minimax, who had been bathing in the river when the fire had begun. So she knows that he could not have caused the fire. In fact, he helps extinguish part of the fire and then carries Hilde to his cave since he prefers to roast potatoes with his flames and sleep for long hours rather than burn down towns. The knight pretends to fight in the interests of the town and accuses Minimax of starting the fire and kidnapping Hilde. He darns his armor and goes in search of the dragon, but he is no contest for Minimax, who overwhelms him. The knight expects the dragon to kill him, but Minimax tells him instead to take Hilde home since her parents might be worried about her. Again the knight lies to the townspeople and tells them that he has rescued Hilde and killed the dragon. Hilde tries to convince the people that he is lying, but she is only believed by a handful of people who fortunately decide to see if Minimax is alive or dead. Upon finding him, they realize the truth and bring Minimax back to town. This causes the knight to flee in fear. Minimax is welcomed by the townspeople, and he helps them rebuild the town. Thereafter, he remains in the town, roasts potatoes for the children or takes them on rides in the sky. Hilde is his favorite, and he flies highest with her and often tells her fairy tales about dragons. Obviously the Hopfs are concerned with racism and militarism in this tale. The dragon represents the weird-looking alien figure, who acts differently from the 'normal' people. And the Hopfs show how the strange and different creature is often used by people in power as a scapegoat to distract attention from the real enemy, namely the people in power. In contrast to the dominant master/slave relationship established in the medieval community, Hilde and the dragon form a friendship based on mutual recognition. Their relationship is opposed to the dominant power relationship of male patriarchy in the town. In terms of problems in today's late capitalist society, the tale also relates to feminism and the prevention of cruelty to animals. The activism of Hilde on behalf of the dragon sets norms of behavior for young girls, when she asserts herself and uses her talents for the benefit of oppressed creatures in the community. As in Waechter's politicized fairy tale, the textual symbols of goal-oriented behavior are aimed at cooperation and collectivism, not domination and private control.

The publishing house which has been most outspoken in behalf of such general socialist goals in children's culture has been Basis Verlag in West Berlin. Working in a collective manner, the people in this group have produced a number of excellent studies on fairy tales and children's literature,[33] as well as a series of different types of books for young readers. Here I want to remark on just one of their fairy-tale experiments entitled *Zwei Korken für Schlienz* (*Two Corks for Schlienz*, 1972) by Johannes Merkel based on the Grimms' tale *How Six Travelled through the World*. The reutilized fairy tale deals with housing difficulties in large cities, and the text is accompanied by amusing photos with superimposed drawings. Four young people with extraordinary powers seek to organize tenants to fight against an exploitative landlord. Ultimately, they fail, but in the process they learn, along with the readers, to recognize their mistakes. The open ending suggests that the four will resume their struggle in the near future – this time without false illusions.

Most of the tales in *Janosch erzählt Grimm's Märchen* (*Janosch Tells Grimm's Fairy Tales*, 1972) are intended to smash false illusions, too, but it is not so apparent that Janosch has a socialist goal in mind, i.e., that he envisions collective living and sharing as a means to eliminate the evils in the world.[34] He is mainly concerned with the form and contents of fifty Grimms' tales which he wants to parody to the point of bursting their seams. He retells them in a caustic manner using modern slang, idiomatic expressions, and pointed references to deplorable living conditions in affluent societies. Each tale endeavors to undo the socialization of a Grimms' tale by inverting plots and characters and adding new incidents. Such inversion does not necessarily amount to a 'happier' or more 'emancipatory' view of the world. If Janosch is liberating, it is because he is so humanely candid, often cynical, and disrespectful of conditioned and established modes of thinking and behavior. For instance, in *The Frog Prince* it is the frog who loses his ball and is pursued by a girl. The frog is forced by his father to accept the annoying girl in the subterranean water palace. Her pestering, however, becomes too much for him, and he suffocates her. This causes her transformation into a frog princess whereupon she marries the frog prince and explains to him how she had been captured by human beings and changed herself into an ugly girl to escape malicious treatment by humans. Her ugliness prevented other humans from marrying her and allowed her to return to her true form.

Such an inversion makes a mockery of the Grimms' tale and perhaps makes the reader aware of the potential threat which humans pose to nature and the animal world. This point can be argued. But what is clear from the story is that Janosch fractures the social framework of audience expectations, whether or not the readers are familiar with the original Grimms' tales. The numerous illustrations by Janosch are just as upsetting, and the tales derive their power by not conforming to the socialization of reading the Grimms' tales as harmless stories. His anarchistic, somewhat cynical rejection of the Grimms and the norms they represent is related to his rejection of the hypocritical values of the new rich in post-war Germany created by a so-called 'economic miracle'. For instance, in *Puss 'n Boots*, a marvelous cat exposes his young master Hans to the emptiness and meaninglessness of high society. When Hans experiences how rich people place more stock in objects than in the lives of other people, he decides to abandon his dreams of wealth and success and to lead a carefree life on a modest scale with the cat. This is not to say that the cat or Hans are model characters or point to models for creating a new society. They are symbols of refusal, and by depicting such refusal, Janosch seeks to defend a 'questioning spirit,' which is totally lacking in the Grimms tales and very much alive in his provocative *re-visions*, where everything depends on a critical new viewpoint.

One of Janosch's major supporters of re-visions is Hans-Joachim Gelberg, who has been one of the most important proponents for the reutilization of the Grimms' tales and the creation of more politicized and critical stories for children and adults. Gelberg edits special yearbooks, which include various types of experimental fairy tales and have received prestigious awards in West Germany,[35] for Gelberg has pointed in new directions for a children's literature that refuses to be infantile and condescending. In addition to the yearbooks, Gelberg has published a significant volume of contemporary fairy tales entitled *Neues vom Rumpelstilzchen und andere Haus-Märchen von 43 Autoren*, 1976.[36] Since there are fifty-eight different fairy tales and poems, it is difficult to present a detailed discussion of the reutilization techniques in regard to socialization in the tales. Generally speaking, the direction is the same: a wholesale rethinking and reconceptualization of traditional fairy-tale motifs to question standard reading and rearing processes. Since the title of the book features *Rumpelstiltskin*, and since the motto of the book – 'No, I would rather have something living than all the treasures of the world' – is taken from his tale, I shall deal with the two versions of *Rumpelstiltskin* by Rosemarie Künzler and Irmela Brender[37] since they represent the basic critical attitude of most of the authors.

Both Künzler and Brender shorten the tale drastically and take different approaches to the main characters. Künzler begins by stressing the boastful nature of the miller who gets his daughter into a terrible fix. She is bossed around by the king and then by some little man who promises to help her by using extortion. When the little man eventually barters for her first-born child, the miller's daughter is shocked into her senses. She screams and tells the little man that he is crazy, that she will never marry the horrid king, nor would she ever give her child away. The angry little man stamps so hard that he causes the door of the room to spring open, and the miller's daughter runs out into the wide world and is saved. This version is a succinct critique of male exploitation and domination of women. The miller's daughter allows herself to be pushed around until she has an awakening. Like Janosch, Künzler projects the refusal to conform to socialization as the first step toward actual emancipation.

Brender's version is different. She questions the justice in the Grimms' tale from Rumpelstiltskin's point of view, for she has always felt that the poor fellow has been treated unfairly. After all, what he wanted most was something living, in other words, some human contact. She explains that Rumpelstiltskin did not need money since he was capable of producing gold any time he wanted it. He was also willing to work hard and save the life of the miller's daughter. Therefore, the miller's daughter could have been more understanding and compassionate. Brender does not suggest that the miller's daughter should have given away the child, but as the young queen, she could have invited

Rumpelstiltskin to live with the royal family. This way Rumpelstiltskin would have found the human companionship he needed, and everyone would have been content. The way things end in the Grimms' version is for Brender totally unjust. Her technique is a play with possibilities to open up rigid social relations and concern about private possession. Through critical reflection her narrative shifts the goal of the Grimms' story from gold and power to justice and more humane relations based on mutual consideration and cooperation.

Both Künzler and Brender seek a humanization of the socialization process by transforming the tales and criticizing commodity exchange and male domination, and they incorporate a feminist perspective which is at the very basis of an entire book entitled *Märchen für tapfere Mädchen* (*Fairy Tales for Girls with Spunk*, 1978) by Doris Lerche, illustrator, and O.F. Gmelin, writer.[38] They use two fictitious girls named Trolla and Svea and a boy named Bror from the North to narrate different types of fairy tales which purposely seek to offset our conditioned notions of sexual roles and socialization. For instance, the very beginning of *Little Red Cap* indicates a markedly different perspective from the Grimms' version: 'There was once a fearless girl. . . .'[39] She is not afraid of the wolf, and, even though she is swallowed by him in her grandmother's bed, she keeps her wits about her, takes out a knife, cuts herself a hole in his stomach while he sleeps, and rescues herself and granny. In Gmelin's rendition of *Hans and Gretel*, the poor parents are not the enemies of the children, rather poverty is the source of trouble. To help the parents, the children go into the woods in search for food and eventually they become lost. Then they encounter a woman who is no longer a witch, but an outcast who has learned to live by the brutal rule of the land set by others. Hans and Gretel overcome the obstacles which she places in their quest for food, but they do not punish her. They are more concerned in re-establishing strong bonds of cooperation and love with their parents. The children return home without a treasure, and the ending leaves the future fate of the family open.

IV

The open endings of many of the reutilized fairy tales from West Germany indicate that the future for such fairy tales may also be precarious. Given the social import and the direct political tendency of the tales to contradict and criticize the dominant socialization process in West Germany, these tales are not used widely in schools, and their distribution is limited more to groups partial to the tales among the educated classes in West Germany. They have also been attacked by the conservative press because of their 'falsifications' and alleged harmfulness to children. Nevertheless, the production of such tales has not abated in recent years, and such continuous publication may reflect something about the diminishing appeal of the Grimms' tales and the needs of young and adult readers to relate to fantastic projections which are connected more to the concrete conditions of their own reality.

Folk tales and fairy tales have always been dependent on customs, rituals, and values in the particular socialization process of a social system. They have always symbolically depicted the nature of power relationships within a given society. Thus, they are strong indicators of the level of civilization, that is, the essential quality of a culture and social order. The effectiveness of emancipatory and reutilized tales has not only depended on the tales themselves but also on the manner in which they have been received, their use and distribution in society. The fact that West German writers are arguing that it is time for the Brothers Grimm to stop looking over our shoulders may augur positive changes for part of the socialization process. At the very least, they compel us to reconsider where socialization through the reading of the Grimms' tales has led us.

Notes

1   It has always been fashionable to try to rewrite folk tales and the classical ones by the Grimms. However, the recent trend is more international in scope, not just centered in Germany, and more political in intent. For some examples see, Jay Williams *The Practical Princess and other Liberating Fairy Tales* (London: Chatto & Windus, 1979); Astrid Lindgren, *Märchen* (Hamburg: Oetingen, 1978), which first appeared in Swedish; *The Prince and the Swineherd, Red Riding Hood, Snow White* by the Fairy Story Collective (Liverpool, 1976), three different publications by four women from the Merseyside Women's Liberation Movement. I shall discuss this international trend in my final chapter, 'The liberating potential of the fantastic in contemporary fairy tales for children.'

2   My focus is on the development in West Germany only. The official attitude toward fairy tales in East Germany has gone through different phases since 1949. At first they were rejected, but more recently there has been a favorable policy, so long as the tales do not question the existing state of affairs. Thus, the older fairy tales by the Grimms are accorded due recognition while reutilization of the tales in a manifest political manner critical of the state and socialization is not condoned. See Sabine Brandt. 'Ropkäppchen und der Klassenkampf,' *Der Monat*, **12** (1960), pp. 64–74.

3   See Dieter Richter and Jochen Vogt (eds), *Die heimlichen Erzieher, Kinderbücher und politisches Lernen* (Reinbek bei Hamburg: Rowohlt, 1974) and Linda Dégh, 'Grimms' household tales and its place in the household: the social relevance of a controversial classic,' *Western Folklore*, **38** (April 1979), pp. 83–103.

4   See Erich Kaiser, ' "Ent-Grimm-te" Märchen,' *Westermanns Pädagogische Beiträge*, **8** (1975), pp. 448–59, and Hildegard Pischke, 'Das veränderte Märchen,'

Literatur für Kinder, ed. by Maria Lypp (Göttingen: Vandenhoeck & Ruprecht, 1977), pp. 94–113.

5 See Heinz Rölleke's introduction and commmentaries to the 1810 manuscript written by the Grimms in *Die älteste Märchensammlung der Brüder Grimm* (Cologny-Geneva: Fondation Martin Bodmer, 1975); Werner Psaar and Manfred Klein, *Wer hat Angst vor der bösen Geiss?* (Braunschweig: Westermann, 1976), pp. 9–30; Ingeborg Weber-Kellermann's introduction to *Kinder- und Hausmärchen gesammelt durch die Brüder Grimm*, Vol. I (Frankfurt am Main: Insel, 1976), pp. 9–18.

6 Weber-Kellermann, *Kinder-und Hausmärchen gesammelt durch die Brüder Grimm*, Vol. I, p. 14.

7 *Ibid.*, pp. 23–4. This is taken from the 1819 preface by the Brothers Grimm.

8 *Ibid.*, p. 24.

9 Rölleke (ed.), *Die älteste Marchensammlung der Brüder Grimm*, p. 144. Unless otherwise indicated, all the translations in this chapter are my own. In most instances I have endeavored to be as literal as possible to document the historical nature of the text.

10 *Ibid.*, p. 145.

11 *Kinder- und Hausmärchen gesammelt durch die Brüder Grimm*, pp. 35–6.

12 *Contes de Perrault*, ed. by Gilbert Rouger (Paris: Garnier 1967), p. 113.

13 Brüder Grimm, *Kinder- und Hausmärchen. In der ersten Gestalt.* (Frankfurt am Main, 1962), p. 78.

14 'Perrault's "Little Red Riding Hood"': victim of revision,' *Children's Literature*, 7 (1978), p. 68.

15 For the best analysis of Perrault and his times, see Marc Soriano, *Les Contes de Perrault* (Paris: Gallimard, 1968).

16 The word *sittsam* is used in the 1857 edition and carries with it a sense of chastity, virtuousness, and good behavior.

17 *Die älteste Sammlung der Brüder Grimm*, pp. 246, 248 (op. cit., note 5).

18 *Ibid.*, pp. 249, 251.

19 *Ibid.*, p. 250.

20 Psaar and Klein, *Wer hat Angst vor der bösen Geiss?* pp. 112–36.

21 See *The Uses of Enchantment: The Meaning and Importance of Fairy Tales* (New York: Knopf, 1976). For a critique of Bettelheim's position, see James W. Heisig, 'Bruno Bettelheim and the fairy tales,' *Children's Literature*, 6 (1977). pp. 93–114, and my own criticism in the chapter, 'On the use and abuse of folk and fairy tales: Bruno Bettelheim's moralistic magic wand,' in *Breaking the Magic Spell: Radical Theories of Folk and Fairy Tales* (London: Heinemann, 1979), pp. 160–82.

22 Helmut Fend, *Sozialisation durch Literatur* (Weinheim: Beltz, 1979), p. 30, remarks:

'Socialization proves itself to be a process of resubjectification of cultural objectifications. In highly complex cultures and societies this involves the learning of complex sign systems and higher forms of knowledge as well as the general comprehension of the world for dealing with natural problems and the general self-comprehension of human beings. Through the process of resubjectification of cultural objectifications, structures of consciousness, that is, subjective worlds of meaning, are constructed. Psychology views this formally as abstraction from particular contents and speaks about the construction of cognitions, about the construction of a 'cognitive map,' or a process of internalization. In a depiction of how cultural patterns are assumed in a substantive way, the matter concerns what conceptions about one's own person, which skills and patterns or interpretations, which norms and values someone takes and accepts in a certain culture relative to a sub-sphere of a society. Generally speaking, what happens in the socialization process is what hermeneutical research defines as 'understanding'. Understanding is developed and regarded here as an interpretative appropriation of linguistically transmitted meanings which represent socio-historical forms of life. To be sure, this understanding has a differentiated level of development which is frequently bound by social class.'

23 See Richard Hoggart, *The Uses of Literacy* (London: Chatto & Windus, 1957).

24 Frankfurt am Main: Klostermann, 1970.

25 Emanuel K. Schwartz, 'A psychoanalytical study of the fairy tale,' *American Journal of Psychotherapy*, 10 (1956), p. 755. See also Julius E. Heuscher, *A Psychiatric Study of Fairy Tales* (Springfield, Illinois: Thomas, 1963).

26 The terms are from Victor Laruccia's excellent study, 'Little Red Riding Hood's metacommentary: paradoxical injunction, semiotics and behavior,' *Modern Language Notes*, 90 (1975), pp. 517–34. Laruccia notes (p. 520) that,

all messages have two aspects, a command and a report, the first being a message about the nature of the relationship between sender and receiver, the second the message of the content. The crucial consideration is how these two messages relate to each other. This relationship is central to all goal-directed activity in any community since all human goals necessarily involve a relation with others.

Laruccia's essay includes a discussion of the way male domination and master/slave relationships function in the Grimms' tales.

27 See Dieter Richter (ed.), *Das politische Kinderbuch* (Darmstadt: Luchterhand, 1973). A writer such as Kurd Lasswitz began creating political fairy tales at the end of the nineteenth century. One of the first collections of political fairy tales published during the Weimar period is Ernst Friedrich (ed.), *Proletarischer Kindergarten* (Berlin: Buchverlag der Arbeiter-Kunst-Ausstellung, 1921), which contains stories and poems as well.

28 All these writers either wrote political fairy tales or wrote about them during the 1920s and early part of the 1930s. One could add many other names to this list, such as Ernst Bloch, Bruno Schönlank, Berta Lask, Oskar Maria Graf, Kurt Held, Robert Grötzsch, and even Bertolt Brecht. The most important fact to bear in mind, aside from the unwritten history of this development, is that the present-day writers began to hark back to this era.

29 See my article 'Down with Heidi, down with Struwwelpeter, three cheers for the revolution: towards a new children's literature in West Germany,' *Children's Literature*, 5 (1976), pp. 162–79.

30 Waechter is one of the most gifted writers and illustrators for children in West Germany today. He is particularly known for the following books: *Der Anti-Struwwelpeter* (1973), *Wir können noch viel zusammenmachen* (1973), *Die Kronenklauer* (1975), and *Die Bauern im Brunnen* (1978).

31 The publisher of *Der Feuerdrache Minimax* is Rowohlt in Reinbek bei Hamburg. Angela Hopf has written several interesting books which are related to political fairy tales: *Fabeljan* (1968), *Die grosse Elefanten-Olympiade* (1972), *Die Minimax-Comix* (1974), and *Der Regentropfen Pling Plang Pling* (1981).

32 For a thorough and most perceptive analysis of this book, see Hermann Hinkel and Hans Kammler, 'Der Feuerdrache Minimax – ein Märchen? – ein Bilderbuch,' *Die Grundschule*, 3 (1975), pp. 151–60.

33 Among the more interesting studies related to the fairy tale are: Dieter Richter and Johannes Merkel, *Märchen, Phantasie und soziales Lernen* (Berlin: Basis, 1974); Andrea Kuhn, *Tugend und Arbeit. Zur Sozialisation durch Kinder- und Jugendliteratur im 18. Jahrhundert* (Berlin: Basis, 1975); Andrea Kuhn und Johannes Merkel, *Sentimentalität und Geschäft. Zur Sozialisation durch Kinder- und Jugendliteratur im 19. Jahrhundert* (Berlin: Basis, 1977).

34 The publisher of *Janosch erzählt Grimms Märchen* is Beltz & Gelberg in Weinheim.

Janosch, whose real name is Horst Eckert, is considered one of the most inventive and provocative illustrators and writers for young people in West Germany. Among his many titles, the most important are: *Das Auto heisst Ferdinand* (1964), *Wir haben einen Hund zu Haus* (1968), *Flieg Vogel flieg* (1971), *Mein Vater ist König* (1974), *Das grosse Janosch-Buch* (1976), *Ich sag, du bist ein Bär* (1977), *Oh, wie schön ist Panama* (1978), *Die Maus hat rote Strümpfe an* (1978).

35 A good example is *Erstes Jahrbuch der Kinderliteratur. 'Geh und spiel mit dem Riesen,'* ed. by Hans-Joachim Gelberg (Weinheim: Beltz, 1971), which won the German Youth Book Prize of 1972.

36 Many of the tales were printed in other books edited by Gelberg, or they appeared elsewhere, indicative of the great trend to reutilize fairy tales.

37 Translations of the tales by Brender and Künzler have been published in my book *Breaking the Magic Spell*, pp. 180-2.

38 Gmelin, in particular, has been active in scrutinizing the value of fairy tales and has changed his position in the course of the last eight years. See Otto Gmelin, 'Böses kommt aus märchen,' *Die Grundschule*, 3 (1975), pp. 125-32.

39 Lerche and Gmelin, *Märchen für tapfere Mädchen* (Giessen: Schlot, 1978), p. 16.

4 Hans Christian Andersen and the Discourse of the Dominated

Andersen visited me here several years ago. He seemed to me like a tailor. This is the way he really looks. He is a haggard man with a hollow, sunken face, and his demeanour betrays an anxious, devout type of behavior which kings love. This is the reason why they give Andersen such a brilliant reception. He is the perfect representation of all poets, just the way kings want them to be.
Heinrich Heine (1851)

If the Grimm Brothers were the first writers in the nineteenth century to distinguish themselves by remolding oral folk tales explicitly for a bourgeois socialization process, then Hans Christian Andersen completed their mission so to speak and created a canon of literary fairy tales for children between 1835 and 1875 in praise of essentialist ideology. By infusing his tales with general notions of the Protestant Ethic and essentialist ideas of natural biological order, Andersen was able to receive the bourgeois seal of good housekeeping. From the dominant class point of view his tales were deemed useful and worthy enough for rearing chidren of all classes, and they became a literary staple in western culture. Fortunately for Andersen he appeared on the scene when the original middle-class prejudice against imaginative fairy tales was receding. In fact, there was gradual recognition that fantasy could be employed for the utilitarian needs of the bourgeoisie, and Andersen proved to be a most humble servant in this cause.

But what was at the heart of Andersen's mode of service? In what capacity did his tales serve children and adults in Europe and America? What is the connection between Andersen's achievement as a fairy-tale writer, his servile demeanour, and our cultural appreciation of his tales? It seems to me that these questions have to be posed even more critically if we are to understand the underlying reasons behind Andersen's rise to fame and general acceptance in the nineteenth century. In fact, they are crucial if we want to grasp the continual reception, service, and use of the tales in the twentieth century, particularly in regard to socialization through literature.

Despite the fact that Andersen wrote a great deal about himself and his tales and was followed by scholars who have investigated every nook and cranny of his life and work, there have been very few attempts to study his tales ideologically and to analyze their function in the acculturation process. This is all the more surprising when one considers that they were written with a plump didactic purpose and were overloaded with references to normative behavior and ideal political standards. Indeed, the discourse of his narratives has a distinct ideological bias peculiarly 'marred' by his ambivalent feelings toward his social origins and the dominant classes in Denmark that controlled his fortunes. It is this 'marred ambivalence' which is subsumed in his tales and lends them their dynamic tension. Desirous of indicating the way to salvation through emulation of the upper classes and of paying reverence to the Protestant Ethic, Andersen also showed that this path was filled with suffering, humiliation, and torture – and that it could even lead to crucifixion. It is because of his ambivalent attitude, particularly toward the dominance of essentialist ideology, that his tales have retained their basic appeal up through the present day. But before we re-evaluate this appeal as constituted by the socializing elements of the tales, we must first turn to reconsider Andersen in light of the class conflict and conditions of social assimilation in his day.

I

Son of a poor cobbler and a washerwoman, Andersen was embarrassed by his proletarian background and grew to insist on notions of natural nobility. Once he became a successful writer, he rarely mingled with the lower classes. If anything, the opposite was the case: he was known to cowtow to the upper classes throughout *all* of Europe – quite an achievement when one considers his fame! However, his success then and now cannot be attributed to his opportunism and conformism. That is, he cannot simply be dismissed as a class renegade who catered to the aesthetic and ideological interests of the dominant classes. His case is much more complex, for in many respects his tales were innovative narratives which explored the limits of assimilation in a closed social order to which he aspired. Despite all the recognition and acceptance by the nobility and bourgeoisie in the western world, Andersen never felt himself to be a fully fledged member of any group. He was the outsider, the loner, who constantly travelled in his mature years, and his wanderings were symptomatic (as the wanderers and birds in his tales) of a man who hated to be dominated though he loved the dominant class.

As Elias Bredsdorff, the leading contemporary biographer of Andersen, maintains:

> Speaking in modern terms Andersen was a man born in the 'Lumpenproletariat' but completely devoid of class 'consciousness'. In his novels and tales he often expresses an unambiguous sympathy for 'the underdog,' especially for people who have been deprived of their chance of success because of their humble origins, and he pours scorn on haughty people who pride themselves on their noble birth or their wealth and who despise others for belonging to, or having their origin in, the lower classes. But in his private life Andersen accepted the system of absolutism and its inherent class structure, regarded royalty with awe and admiration and found a special pleasure in being accepted by and associating with kings, dukes and princes, and the nobility at home and abroad.[1]

Though Andersen's sympathy did lay with the downtrodden and disenfranchised in his tales, it was not as unambiguous as Bredsdorff would have us believe, for Andersen's fawning servility to the upper classes also manifested itself in his fiction. In fact, as I have maintained, the ambivalent feelings about both his origins and the nobility constitute the appeal of the tales. Andersen prided himself on his 'innate' gifts as poet (*Digter*), and he devoutly believed that certain biologically determined people were chosen by divine providence to rise above others. This belief was his rationalization for aspiring toward recognition and acceptance by the upper classes. And here an important distinction must be made. More than anything else Andersen sought the blessing and recognition of Jonas Collin and the other members of this respectable, wealthy, patriarchal family as well as other people from the educated bureaucratic class in Denmark like Henriette Wulff. In other words, Andersen endeavored to appeal to the Danish bourgeois elite, cultivated in the arts, adept at commerce and administration, and quick to replace the feudal caste of aristocrats as the leaders of Denmark.

The relationship to Jonas Collin was crucial in his development, for Collin took him in hand, when he came to Copenhagen, and practically adopted him as a son. At first he tried to make a respectable bourgeois citizen out of the ambitious 'poet' but gradually relented and supported Andersen's artistic undertakings. In due course Andersen's primary audience came to be the Collin family and people with similar attitudes. All his artistic efforts throughout his life were aimed at pleasing them. For instance, on Jonas Collin's birthday in 1845 he wrote the following:

You know that my greatest vanity, or call it rather joy, consists in making you realize that I am worthy or you. All the kind of appreciation I get makes me think of you. I am truly popular, truly appreciated abroad, I am famous – all right, you're smiling. But the cream of the nations fly towards me, I find myself accepted in all families, the greatest compliments are paid to me by princes and by the most gifted of men. You should see the way people in so-called High Society gather round me. Oh, no one at home thinks of this among the many who entirely ignore me and might be happy to enjoy even a drop of the homage paid to me. My writings must have greater value than the Danes will allow for. Heiberg has been translated too, but no one speaks of his work, and it would have been strange if the Danes were the only ones to be able to make judgments in this world. You must know, you my beloved father must understand that you did not misjudge me when you accepted me as your son, when you helped and protected me.[2]

Just as important as his relationship to the father Collin was his relationship to his 'adopted' brother Edvard, who served as Andersen's super-ego and most severe critic. Not only did Edvard edit Andersen's manuscripts and scold him for writing too fast and too much to gain fame, but he set standards of propriety for the writer through his cool reserve, social composure, and business-like efficiency. In his person Edvard Collin, a Danish legal administrator like his father, represented everything Andersen desired to become, and Andersen developed a strong homo-erotic attachment to Edvard which remained visibly powerful during his life. In 1838 Andersen wrote a revealing letter which indicates just how deep his feelings for Edvard were:

I'm longing for you, indeed, at this moment I'm longing for you as if you were a lovely Calabrian girl with dark blue eyes and a glance of passionate flames. I've never had a brother, but if I had I could not have loved him the way I love you, and yet – you do not reciprocate my feelings! This affects me painfully or maybe this is in fact what binds me even more firmly to you. My soul is proud, the soul of a prince cannot be prouder. I have clung to you, I have – *bastare*! which is a good Italian verb to be translated in Copenhagen as 'shut up!' . . . Oh, I wish to God that you were poor and I rich, distinguished, a nobleman. In that case I should initiate you into the mysteries, and you would appreciate me more than you do now. Oh! If there is an eternal life, as indeed there must be, then we shall truly understand and appreciate one another. Then I shall no longer be the poor person in need of kind interest and friends, then we shall be equal.[3]

The fact is that Andersen never felt himself equal to any of the Collins and that he measured his worth by the standards *they* set. Their letters to him prescribe humility, moderation, asceticism, decorum, economy of mind and soul, devotion to God, loyalty to Denmark. On the one hand, they provided Andersen with a home, and on the other, their criticism and sobriety made him feel insecure. They were too classical and refined, too 'grammatically' correct, and he knew he could never achieve full recognition as *Digter* in their minds. Yet that realization did not stop him from trying to prove his moral worth and aesthetic talents to them in his tales and novels. This is not to suggest that all the fairy tales are totally informed by Andersen's relationship to the Collins. However, to understand their vital aspect – the ideological formation in relationship to the linguistic and semantic discourse – it is important to grasp how Andersen approached and worked through notions of social domination.

Here Noëlle Bisseret's study, *Education, Class Language and Ideology*, is most useful for my purposes since she endeavors to understand the historical origins of essentialist ideology and concepts of natural aptitudes which figure prominently in Andersen's tales. According to her definition,

> essentialist ideology, which originates along with the establishment of those structures constituting class societies, is a denial of the *historical relations* of an economic, political, juridical and ideological order which preside over the establishment of labile power relationships. Essentialist ideology bases all social hierarchy on the transcendental principle of a natural biological order (which took over from a divine principle at the end of the eighteenth century). A difference in essence among human beings supposedly predetermines the diversity of a psychic and mental phenomena ('intelligence,' 'language,' etc.) and thus the place of individual in a social order considered as immutable.[4]

By analyzing how the concepts of aptitude and disposition were used to designate a contingent reality in the late feudal period, Bisseret is able to show a transformation in meaning to legitimize the emerging power of the bourgeoisie in the nineteenth century: aptitude becomes an *essential* hereditary feature and is employed to justify social inequalities. In other words, the principle of equality developed by the bourgeoisie was gradually employed as a socializing agent to demonstrate that there are certain select people in a free market system, people with innate talents who are destined to succeed and rule because they 'possess or own' the essential qualities of intelligence, diligence, and responsibility.

We must remember that the nineteenth century was the period in which the interest in biology, eugenics, and race became exceedingly strong.[5] Not only did Charles Darwin and Herbert Spencer elaborate their theories at this time, but Arthur de Gobineau wrote his *Essai sur l'inegalité des races humaines* (1852) and Francis Galton wrote

Hereditary Genius (1869) to give a seemingly scientific veneer to the middle-class social selection process. Throughout the western world a more solidified bourgeois public sphere was establishing itself and replacing feudal systems, as was clearly the case in Denmark.[6] Along with the new institutions designed for rationalization and maximation of profit, a panoptic principle of control, discipline, and punishment was introduced into the institutions of socialization geared to enforce the interests and to guarantee the domination of the propertied classes. This is fully demonstrated in Michel Foucault's valuable study *Discipline and Punish*,[7] which supports Bisseret's thesis of how the ideological concept of attitudes became the 'scientific' warrant of a social organization which it justified.

> The ideology of natural inequalities conceived and promoted by a social class at a time when it took economic, and later on political, power gradually turned into a scientific truth, borrowing from craniometry, then from anthropometry, biology, genetics, psychology, and sociology (the scientific practice of which it sometimes oriented); the elements enabling it to substantiate its assertions. And by this very means, it was able to impose itself upon all the social groups which believed in the values presiding over the birth of aptitude as an ideology: namely Progress and Science. It now appears that well beyond the controversies, which oppose the different established groups, this general ideology directs the whole conception of selection and educational guidance: the educational system aims at selecting and training an 'elite,' which by its competence, merit, and aptitude is destined for high functions, the responsibility of which entails certain social and economic advantages.[8]

If we look at the case of Andersen in light of Bisseret's thesis at this point, two factors are crucial for his personal conception of an essentialist ideology. First, Denmark was a tiny country with a tightly knit bureaucratic feudal structure which was rapidly undergoing a transformation into a bourgeois dominated society. There were less than 200,000 people in the country, and 120,000 in Copenhagen. Among the educated bourgeoisie and nobility everyone knew everyone else who was of importance, and, though the country depended on the bourgeois bureaucratic administrators and commercial investors, the king and his advisors made most of the significant decisions up until the early 1840s when constitutive assemblies representing the combined interests of industry, commerce, and agriculture began assuming more control. Essentially, as Bredsdorff has aptly stated, 'in Danish society of the early nineteenth century it was almost impossible to break through class barriers. Almost the only exceptions were a few individuals with unusual artistic gifts: Bertel Thorvaldsen, Fru Heiberg and Hans

Christian Andersen. And even they had occasionally to be put in their place and reminded of their low origin.'⁹ Here it is difficult to talk about a *real* breakthrough. Throughout his life Andersen was obliged to act as a dominated subject within the dominant social circles despite his fame and recognition as a writer.

Even to reach this point – and this is the second crucial factor – he had to be strictly supervised, for admission to the upper echelons had to be earned and constantly proved. And, Andersen appeared to be a 'security risk' at first. Thus, when he came to Copenhagen in 1819 from the lower-class and provincial milieu of Odense, he had to be corrected by his betters so that he could cultivate proper speech, behavior, and decorum. Then for polishing he was also sent to elite private schools in Slagelse and Helsingör at a late age from 1822 to 1827 to receive a thorough formal and classical education. The aim of this education was to curb and control Andersen, especially his flamboyant imagination, not to help him achieve a relative amount of autonomy.

> Jonas Collin's purpose in rescuing Andersen and sending him to a grammar school was not to make a great writer out of him but to enable him to become a useful member of the community in a social class higher than the one into which he was born. The grammar-school system was devised to teach boys to learn properly, to mould them into the desired finished products, to make them grow up to be like their fathers.[10]

As Bredsdorff remarks, the system was not so thorough that Andersen was completely broken. But it left its indelible marks. What Andersen was to entitle *The Fairy Tale of My Life* – his autobiography, a remarkable mythopoeic projection of his life[11] – was in actuality a process of self-denial which was cultivated as individualism. Andersen was ashamed of his family background and did his utmost to avoid talking or writing about it. When he did, he invariably distorted the truth. For him, home was the Collin family, but home, as Andersen knew quite well, was unattainable because of social differences.

It was through his writings and literary achievement that Andersen was able to veil his self-denial and present it as a form of individualism. At the beginning of the nineteenth century in Denmark there was a literary swing from the universality of classicism to the romantic cult of genius and individuality, and Andersen benefited from this greatly. As a voracious reader, Andersen consumed all the German romantic writers of fairy tales along with Shakespeare, Scott, Irving, and other writers who exemplified his ideal of individualism. Most important for his formation in Denmark, the romantic movement was

> accompanied by what is known as the Aladdin motif, after the idea which

Oehlenschläger expressed in his play Aladdin. This deals with the theory that certain people are chosen by nature, or God, or the gods, to achieve greatness, and that nothing can succeed in stopping them, however weak and ill-suited they may otherwise seem. . . . The twin themes of former national greatness and of the possibility of being chosen to be great, despite all appearances, assumed a special significance for Denmark after 1814. Romantic-patriotic drama dealing with the heroic past appealed to a population looking for an escape from the sordid present, and served as a source of inspiration for many years. At the same time the Aladdin conception also took on new proportions: it was not only of use as a literary theme, but it could be applied to individuals – Oehlenschläger felt that he himself exemplified it, as did Hans Christian Andersen – and it was also possible to apply it to a country.[12]

Andersen as Aladdin. Andersen's life as a fairy tale. There is something schizophrenic in pretending that one is a fairy-tale character in reality, and Andersen was indeed troubled by nervous disorders and psychic disturbances throughout his life. To justify his schizophrenic existence, he adopted the Danish physicist Hans Christian Orsted's ideas from *The Spirit of Nature* and combined them with his animistic belief in Christianity.[13] Orsted believed that the laws of nature are the thoughts of God, and, as the spirit of nature becomes projected, reality assumes the form of a miracle. Moreover, Andersen felt that, if life is miraculous, then God protects 'His elect' and gives them the help they need. Such superstition – his mother was extraordinarily superstitious – only concealed Andersen's overwhelming desire to escape the poverty of his existence and his indefatigable efforts to gain fame as a writer. Certainly, if providence controlled the workings of the world, genius was a divine and natural gift and would be rewarded regardless of birth. Power was located in the hands of God, and only before Him did one have to bow. However, Andersen did in fact submit more to a temporal social system and had to rationalize this submission adequately enough so that he could live with himself. In doing so, he inserted himself into a socio-historical nexus of the dominated denying his origins and needs to receive applause, money, comfort, and space to write about social contradictions that he had difficulty resolving for himself. Such a situation meant a life of self-doubt and anxiety for Andersen.

Again Bisseret is useful in helping us understand the socio-psychological impact on such ego formation and perspectives:

Dominant in imagination (who am I?), dominated in reality (what am I?), the ego lacks cohesion, hence the contradiction and incoherence of the practices. Dominated-class children think in terms of aptitudes, tastes and interests because at each step in their education their success has progressively convinced them that they are not 'less than nothing' intellectually; but at the same time they profoundly doubt themselves. This doubt is certainly not unrelated to the split, discontinuous aspects of their orientations, as measured by the standards of a parsimonious and fleeting time. Their day-to-day projects which lead them into dead ends or which build up gaps in knowledge which are inhibitory for their educational future, reinforce their doubts as to their capacities.[14]

In the particular case of Andersen, the self-doubts were productive insofar as he constantly felt the need to prove himself, to show that his aptitude and disposition were noble and that he belonged to the elect. This is apparent in the referential system built into most of his tales which are discourses of the dominated. In analyzing such discourse, Bisseret makes the point that

> the relationship to his social being simultaneously lived and conceived by each agent is based on unconscious knowledge. What is designated as the 'subject' (the 'I') in the social discourse is the social being of the dominant. Thus in defining his identity the dominated cannot polarize the comparison between the self/the others on his 'me' in the way the dominant does. . . There cannot be a cohesion except on the side of power. Perhaps the dominated ignore that less than the dominant, as is clear through their accounts. Indeed, the more the practices of the speaker are the practices of power, the more the situation in which he places himself in the conceptual field is the mythical place where power disappears to the benefit of a purely abstract creativity. On the other hand, the more the speaker is subjected to power, the more he situates himself to the very place where power is concretely exercised.[15]

Though Bisseret's ideas about the dominated and dominant in regard to essentialist ideology are concerned with linguistic forms in everyday speech, they also apply to modes of narration used by writers of fiction. For instance, Andersen mixed popular language or folk linguistic forms with formal classical speech in creating his tales, and this stylistic synthesis not only endowed the stories with an unusual tone but also reflected Andersen's efforts to unify an identity which dominant discourse kept dissociating. Andersen also endeavored to ennoble and synthesize folk motifs with the literary motifs of romantic fairy tales, particularly those of Hoffmann, Tieck, Chamisso, Eichendorff, and Fouqué. His stylization of lower-class folk motifs was similar to his personal attempt to rise in society: they were aimed at meeting the standards of 'high art' set by the middle classes. In sum, Andersen's linguistic forms and stylized motifs reveal the structure of relationships as they were being formed and solidified around emerging bourgeois domination in the nineteenth century.

With a few exceptions, most of the 156 fairy tales written by Andersen contain no 'I,' that is, the 'I' is sublimated through the third person, and the narrative discourse becomes dominated by constant reference to the location of power. The identification of the third-person narrator with the underdog or dominated in the tales is consequently misleading. On one level, this occurs, but the narrator's voice always seeks approval and identification with a higher force. Here, too, the figures representing dominance or nobility are not always at the seat of power. Submission to power beyond the aristocracy constituted and constitutes the real appeal of Andersen's tales for middle-class audiences: Andersen placed power in divine providence, which invariably acted in the name of bourgeois essentialist ideology. No other writer of literary fairy tales in the early nineteenth century introduced so many Christian notions of God, the Protestant Ethic, and bourgeois enterprise in his narratives as Andersen did. All his tales make explicit or implicit reference to a miraculous Christian power which rules firmly but justly over His subjects. Such patriarchal power would appear to represent a feudal organization but the dominant value system represented by providential action and the plots of the tales is thoroughly bourgeois and justifies essentialist notions of aptitude and disposition. Just as aristocratic power was being transformed in Denmark, so Andersen reflected upon the meaning of such transformation in his tales.

There are also clear strains of social Darwinism in Andersen's tales mixed with the Aladdin motif. In fact, survival of the fittest is the message of the very first tale he wrote for the publication of his anthology – *The Tinderbox*. However, the fittest is not always the strongest but the chosen protagonist who proves himself or herself worthy of serving a dominant value system. This does not mean that Andersen constantly preached one message in all his tales. As a whole, written from 1835 to 1875, they represent the creative process of a dominated ego endeavoring to establish a unified self while confronted with a dominant discourse which dissociated this identity. The fictional efforts are variations on a theme of how to achieve approbation, assimilation, and integration in a social system which does not allow for real acceptance or recognition if one comes from the lower classes. In many respects Andersen is like a Humpty-Dumpty figure who had a great fall when he realized as he grew up that entrance into the educated elite of Denmark did not mean acceptance and totality. Nor could all the king's men and horses put him back together when he was humiliated and perceived the inequalities. So his fairy tales are variegated and sublimated efforts to achieve wholeness, to gain vengeance, and to depict the reality of class struggle. The dominated voice, however, remains constant in its reference to real power.

Obviously there are other themes than power and domination in the tales and other valid approaches to them, but I believe that the widespread, continuous reception of Andersen's fairy tales in western culture can best be explained by understanding how the discourse of the dominated functions in the narratives. Ideologically speaking Andersen furthered bourgeois notions of the self-made man or the Horatio Alger myth, which was becoming so popular in America and elsewhere, while reinforcing a belief in the existing power structure that meant domination and exploitation of the lower classes. This is why we must look more closely at the tales to analyze how they embody the dreams of social rise and individual happiness which further a powerful, all-encompassing bourgeois selection process.

II

Bredsdorff notes that, among the 156 tales written by Andersen, there are 30 which have proven to be the most popular throughout the world.[16] My analysis will concentrate first on these tales in an effort to comprehend the factors which might constitute their popularity in reception. Since they form the kernel of Andersen's achievement, they can be considered the ultimate examples of how the dominated discourse can rationalize power in fairy tales written for children and adults as well. Aside from examining this aspect of these tales, I shall also analyze those features in other significant tales that reveal the tensions of a life which was far from the fairy tale Andersen wanted his readers to believe it was. Ironically, the fairy tales he wrote are more 'realistic' than his own autobiographies, when understood as discourses defined by dominance relationships in which the narrator defines what he would like to be according to definitions of a socially imposed identity.

Since there is no better starting point than the beginning, let us consider Andersen's very first tale *The Tinderbox* as an example of how his dominated discourse functions. As I have already mentioned, the basic philosophy of *The Tinderbox* corresponds to the principles of social Darwinism, but this is not sufficient enough to understand the elaboration of power relations and the underlying message of the tale. We must explore further.

As the tale unfolds, it is quite clear that the third-person narrative voice and providence are on the young soldier's side, for without any ostensible reason he is chosen by the witch to fetch a fortune. Using his talents, he not only gains a treasure but immense power, even if he must kill the witch to do so. Here the murder of the witch is not viewed as immoral since witches are evil *per se*. The major concern of Andersen is to present a young soldier who knows how to pull himself up by the bootstraps when fortune shines upon him to become a 'refined gentleman.'[17] The word refined has nothing to do with culture but more with money and power. The soldier learns this when he runs out of coins, is forgotten by fair-weather friends, and sinks in social status. Then he discovers the magic of the tinderbox and the power of the three dogs which means endless provision. Here Andersen subconsciously concocted a socio-political formula which was the keystone of bourgeois progress and success in the nineteenth century: use of talents for the acquisition of money, establish a system of continual recapitalization (tinderbox and three dogs) to guarantee income and power, employ money and power to achieve social and political hegemony. The soldier is justified in his use of power and money because he is *essentially* better than anyone else – chosen to rule. The king and queen are dethroned, and the soldier rises through the application of his innate talents and fortune to assume control of society.

Though it appears that the soldier is the hero of the story, there is a hidden referent of power in this dominated narrative discourse. Power does not reside in the soldier but in the 'magical' organization of social relations that allows him to pursue and realize his dreams. Of course, these social relations were not as magical as they appear since they were formed through actual class struggle to allow for the emergence of a middle class which set its own rules of the game and established those qualities necessary for leadership: cleverness, perseverance, cold calculation, respect for money and private property. Psychologically Andersen's hatred for his own class (his mother) and the Danish nobility (king and queen) are played out bluntly when the soldier kills the witch and has the king and queen eliminated by the dogs. The wedding celebration at the end is basically a celebration of the solidification of power by the bourgeois class in the nineteenth century: the unification of a middle-class soldier with a royal princess. In the end the humorous narrative voice appears to gain deep pleasure and satisfaction in having related this tale, as though it has been ordained from above.

In all the other tales published in 1835 there is a process of selection and proving one's worth according to the hidden referent of bourgeois power. In *Little Claus and Big Claus* the small farmer must first learn the lesson of humility before providence takes his side and guides him against the vengeful big farmer. Again, using his wits without remorse, an ordinary person virtually obliterates a rich arrogant landowner and amasses a small fortune. *The Princess and the Pea* is a simple story about the *essence* of true nobility. A *real* prince can only marry a *genuine* princess with the right sensitivity. This sensitivity is spelled out in different ways in the other tales of 1835: *Little Ida's Flowers*, *Thumbelina*, and *The Travelling Companion* portray 'small' or oppressed people who cultivate their special talents and struggle to realize their goals despite the forces of adversity. Ida retains and fulfills her dreams of flowers despite the crass professor's vicious attacks. Thumbelina survives many adventures to marry the king of the angels and become a queen. Johannes, the poor orphan, promises to be good so that God will protect him, and indeed his charitable deeds amount to a marriage with a princess. The *Taugenichts* who trusts in God will always be rewarded. All the gifted but disadvantaged characters, who are God-fearing, come into their own in Andersen's tales, but they never take possession of power which resides in the shifting social relations leading to bourgeois hegemony.

In all of these early tales Andersen focuses on lower-class or disenfranchised protagonists, who work their way up in society.[18] Their rise is predicated on their proper behavior which must correspond to a higher power that elects and tests the hero. Though respect is shown for feudal patriarchy, the correct normative behavior reflects the values of the bourgeoisie. If the hero comes from the lower classes, he or she must be humbled if not humiliated at one point to test obedience. Thereafter, the natural aptitude of a successful individual will be unveiled through diligence, perseverence, and adherence to an ethical system which legitimizes bourgeois domination. Let me be more specific by focusing on what I consider the major popular tales written after 1835: *The Little Mermaid* (1837), *The Steadfast Tin Soldier* (1838), *The Swineherd* (1841), *The Nightingale* (1843), *The Ugly Duckling* (1843), *The Red Shoes* (1845), and *The Shadow* (1847).

There are two important factors to bear in mind when considering the reception of these tales in the nineteenth century and the present in regard to the narrative discourse of the dominated. First, as a member of the dominated class, Andersen could only experience dissociation despite entrance into upper-class circles. Obviously this was because he measured his success as a person and artist by standards which were not of his own social group's making. That ultimate power which judged his efforts and the destiny of his heroes depended on the organization of hierarchical relations at a time of socio-political transformation which was to leave Denmark and most of Europe under the control of the bourgeoisie. This shift in power led Andersen to identify with the emerging middle-class elite, but he did not depict the poor and disenfranchised in a negative way. On the contrary, Andersen assumed a humble, philanthropic stance – the fortunate and gifted are obliged morally and ethically to help the less fortunate. The dominated voice of all his narratives does not condemn his former social class, rather Andersen loses contact with it by denying the rebellious urges of his class within himself and making compromises that affirmed the rightful domination of the middle-class ethic.

A second factor to consider is the fundamental ambiguity of the dominated discourse in Andersen's tales: this discourse cannot represent the interests of the dominated class; it can only rationalize the power of the dominant class so that this power becomes legitimate and acceptable to those who are powerless. As I have noted before, Andersen depersonalizes his tales by using the third-person stance which appears to universalize his voice. However, this self-denial is a recourse of the dominated, who always carry references and appeal to those forces which control their lives. In Andersen's case he mystifies power and makes it appear divine. It is striking, as I have already stressed, when one compares Andersen to other fairy-tale writers of his time, how he constantly appeals to God and the Protestant Ethic to justify and sanction the actions and results of his tales. Ironically, to have a soul in Andersen's tales one must sell one's soul either to the aristocracy or to the bourgeoisie. In either case it was the middle-class moral and social code which guaranteed the success of his protagonists, guaranteed his own social success, and ultimately has guaranteed the successful reception of the tales to the present.

Speaking about lost souls, then, let us turn to *The Little Mermaid* to grasp how the dominated seemingly gains 'happiness and fulfillment' while losing its voice and real power. This tale harks back to the folk stories of the water urchin who desires a soul so she can marry a human being whom she loves. Andersen was certainly familiar with Goethe's *Melusine* and Fouqué's *Undine*, stories which ennobled the aspirations of pagan sprites, but his tale about the self-sacrificing mermaid is distinctly different from the narratives of Goethe and Fouqué, who were always part of the dominant class and punished upper-class men for forgetting their Christian manners. Andersen's perspective focuses more on the torture and suffering which a member of the dominated class must undergo to establish her true nobility and virtues. Characteristically, Andersen only allows the mermaid to rise out of the water and move in the air of royal circles after her tongue is removed and her tail is transformed into legs described as 'sword-like' when she walks or dances. Voiceless and tortured, deprived physically and psychologically, the mermaid serves a prince who never fully appreciates her worth. Twice she saves his life. The second time is most significant: instead of killing him to regain her identity and rejoin her sisters and grandmother, the mermaid forfeits her own life and becomes an ethereal figure, blessed by God. If she does good deeds for the next 300 years, she will be endowed with an immortal soul. As she is told, her divine mission will consist of flying through homes of human beings as an invisible spirit. If she finds a good child who makes his parents happy and deserves their love, her sentence will be shortened. A naughty and mean child can lengthen the 300 years she must serve in God's name.

However, the question is whether the mermaid is really acting in God's name. Her falling in love with royalty and all her future actions involve self-denial and a process of rationalizing self-denial. The mermaid's ego becomes dissociated because she is attracted to a class of people who will never accept her on her own terms. To join her 'superiors' she must practically cut her own throat, and, though she realizes that she can never express truthfully who she is and what her needs are, she is unwilling to return to her own species or dominated class. Thus she must somehow justify her existence to herself through abstinence and self-abnegation – values preached by the bourgeoisie and certainly not practiced by the nobility and upper classes. Paradoxically Andersen seems to be preaching that true virtue and self-realization can be obtained through self-denial. This message, however, is not so paradoxical since it comes from the voice of the dominated. In fact, it is based on Andersen's astute perception and his own experience as a lower-class clumsy youth who sought to cultivate himself: by becoming voiceless, walking with legs like knives, and denying one's needs, one (as a non-entity) gains divine recognition.

Andersen never tired of preaching self-abandonment and self-deprivation in the name of bourgeois laws. The reward was never power over one's life but security in adherence to power. For instance, in *The Steadfast Tin Soldier*, the soldier falls in love with a ballerina and remarks: 'She would be a perfect wife for me. . . but I am afraid she is above me. She has a castle, and I have only a box that I must share with twenty-four soldiers; that wouldn't do for her. Still, I would like to make her acquaintance.'[19] He must endure all sorts of hardships in pursuit of his love and is finally rewarded with fulfillment – but only after he and the ballerina are burned and melted in a stove. Again, happiness is predicated on a form of self-effacement.

This does not mean that Andersen was always self-denigrating in his tales. He often attacked greed and false pride. But what is interesting here is that vice is generally associated with the pretentious aristocracy and hardly ever with bourgeois characters. Generally speaking, Andersen punished overreachers, that is, the urge within himself to be rebellious. Decorum and balance became articles of faith in his philosophical scheme of things. In *The Swineherd* he delights in depicting the poor manners of a princess who has lost her sense of propriety. Andersen had already parodied the artificiality and pretentiousness of the nobility in *The Tinderbox* and *The Emperor's Clothes*. Similar to the 'taming of the shrew' motif in the folk tale *King Thrushbeard*, Andersen now has the dominant figure of the fickle, proud princess humiliated by the dominated figure of the prince disguised as swineherd. However, there is no happy end here, for the humor assumes a deadly seriousness when the prince rejects the princess after accomplishing his aim: ' "I have come to despise you", said the prince, "You did not want an honest prince. You did not appreciate the rose of the nightingale, but you could kiss a swineherd for the sake of a toy. Farewell!" '[20]

The oppositions are clear: honesty vs. falseness, genuine beauty (rose/nightingale) vs. manufactured beauty (toys), nobility of the soul vs. soulless nobility. Indirectly Andersen argues that the nobility must adapt to the value system of the emerging bourgeoisie or be locked out of the kingdom of happiness. Without appreciating the beauty and power of genuine leaders – the prince is essentially middle-class – the monarchy will collapse.

This theme is at the heart of *The Nightingale*, which can also be considered a remarkable treatise about art, genius, and the role of the artist. The plot involves a series of transformations in power relations and service. First the Chinese Emperor, a benevolent patriarch, has the nightingale brought to his castle from the forest. When the chief courtier finds the nightingale, he exclaims: 'I had not imagined it would look like that. It looks so common! I think it has lost its color from shyness and out of embarrassment at seeing so many noble people at one time.'[21] Because the common-looking bird (an obvious reference to Andersen) possesses an inimitable artistic genius, he is engaged to serve the Emperor. The first phase of the dominant–dominated relationship based on bonded servitude is changed into neglect when the Emperor is given a jeweled mechanical bird that never tires of singing. So the nightingale escapes and returns to the forest, and eventually the mechanical bird breaks down. Five years later the Emperor falls sick and appears to be dying. Out of his own choice the nightingale returns to him and chases death from his window. Here the relationship of servitude is resumed with the exception that the nightingale has assumed a different market value: he agrees to be the emperor's songbird forever as long as he can come and go as he pleases. Feudalism has been replaced by a free market system; yet, the bird/artist is willing to serve loyally and keep the autocrat in power. 'And my song shall make you happy and make you thoughtful. I shall sing not only of the good and of the evil that happen around you, and yet are hidden from you. For a little songbird flies far. I visit the poor fisherman's cottages and the peasant's hut, far away from your palace and your court. I love your heart more than your crown, and I feel that the crown has a fragrance of something holy about it. I will come! I will sing for you!'[22]

As we know, Andersen depended on the patronage of the King of Denmark and other upper-class donors, but he never felt esteemed enough, and he disliked the strings which were attached to the money given to him. Instead of breaking with such patronage, however, the dominated voice of this discourse seeks to set new limits which continue servitude in marketable conditions more tolerable for the servant. Andersen reaffirms the essentialist ideology of this period and reveals how gifted 'common' individuals are the pillars of power – naturally in service to the state. Unfortunately, he never bothered to ask why 'genius' cannot stand on its own and perhaps unite with like-minded people.

In *The Ugly Duckling* genius also assumes a most awe-inspiring shape, but it cannot fly on its own. This tale has generally been interpreted as a parable of Andersen's own success story because the naturally gifted underdog survives a period of 'ugliness' to reveal its innate beauty. Yet, more attention should be placed on the *servility of genius*. Though Andersen continually located real power in social conditions which allowed for the emergence of bourgeois hegemony, he often argued – true to conditions in Denmark – that power was to be dispensed in servitude to appreciate rulers, and naturally these benevolent rulers were supposed to recognize the interests of the bourgeoisie. As we have seen in *The Nightingale*, the artist returns to serve royalty after he is neglected by the emperor. In *The Ugly Duckling*, the baby swan is literally chased by coarse lower-class animals from the henyard. His innate beauty cannot be recognized by such crude specimens, and only after he survives numerous ordeals, does he realize his essential greatness. But his self-realization is ambivalent, for right before he perceives his true nature, he wants to kill himself: 'I shall fly over to them, those royal birds! And they can hack me to death because I, who am so ugly, dare to approach them! What difference does it make! It is better to be killed by them than to be bitten by the other ducks, and pecked by the hens, and kicked by the girl who tends the henyard; or to suffer through the winter.'[23]

Andersen expresses a clear disdain for the common people's lot and explicitly states that to be humiliated by the upper class is worth more than the trials and tribulations one must suffer among the lower classes. And, again, Andersen espouses bourgeois essentialist philosophy when he saves the swan and declares as narrator: 'It does not matter that one has been born in the henyard as long as one has lain in a swan's egg.'[24] The fine line between eugenics and racism fades in this story where the once-upon-a-time dominated swan reveals himself to be a tame but noble member of a superior race. The swan does not return 'home' but lands in a beautiful garden where he is admired by children, adults, and nature. It appears as though the swan has finally come into his own, but, as usual, there is a hidden reference of power. The swan measures himself by the values and aesthetics set by the 'royal' swans and by the proper well-behaved children and people in the beautiful garden. The swans and the beautiful garden are placed in opposition to the ducks and the henyard. In appealing to the 'noble' sentiments of a refined audience and his readers, Andersen reflected a distinct class bias if not classical racist tendencies.

What happens, however, when one opposes the structures of the dominant class? Here Andersen can be merciless, just as merciless as the people who reprimanded and scolded him for overreaching himself. In *The Red Shoes*, Karen, a poor little orphan, mistakenly believes that she is adopted by a generous old woman because she wears red shoes, a symbol of vanity and sin. This red stigma is made clear as she is about to be baptized in church: 'When the bishop laid his hands on her head and spoke of the solemn promise she was about to make – of her convenant with God to be a good Christian – her mind was not on his words. The ritual music was played on the organ; the old cantor sang, and the sweet voices of the children could be heard, but Karen was thinking of her red shoes.'[25] Although she tries to abandon the red shoes, she cannot resist their red lure. So she must be taken to task and is visited by a stern angel who pronounces sentence upon her: ' "You shall dance," he said, "dance in your red shoes until you become red and thin. Dance till the skin on your face turns yellow and clings to your bones as if you were a skeleton. Dance you shall from door to door, and when you pass a house where proud and vain children live, there you shall knock on the door so they will see you and fear your fate." '[26]

The only way Karen can overcome the angel's curse is by requesting the municipal executioner to cut off her feet. Thereafter, she works diligently for the minister of the church. Upon her death, Karen's devout soul 'flew on a sunbeam up to God.'[27] This ghastly tale – reminiscent of the gory German pedagogical best-seller of this time, Heinrich

Hoffmann's *Struwwelpeter* (1845) – is a realistic description of the punishment which awaited anyone who dared oppose the powers that be.

Though Andersen acknowledged the right of the Danish ruling class to exercise its power, he knew how painful it was to be at their mercy. The most telling tale about the excrutiating psychological effects of servility, the extreme frustration he felt from his own obsequious behavior, was *The Shadow*. As many critics have noted, this haunting narrative is highly autobiographical; it stems from the humiliation that Andersen suffered when Edvard Collin adamantly rejected his proposal to use the 'familiar you' (*du*) in their discourse – and there was more than one rejection. By retaining the 'formal you' (De), Collin was undoubtedly asserting his class superiority, and this distance was meant to remind Andersen of his humble origins. Though they had come to regard each other as brothers during their youth, Collin lorded his position over Andersen throughout their lives and appeared to administrate Andersen's life – something which the writer actually desired but feared. In *The Shadow* Andersen clearly sought to avenge himself through his tale about a philosopher's shadow who separates himself from his owner and becomes immensely rich and successful. When the shadow returns to visit the scholar, his former owner wants to know how he achieved such success. To which the shadow replies that he will reveal 'everything! And I'll tell you about it, but . . . it has nothing whatsoever to do with pride, but out of respect to my accomplishments, not to speak of my social position, I wish you wouldn't address me familiarly.'

' "Forgive me!" exclaimed the philosopher. "It is an old habit, and they are the hardest to get rid of. But you are quite right, and I'll try to remember." '[28]

Not only does the shadow/Andersen put the philosopher/Collin in his place, but he explains that it was *Poetry* which made a human being out of him and that he quickly came to understand his 'innermost nature, that part of me which can claim kinship to poetry.'[29] Humanlike and powerful, the shadow can control other people because he can see their evil sides. His own sinister talents allow him to improve his fortunes, while the philosopher, who can only write about the beautiful and the good, becomes poor and neglected. Eventually, the philosopher is obliged to travel with his former shadow – the shadow now as master and the master as shadow. When the shadow deceives a princess to win her hand in marriage, the philosopher threatens to reveal the truth about him. The crafty shadow, however, convinces the princess that the old man himself is a deranged shadow, and she decides to have him killed to end his misery.

The reversal of fortunes and of power relations is not a process of liberation but one of revenge. Nor can one argue that the shadow possesses power, for power cannot be possessed in and of itself but is constituted by the organization of social classes and property. One can gain access to power and draw upon it, and this is what the shadow does. Aside from being Andersen's wish-fulfillment, the fantastic projection in this story is connected to the Hegelian notion of master/slave (*Herr/Knecht*). The shadow/slave, who is closer to material conditions, is able to take advantage of what he sees and experiences – the underpinnings of social life – to overthrow his master, whereas the master, who has only been able to experience reality through the mediation of his shadow, is too idealistic and cannot defend himself. In Andersen's tale it should be noted that the shadow does not act in the interests of the dominated class but rather *within* the framework of institutionalized power relationships. Therefore, he still remains servile and caters to the dominant class despite the reversal of his circumstances. In this regard Andersen's heroes, who rise in class, do not undergo a qualitative change in social existence but point more to manifold ways one can accede to power.

As we have seen, the major theme and its variations in Andersen's most popular tales pertain to the rise of a protagonist under conditions of servitude. Only if the chosen hero complies with a code based on the Protestant Ethic and reveres divine providence does he advance in society or reach salvation. Though this is not explicitly spelled out, the references to real power reveal that it resides in the social organization of relations affirming bourgeois hegemony of a patriarchal nature. Even the benevolent feudal kings cannot maintain power without obeying sacrosanct bourgeois moral laws. Obviously this applies to the members of the lower classes and circumscribes their rise in fortunes. Limits are placed on their position in acceptable society. In most of the other 126 tales, which are not as widely circulated as the best known Andersen narratives, the dominated voice remains basically the same: it humbly recognizes the bourgeois rules of the game, submits itself to them as loyal subject and has the fictional protagonists do the same.

III

What saves Andersen's tales from simply becoming sentimental homilies (which many of them are) was his extraordinary understanding of how class struggle affected the lives of people in his times, and some tales even contain a forthright criticism of abusive domination – though his critique was always balanced by admiration for the upper classes and a fear of poverty. For instance, there are some exceptional tales of the remaining 126 which suggest a more rebellious position. Such rebelliousness, perhaps, accounts for the fact that they are not among the 30 most popular. Indeed, the dominated discourse is not homogenous or univocal, though it constantly refers to bourgeois power and never seeks to defy it. In 1853, shortly after the revolutionary period of 1848–1850 in Europe, Andersen reflected upon the thwarted rebellions in a number of tales, and they are worth discussing because they show more clearly how Andersen wavered when he subjected himself to bourgeois and aristocratic domination.

In *Everything in its Right Place* (1853) the arrogant aristocratic owner of a manor takes pleasure in pushing a goose-girl off a bridge. The peddler, who watches this and saves the girl, curses the master by exclaiming 'everything in its right place.'[30] Sure enough, the aristocrat drinks and gambles away the manor in the next six years. The new owner is none other than the peddler, and, of course, he takes the goose girl for his bride and the Bible as his guide. The family prospers for the next hundred years with its motto 'everything in its right place.' At this point the narrator introduces us to a parson's son tutoring the humble daughter of the now wealthy enobled house. This idealistic tutor discusses the differences between the nobility and bourgeoisie and surprises the modest baronness by stating:

'I know it is the fashion of the day – and many a poet dances to that tune – to say that everything aristocratic is stupid and bad. They claim that only among the poor – and the lower you descend the better – does pure gold glitter. But that is not my opinion; I think it is wrong, absolutely false reasoning. Among the highest classes one can often observe the most elevated traits. . . But where nobility has gone to a man's head and he behaves like an Arabian horse that rears and kicks, just because his blood is pure and he has a degree, there nobility has degenerated. When noblemen sniff the air in a room because a plain citizen has been there and say, "It smells of the street," why then Thespis should exhibit them to the just ridicule of satire.'[31]

This degradation is, indeed, what occurs. A cavalier tries to mock the tutor at a music soiree, and the tutor plays a melody on a simple willow flute which suddenly creates a storm with the wind howling 'everything in its right place!' In the house and throughout the countryside the wind tosses people about, and social class positions are reversed until the flute cracks and everyone returns to their former place. After this scare, Andersen still warns that 'eventually everything is put in its right place. Eternity is long, a lot longer than this story.'[32] Such a 'revolutionary' tone was uncharacteristic of Andersen, but given the mood of the times, he was prompted time and again in the early 1850s to voice his critique of the upper classes and question not only aristocratic but also bourgeois hegemony.

In *The Pixy and the Grocer* (1853) a little imp lives in a grocer's store and receives a free bowl of porridge and butter each Christmas. The grocer also rents out the garret to a poor student who would rather buy a book of poetry and eat bread for supper instead of cheese. The pixy visits the student in the garret to punish him for calling the grocer a boor with no feeling for poetry. Once in the garret, however, the pixy discovers the beauty and magic of poetry and almost decides to move in with the student. Almost, for he remembers that the student does not have much food, nor can he give him porridge with butter. So he continues to visit the garret from time to time. Then one night a fire on the street threatens to spread to the grocer's house. The grocer and his wife grab their gold and bonds and run out of the house. The student remains calm while the pixy tries to save the most valuable thing in the house – the book of poetry. 'Now he finally understood his heart's desire, where his loyalty belonged! But when the fire in the house across the street had been put out, then he thought about it again. "I will share myself between them," he said, "for I cannot leave the grocer altogether. I must stay there for the sake of the porridge." '33 'That was quite human,' the dominated narrator concludes, 'after all, we, too, go to the grocer for the porridge's sake.'34

This tale is much more ambivalent in its attitude toward domination than *Everything in Its Right Place*, which is open-ended and allows for the possibility of future revolutions. Here, Andersen writes more about himself and his own contradictions at the time of an impending upheaval (i.e., fire = revolution). Faced with a choice, the pixy/Andersen leans toward poetry or the lower classes and idealism. But, when the fire subsides, he makes his usual compromise, for he knows where his bread is buttered and power resides. The narrative discourse is ironic, somewhat self-critical but ultimately rationalizing. Since everyone falls in line with the forces that dominate and provide food, why not the pixy? Who is he to be courageous or different? Nothing more is said about the student, nor is there any mention of those who do not make compromises. Andersen makes it appear that servility is most human and understandable. Rarely does he suggest that it is just as human to rebel against inequality and injustice out of need as it is to bow to arbitrary domination.

The tales of 1853 demonstrate how Andersen was not unaware of possibilities for radical change and questioned the conditions of bourgeois/aristocratic hegemony. In one of his most remarkable tales *The*

Gardener and His Master, written toward the very end of his life in 1871, he sums up his views on servitude, domination, and aptitude in his brilliantly succinct, ambivalent manner. The plot is simple and familiar. A haughty aristocrat has an excellent plain gardener who tends his estate outside of Copenhagen. The master, however, never trusts the advice of the gardener nor appreciates what he produces. He and his wife believe that the fruits and flowers grown by other gardeners are better, and, when they constantly discover, to their chagrin, that their very own gardener's work is considered the best by the royal families, they hope he won't think too much of himself. Then, the storyteller Andersen comments, 'he didn't; but the fame was a spur, he wanted to be one of the best gardeners in the country. Every year he tried to improve some of the vegetables and fruits, and often he was successful. It was not always appreciated. He would be told that the pears and apples were good but not as good as the ones last year. The melons were excellent but not quite up to the standard of the first ones he had grown.'[35]

The gardener must constantly prove himself, and one of his great achievements is his use of an area to plant 'all the typical common plants of Denmark, gathered from forests and fields'[36] which flourish because of his nursing care and devotion. So, in the end, the owners of the castle must be proud of the gardener because the whole world beat the drums for his success. 'But they weren't really proud of it. They felt that they were the owners and that they could dismiss Larsen if they wanted to. They didn't, for they were decent people, and there are lots of their kind, which is fortunate for the Larsens.'[37]

In other words, Andersen himself had been fortunate, or, at least this was the way he ironically viewed his career at the end of his life. Yet, there is something pathetically sad about this story. The gardener Larsen is obviously the storyteller Andersen, and the garden with all its produce is the collection of fairy tales which he kept cultivating and improving throughout his life. The owners of the garden are Andersen's patrons and may be associated with the Collin family and other upper-class readers in Denmark. We must remember that it was generally known that the Collin family could never come to recognize Andersen as a *Digter* but thought of him as a fine popular writer. Andersen, whose vanity was immense and unquenchable, was extremely sensitive to criticism, and he petulantly and consistently complained that he felt unappreciated in Denmark while other European countries recognized his genius. Such treatment at home despite the fact he considered himself a most loyal servant, whether real or projected, became symbolized in this tale. The reference to the *common plants*, which the gardener cultivates, pertains to the folk motifs he employed and enriched so they would bloom aesthetically on their own soil. Andersen boasts that he, the gardener, has made Denmark famous, for pictures are taken of this garden and circulated throughout the world. Yet, it is within the confines of servitude and patronage that the gardener works, and the dominated voice of the narrator, even though ironic, rationalizes the humiliating ways in which his masters treat Larsen: they are 'decent' people. But, one must wonder – and the tension of the discourse compels us to do so – that, if the gardener is superb and brilliant, why doesn't he rebel and quit his job? Why does the gardener suffer such humiliation and domination?

Andersen pondered these questions often and presented them in many of his tales, but he rarely suggested alternatives or rebellion. Rather he placed safety before idealism and chose moral compromise over moral outrage, individual comfort and achievement over collective struggle and united goals. He aimed for identification with the power establishment that humiliates subjects rather than opposition to autocracy to put an end to exploitation through power. The defects in Andersen's ideological perspective are not enumerated here to insist that he should have learned to accept squalor and the disadvantages of poverty and struggle. They are important because they are the telling marks in the historical reception of his tales. Both the happy and sad endings of his narratives infer that there is an absolute or a divine, harmonious power, and that unity of the ego is possible under such power. Such a projection, however, was actually that of a frustrated and torn artist who was obliged to compensate for an existence which lacked harmonious proportions and a center of autonomy. Andersen's life was one based on servility, and his tales were endeavors to justify a false consciousness: literary exercises in the legitimation of a social order to which he subscribed.

Whether the discourse of such a dominated writer be a monologue with himself or dialogue with an audience who partakes of his ideology, he still can never feel at peace with himself. It is thus the restlessness and the dissatisfaction of the dominated artist which imbues his work ultimately with the qualitative substance of what he seeks to relate. Ironically, the power of Andersen's fairy tales for him and for his readers has very little to do with the power he respected. It emanates from the missing gaps, the lapses, which are felt when the compromises are made under compulsion, for Andersen always painted happiness as adjusting to domination no matter how chosen one was. Clearly, then, Andersen's genius, despite his servility, rested in his inability to prevent himself from loathing all that he admired.

Notes

1 *Hans Christian Andersen. The Story of his Life Work* (London: Phaidon, 1975), p. 152.

2 *Ibid.*, p. 179. Many more statements like this can be found in Andersen's letters and journals. See Hans Christian Andersen, *Das Märchen meines Lebens. Briefe. Tagebucher*, ed. by Erling Nielsen (Munich: Winkler, 1961). Unfortunately, the letters and journals have not been translated into English.

3 *Ibid.*, pp. 132–3.

4 London: Routledge & Kegan Paul, 1979, pp. 1–2.

5 See Jeffrey M. Blum, *Pseudoscience and Mental Ability* (New York: Monthly Review Press, 1978) and Stephan L. Chorover, *From Genesis to Genocide: The Meaning of Human Nature and the Power of Behavior Control* (Cambridge: MIT Press, 1979).

6 For the general development in Europe, see Jürgen Habermas, *Strukturwandel der Öffentlichkeit. Untersuchungen zu einer Kategorie der bürgerlichen Gesellschaft.* (Neuwied: Luchterhand, 1962) and Charles Morazé, *The Triumph of the Middle Classes. A Political and Social History of Europe in the Nineteenth Century* (London: Weidenfeld and Nicolson, 1966). For Denmark, see W. Glyn Jones, *Denmark* (New York: Praeger, 1970), pp. 17–129.

7 New York: Pantheon, 1968.

8 *Education, Class Language and Ideology*, p. 26.

9 *Hans Christian Audersen*, p. 154.

10 *Ibid.*, p. 69.

11 Cf. *The Fairy Tale of My Life*, trans. by W. Glyn Jones (New York: British Book Centre, 1955.) Andersen wrote three major autobiographies during his life, and each one is filled with distortions and amplifications of fact.

12 *Denmark*, pp. 66–7.

13 Cf. Paul V. Rubow, 'Idea and form in Hans Christian Andersen's fairy tales,' in *A Book on the Danish Writer Hans Christian Andersen*, ed. by Svend Dahl and H.G. Topsoe-Jensen (Copenhagen: Det Berlingske Bogtrykkeri, 1955), pp. 97–136.

14 *Education, Class Language and Ideology*, pp. 63–4.

15 *Ibid.*, p. 65.

16 *Hans Christian Andersen*, p. 308. They are as follows: *The Tinder Box, Little Claus and Big Claus, The Princess and the Pea, Little Ida's Flowers, Thumbelina, The Travelling Companion* (1835); *The Little Mermaid, The Emperor's New Clothes* (1837); *The Steadfast Tin Soldier, The Wild Swans* (1838); *The Garden of Eden, The Flying Trunk, The Storks* (1839); *Willie Winkie, The Swineherd, The Buckwheat* (1841); *The Nightingale, The Top and the Ball, The Ugly Duckling*, (1843); *The Fir Tree, The Snow Queen* (1844); *The Darning Needle, The Elf Hill, The Red Shoes, The Shepherdess and the Chimney-Sweep, The Little Match Girl* (1845); *The Shadow* (1847); *The Old House, The Happy Family, The Shirt Collar* (1848). Interestingly, the most popular tales are the earlier tales when Andersen tended to be less critical of social conditions and wrote more expressly for children.

17 Hans Christian Andersen, *The Complete Fairy Tales and Stories*, trans. by Erik Christian Haugaard (New York: Doubleday, 1974), p. 3.

18 This is also true of the novels written during this time: *The Improvisatore* (1835), *O.T.* (1836), and *Only a Fiddler* (1837).

19 *The Complete Fairy Tales and Stories*, p. 113.

20 *Ibid.*, p. 197.

21 *Ibid.*, p. 205.

22 *Ibid.*, p. 211.

23 *Ibid.*, pp. 223–4.

24 *Ibid.*, p. 224.

25   *Ibid.*, p. 290.
26   *Ibid.*, p. 292.
27   *Ibid.*, p. 294.
28   *Ibid.*, p. 339.
29   *Ibid.*
30   *Ibid.*, p. 417.
31   *Ibid.*, pp. 420–1.
32   *Ibid.*, p. 423.
33   *Ibid.*, p. 427.
34   *Ibid.*
35   *Ibid.*, p. 1018.
36   *Ibid.*, p. 1020.
37   *Ibid.*, p. 1021.

5 Inverting and Subverting the World with Hope: The Fairy Tales of George MacDonald, Oscar Wilde and L. Frank Baum

The only form in which the future presents itself to us is that of possibility, while the imperative, the 'should,' tells us which of these possibilities we should choose. As regards knowledge, the future – in so far as we are not concerned with the purely organized and rationalized part of it – presents itself as an impenetrable medium, an unyielding wall. And when our attempts to see through it are repulsed, we first become aware of the necessity of wilfully choosing our course and, in close connection with it, the need for an imperative (a utopia) to drive us onward. Only when we know what are the interests and imperatives involved are we in a position to inquire into the possibilities of the present situation, and thus to gain our first insights into history.

Karl Mannheim
Ideology and Utopia (1936)

I

Towards the latter part of the nineteenth century the discourse on proper socialization through fairy tales received a jolt. Whereas Perrault, the Grimms, Andersen, some imitators like Benjamin Tabert, Felix Summerly, Gustav Holting, Ludwig Bechstein, and a host of other writers legitimized the normative standards of *civilité* through their symbolical constructs, configurations, and plots of their tales, a new trend became visible in the Anglo-Saxon world, namely in Great Britain and the United States, which reflected sharp criticism of traditional child-rearing and the rationalized means of discipline and punishment employed to make children into good and responsible citizens.

There is a tendency on the part of some literary critics to assume that the fairy tale for children went completely underground during the first half of the nineteenth century because it was considered too pleasurable and entertaining and not instructive and pious enough for young souls. Yet, these critics tend to neglect the tremendous popularity of fairy-tale broadsheets, chapbooks, and the continual favorable reception of Perrault, the Grimms, and Andersen in England, America, and on the Continent. They also forget that the basic discourse of the classical fairy tale was *not* contrary to the civilizing purposes of the bourgeoisie. Perhaps it is true that publication of fairy tales was limited and curtailed in comparison to later years and that the selection and censorship of the tales were severe. In other words, the fairy-tale discourse was controlled by the same sociopolitical tendencies which contributed toward strengthening bourgeois domination of the public sphere in the first half of the nineteenth century.[1] Reason and morality were used perversely to conserve the gains of the rising middle classes. This conservatism, however, was not to last.

By the 1860s, if not earlier, literary conservatism in children's book publishing was challenged by a new wave of innovative fairy tales as Brian Alderson has amply shown in his essay 'Tracts, rewards and fairies'.[2] He points to John Ruskin's *King of the Golden River* (1851), the re-issue of the Grimms' *German Popular Stories* (1868) with Ruskin's introduction, and William Allingham's *In Fairy Land* (1870) as significant breakthroughs in the fairy-tale discourse. There was, in fact, a 'munificent productiveness' in fairy tales which can be gleaned in Jonathan Cott's fine collection *Beyond the Looking Glass*.[3] In discussing the extraordinary works of fantasy and fairy tale, specifically in England, Cott notes that

> writing fairy tales for children had become an acceptable literary activity. Not only had Thackeray, Ruskin, Dickens, and Christina Rossetti done so, but Victorian children's book writers were generally less involved than 'adult' literary writers in the contemporary debates concerning 'moral aesthetics' engaged in by Tennyson, Ruskin, Arnold, Buchanan, and Pater. In some way the Victorian writers for children had transcended the age-old debate concerning the purposes of 'literature' (instruction vs. delight) as well as the equivalent moral tract vs. fairy story argument regarding children's literature. . . Children's literature of this period almost always had a moral or religious basis, but it was often just this conflict between morality and invention (or morality and eroticism in Christina Rossetti's *Goblin Market*) that created some of the era's greatest works.[4]

It is difficult to pinpoint exactly when and where the fairy-tale discourse underwent a profound change, who the chief instigators were, and why this began primarily in England. Certainly the development of a strong proletarian class, industrialization, urbanization, educational reform acts, evangelism, and the struggles against those forces which caused poverty and exploitation led to social and cultural upheavals which affected the fairy-tale works of Dickens, Ruskin, Thackeray, Lewis Carroll, Charles Kingsley, Andrew Lang, William Morris, the neo-Raphaelites, and numerous other well-known authors. However, the truly 'classical' fairy-tale writers, who made a mark not only on their own times but have continued to speak to us today, were George MacDonald, Oscar Wilde, and L. Frank Baum, the American offspring of the British movement. They were the ones who used the fairy tale as a radical mirror to reflect what was wrong with the general discourse on manners, mores, and norms in society, and they commented on this by altering the specific discourse on civilization in the fairy-tale genre.

No longer was the fairy tale to be like the mirror, mirror on the wall reflecting the cosmetic bourgeois standards of beauty and virtue which appeared to be unadulterated and pure. The fairy tale and the mirror cracked into sharp-edged, radical parts by the end of the nineteenth century. This was true for all the tales, those written for children as well as for adults. There was more social dynamite in the contents of the tales, also more subtlety and art. Commenting on the essence of fairy tales, Michel Butor once compared fairyland to a 'world inverted,' an exemplary world, a criticism of ossified reality. 'It does not remain side by side with the latter; it reacts upon it; it suggests that we transform it, that we reinstate what is out of place.'[5] On the one hand, this is an extremely broad and naive statement because we know how the literary fairy tales of Perrault, the Grimms, and Andersen offer a pseudo-criticism of real social conditions to guarantee that children of all classes will mind their manners and preserve the *status quo* – all to the advantage of those who control the dominant discourse. On the other hand, Butor has a keen eye for the subversive potentiality within the fairy-tale genre: he perceives how *certain* fairy tales can disrupt the normative structure and affirmative discourse of the classical fairy-tale tradition that are locked into the bourgeois public sphere. In particular, experimental fairy tales for children are endowed with a subversive potential, but the degree of their 'subversiveness' must be qualified.

In her illuminating study of fantasy as the literature of subversion, Rosemary Jackson argues that

> each fantastic text functions differently, depending upon its particular historical placing, and its different ideological, political and economic determinants, but the most subversive fantasies are those which attempt to *transform* the relations of the imaginary and the symbolic. They try to set up possibilities for radical cultural transformation by making fluid the relations between these realms, suggesting, or projecting, the

dissolution of the symbolic through violent reversal or rejection of the process of the subject's formation.[6]

Jackson views the subversive capacity of fairy tales with some reserve because they belong more to the literature of the marvellous and tend to discourage reader participation: instead of transgressing the values of the 'real' world, they interrogate them only retrospectively or allegorically. In other words, by conceptualizing other worlds and alternatives, presenting ideals, fairy tales do *not* problematize reality or open up space without/outside cultural order. The metaphors are too coherent.[7]

Though the distinctions Jackson draws between fairy tales and fantastic narratives are helpful, she clings too much to a static model of the fairy tale, neglects the radical transformations of the fairy-tale genre, and thus overlooks the close connections to the mode of the fantastic. For instance, Jackson maintains that it is not by chance that the fantastic tended to become a genre in its own right in the nineteenth century in opposition to conventionalized mimesis: 'Subverting this unitary vision, the fantastic introduces confusion and alternatives; in the nineteenth century this meant an opposition to bourgeois ideology upheld through the 'realistic' novel.'[8] Such subversion was also underway within the fairy-tale discourse during the nineteenth century and was directed at adults *and* children. The major breakthrough had been made by the German romantics, who dissolved reader expectations by transforming familiar topoi and motifs into mysterious, symbolic landscapes which lured readers to question the former secure worlds of conservative fairy tales and the very 'real' world of their immediate surroundings. It is true, as Jackson demonstrates, that most fairy tales, even the experimental ones, re-present the world as an 'exemplification of a possibility to be avoided or embraced.'[9] Yet, this imaginary projection does not lessen the subversive potential of the author's symbolical act and the work's constellation. The question of subversion concerns degree and the challenge to reader expectations. Certainly, for children, the historical shift in fairy-tale discourse must be related to a longing by adult writers to open up and subvert traditional socialization by posing infinite textual possibilities for the subjects/readers to define themselves against the background of finite choices proposed by society.

Historically viewed, the first movement of the 'subversion' began at the very moment when the literary fairy tale ironicallly started to find *acceptance* in the well-kempt nurseries, schools, and libraries of nineteenth century Europe and America, and when publishers sought to make their profit by pushing them on the thriving market for children consumers. Many writers of fairy tales catered to the market and the publishers, but the more critical ones recognized that the utopian kernel in the original folk tales, the lust for change and the wish for better living conditions, had been appropriated and cultivated in the classical literary fairy tales to give rise to false hopes. As part of the household, the tales of Perrault, the Grimms, Andersen, and disciples exercised a stranglehold on the topoi of fairy-tale discourse, and more and more writers like MacDonald, Wilde, and Baum sought to break this grip. To be sure, they were in the minority, and they did not boulverize the literary conventions of accepted fairy-tale narration. Yet, they did invert and subvert the real world and classical schemes of Perrault, the Grimms, and Andersen. They expanded the fairy-tale discourse on civilization to conceive alternative worlds and styles of life. This departure from the traditional mode prepared the way for even greater experimentation with fairy tales for children in the twentieth century, and numerous authors began cultivating what might be termed 'the art of subversion' within the fairy-tale discourse.

As is often the case with innovators, even with the most radical, MacDonald, Wilde, and Baum have become known as classical fairy-tale writers. Their 'classicism,' however, is qualitatively different from that of Perrault, the Grimms, and Andersen, and it is most important that we distinguish their singular contributions to the genre because they represent a turning point in the fairy-tale discourse on civilization and set examples for contemporaries and later innovators. All three, MacDonald, Wilde, and Baum, refused to comply with the standard notions of sexuality and sex roles and questioned the restrictions placed on the imagination of children. Moreover, they generally told their stories from the perspective of the oppressed lower classes and added a dimension to their dissatisfaction which resisted the compromises that Andersen had proposed for his protagonists. MacDonald, Wilde, and Baum bring out the need for the alteration and restructuring of social relations by questioning the arbitrariness of authoritarian rule and the profit motives of rulers. Neither one of the writers is revolutionary in the sense that they called for 'violent overthrows' of the government, but it is their intense discontent with domination and the dominant discourse which propelled them to invert and subvert the world with hope in their tales.

If we examine their key works in the history of the literary fairy tale for children, it will become apparent that they were *consciously* inserting themselves into the discourse on civilization in the process of change. They furthered this change with their socially symbolic acts, and we shall see that each one made a unique historical contribution in behalf of children to undo what they ostensibly considered damage done to children through the traditional fairy-tale discourse.

II

George MacDonald's life was filled with struggles against social conservatism, religious orthodoxy, and commercial capitalism.[10] Though the types of socio-religious changes he desired were never realized in his day, he never lost his hope and zest for reform: the beastliness of civilization was to be countered by uncovering and perfecting the divine qualities of humankind – despite the corrupting influences of society.

Raised on a large farm in a rural district of Scotland, MacDonald believed that hard work and diligence would pave the way to success. As a teenager he organized and became president of the local temperance society, and it appeared that his devotion to the clean-cut life would reap benefits. In 1840 he won a scholarship to the University of Aberdeen to pursue his studies mainly in science. It appears, however, that his first long contact with city life almost brought about his ruin. He drank and pursued women rather than his studies and in 1842 had to leave the university for some time. This proved to be one of the turning points in his life. He spent several months working in the library of a nobleman's mansion and discovered German romanticism, classical English poetry, and medieval romances. He also fell in love with the daughter of the house but was spurned because of his lower social status. When he was able to return to the university, he brought with him a distinct hatred for rich aristocrats and a passionate love for literature, especially romanticism.

After receiving a degree in chemistry and physics, he spent the next three years as a private tutor in London and apparently did a great deal of soul-searching, for he decided to become a minister. In 1848 he enrolled in Highbury College, a Congregational Divinity School in London, and he also announced his engagement to Louisa Powell, who would become his wife and companion in 1853 for the rest of his life, undoubtedly the model for many of his admirable female protagonists in his literary works. By the time he graduated from divinity school in 1850 and was ready to assume his first ministry in Sussex, he was brought down by tuberculosis, the disease which haunted his family. It caused the death of his father and some of his own children. From this point on he was beset with physical difficulties and suffered from other ailments such as eczema throughout his life. The struggles against physical diseases actually strengthened his spiritual beliefs and moral character. During his convalescence he wrote a long dramatic poem which was the first manifestation of his non-conformist mystical inclinations. Nor did he hesitate to incorporate his unusual views about God, nature, epiphany, and the perfection of humankind in his sermons and other writings. In 1851 he published a translation of *Twelve Spiritual Songs of Novalis* and began voicing his heterodox views about salvation from the pulpit. Such frankness and intensity were not appreciated by his congregation, and he was forced to resign his position in 1853 and to begin his career as writer. Yet, MacDonald's personal religious mission did not change.

No matter what form his writing took, MacDonald was bent on spreading his socio-religious convictions to large audiences. Indeed, he wrote over forty volumes of prose and poetry and became one of the most successful novelists and popular lecturers of his day. Like Dickens, he wanted to expose the deplorable material conditions and unjust social relations in England during the period of industrialization. Building the Empire meant breaking the backs of common people, and he demanded reforms. However, he never argued for a radical transformation of the hierarchical structure of society and government. Influenced by his agrarian upbringing, his politics were more inclined to take the form of safeguarding the natural rights and autonomy of individuals whose own responsibility was to create the moral and ethical fibre of good government. As Richard H. Reis has remarked,

> this is not to say that MacDonald was insensitive to the problems of the working class. Although he did not recognize the existence of the industrial mass-proletariat, he was convinced that the individual artisan – the shoemaker, blacksmith, carpenter, mason – was the backbone of the English and social economic system. No doubt he was influenced by the social theories of Ruskin and William Morris, who longed for the vanished day of the individual workman's dignity before he was engulfed by mass production and wage slavery; for MacDonald's scattered suggestions toward utopia are usually built along the lines of medieval feudalism.[11]

It is interesting to note that MacDonald's social and political views generally took a more conventional form in his realistic novels than in his fairy tales for children. Writing in the fantastic mode apparently freed him to explore personal and social problems to a degree that fostered his radicalism and innovation. It is generally acknowledged that MacDonald's major historical contribution to literature is in the area of fantasy and children's literature. In particular the fairy tale nurtured his religious mysticism and fundamental beliefs in the dignity of men and women whose mutual needs and talents could only be developed in a community that was not based on exploitation and profit-making. Since MacDonald felt that dreams were like religious epiphanies and that fairy tales were symbolically related to dreams, he endowed their symbolical constellations with social-religious values to convey messages without sermonizing in a laborious manner.

Between 1864 and 1883 MacDonald made his views known to children in various ways. He edited a magazine entitled *Good Words for the Young* (1868–1872), in which several fairy tales appeared including his most famous one *The Light Princess*. He published four book-length fairy tales: *At the Back of the North Wind* (1871), *The Princess and the Goblin* (1872), *A Double Story* (1874–5) also known as *The Lost Princess*, and *The Princess and Curdie* (1883). In addition he incorporated some fairy tales in novels such as *Adela Cathcart* (1864), published them collectively as in *Dealings with Fairies* (1867) or individually as separate books. In each case MacDonald consciously sought to enter into the fairy-tale discourse on manners, norms, and values and to transform it. More than any of the classical writers before him, MacDonald's perspective on the socialization of children contradicted the accepted version of discipline and punishment of the British civilizing process. Indeed, the patterns and configurations of his tales clearly display a tendency to negate the institutionalized and established forms of raising children.

As a Christian mystic, MacDonald believed in the perfection of humankind and maintained that each individual could achieve a supreme state in this world. It is not just 'divine individualism' which MacDonald preached but the necessity to develop compassion for other human beings and nature. Implicit is a notion of utopia in most of his fairy tales: the utopian impulse can be realized in the here and now if one is receptive to God who makes his will known through all earthly creation. 'Nature is brimful of symbolic and analogic parallels to the goings and comings, the growth and changes of the highest nature in man.'[12] There is no *fixed* path to perfection, the equivalent of union with God in MacDonald's mind. Each individual must learn to recognize divine qualities in the immediate surroundings and in him or herself. Through such an epiphany the individual will act according to a conscience that bespeaks God's will. MacDonald placed great significance on developing the creative potential of human beings, and he regarded daydreams, dreams, and mystical experiences as means toward a union with the divine spirit. 'All dreams are not false; some dreams are truer than the plainest facts. Fact at best is but a garment of truth, which has ten thousand changes of raiment woven on the same loom. Let the dreamer only do the truth of his dream and one day he will realize all that was worth realizing it.'[13] Like Novalis, MacDonald felt strongly that the fantastic elements of life and fiction were hieroglyphics of the divine essence. Learning to become a human being in the fullest sense of the word meant becoming a creative artist. The true individual was a self-made autonomous artwork, and MacDonald's fairy tales for children sought to stimulate young readers to recognize their special creative talents so that they could religiously begin their own artful enterprise.

If we compare MacDonald's fairy tales with many of the prudish and pious ones of his day, it becomes apparent that he was arguing against the conventional rules of pedagogy and strict Christian upbringing. He shunned upper-class dictums of an authoritarian nature, and his fairy tales shift and expand attitudes toward children by moving 'God' from a transcendental place to within the child: the divine is to be discovered inside and through the imagination. Such a different perspective on socializing children demanded a reformulation of the norms, values, and social relations, the use of fantasy to mirror the ossification of English social and religious standards. To grasp MacDonald's utopian critique conveyed through his fairy tales, I want to deal with three of his more prominent shorter pieces, *The Light Princess* (1864), *The Golden Key* (1867), and *The Day Boy and the Night Girl* (1879) and two of his major longer narratives, *The Princess and the Goblin* (1872) and *The Princess and Curdie* (1883). The pattern in each one of these fairy tales is similar. There is never one hero, rather there are always male and female protagonists, who learn to follow their deep inclinations, respect each other's needs and talents, and share each other's visions. Together they overcome sinister forces which want to deprive them of possible happiness and the realization of an ideal community. In contrast to all his poems, novels, and essays, MacDonald forgoes the pathos and the rhetoric of sermonizing in the name of God. Though his Christian mysticism may be behind the ideological perspective of each narrative, his very use of unique and bizarre fairy-tale symbols imbue his stories with a touch of the unorthodox. The moral rebel in MacDonald led to a playful experimentation with conventions to undermine them and illuminate new directions for moral and social behavior.

The Light Princess (1864) like his tale *Little Daylight* (1867) is a parody of *Sleeping Beauty* and *Rapunzel*, and, for that matter, it reflects MacDonald's disrespectful attitude toward traditional folk and fairy tales. MacDonald realized that the symbolism of most of the traditional tales points to a dead end and prevents children from glimpsing their special relationship to the divine within and beyond them. It is striking that he does *not* see his point of departure for the fairy-tale discourse in the works of Grimm or Andersen but largely in those of the German romantics, particularly the fascinating stories of Novalis.

Certainly the three tales in Novalis' *Heinrich von Ofterdingen* with their utopian motifs and religious – erotic development of young couples had a great impact on him. In *The Light Princess* MacDonald follows Novalis' tendency to turn an ordered world topsy-turvy so that the conventional social order and relations could be parodied and the possibility of creating new modes of behavior and values could be perceived and designated.

The plot of *The Light Princess*, still in wide circulation today, is well known. A king and queen are without child. When they eventually have one, they insult the king's own sister, Princess Makemnoit, a witch by trade, by not inviting her to the christening. As is to be expected, the insulted witch casts a spell on the baby daughter by destroying her gravity. The princess soars and floats when she wants to walk and is difficult to control because she is light-bodied. When she becomes 17, she learns the pleasure of swimming, gains a sense of gravity, and also meets a young prince, who is willing to sacrifice himself so she can pursue her passion for water. Only by using himself as a plug to stop the water in the lake from disappearing (another spell cast by the witch) will she have enough water to swim. When it dawns upon her that the prince is dying for her, she tries to save him, breaks the spell by bursting into a passion of tears, and finds her gravity.

The irreverent tone of the story not only places the convention of traditional fairy tales in question but also the very style of aristocratic life. For instance, the king is a banal figure, a 'little king with a great throne, like many other kings.'[14] The royal metaphysicians, Hum-Dru and Kopy-Keck, are fools. Even the typical prince is mocked.[15] MacDonald winks his eye and debunks aristocratic language and codes, and yet, there is a serious side to the light comedy. From the beginning, after the bewitchment, the princess, court, and the implied reader of the tale are faced with a problem: how to provide gravity for the princess who does not have her feet on the ground and could cause continual havoc in the kingdom. The major theme of the tale concerns social integration, but – and this is significant – gravity (social responsibility and compassion) cannot be imposed or learned abstractly. It is gained through passion and experience, and it is also liberating. Once the princess touches water, she develops a veritable passion for it because she can control her own movements, and she can share her pleasure with the prince. Moreover, she overcomes her egocentrism by realizing her pleasure is not worth the death of a beloved human being. Through her relation to the prince, who is self-sacrificing and tender in the mold of traditional fairy-tale females, she develops social empathy, and her learning to walk after the spell is broken, though painful, can be equated to the difficult acceptance of social responsibility.

Of course, one could argue that MacDonald leaves the aristocratic social structure unchanged – a system which harbors authoritarianism and that the princess seems to achieve her 'gravity' or identity through the male hero. These were clearly his ideological preferences and weaknesses from a political point of view. It should be pointed out, however, that MacDonald was more interested in the reformation of social character and was convinced that all social change emanated from the development of personal integrity not necessarily through political restructuring and upheaval. This belief is why he stressed ethical choice and action through intense quests and experience. Moreover, in *The Light Princess*, his female protagonist does not become dependent on the prince, who is a 'softy.' Rather she gains certain qualities through her relationship with him just as he benefits from the encounter. There is more sensitive interaction between two unique individuals than traditional role-playing at the end of the tale, a special configuration which MacDonald was to develop in all his narratives.

For instance, in *The Golden Key* the young boy Mossy goes in pursuit of treasure at the end of the rainbow only to learn that the real 'riches' in life are those experiences which amount to self-knowledge. In part he learns this from Tangle, a maltreated 13-year-old girl, who runs away from home out of fear. Both are brought together in the middle of fairyland by the mysterious grandmother (a kind of mother nature), and she instills them with courage so that they bravely embark on a quest for the keyhole of the golden key, which had already been found by Mossy at the end of the rainbow. On their way they become separated and undergo various experiences with the old men of the sea, earth, and fire. Eventually, after enduring all kinds of trials, they are reunited before the country whence the shadows fall. Ageless they move toward their conception of paradise.

At the basis of MacDonald's utopia is the perfect social and sexual relationship. Mossy and Tangle are companions. Once lost in fairyland, as we the readers become lost in this highly symbolical and complex tale, everything depends on how we read the symbols, how receptive and appreciative we are to nature and the challenges of life. Mossy and Tangle have their own unique adventures and impressions while seeking the keyhole (another obvious voyage of sexual exploration).[16] Their mystical and sensual experiences form the bedrock of their growth. Their diligence is rewarded not through material riches but through entrance to another world which promises the fulfillment of their intuitions.

This pattern of self-exploration, symbolical trips toward inner realms that can help create understanding of other people and the outside world is depicted in a variety of intriguing ways in MacDonald's other tales, *The Carasoyn, Little Daylight,* and *Cross Purposes.* The fairy tale, however, which is by far MacDonald's most unusual portrayal of mutual respect and interdependence between men and women is the provocative narrative of *The Day Boy and the Night Girl* (1879). MacDonald creates a witch named Watho, who has a wolf in her mind, and her uncontrollable appetite to know everything leads her to experiment indiscriminately with human beings. She invites two ladies to her castle named Aurora and Vesper, and she uses her magical powers to have them give birth to children. After the births the two women flee the witch in dread. Watho keeps the boy Photogen and the girl Nycteris in separate parts of the castle and exposes one only to darkness and the other only to light. In fact they each develop a respective fear of their opposites, night and day. It is only later during their adolescence that the two of them chance to meet and discover that Watho's means of raising them has crippled them. Therefore, Nycteris offers to be Photogen's eyes in darkness while she teaches him to see, and there is an amusing scene in which MacDonald addresses the entire problem of regimentation and sex-role conditioning:

> He wished she would not make him keep opening his eyes to look at things he could not see; and every other moment would start and grasp tight hold of her, as some fresh pang of terror shot into him.
> 'Come, come, dear!' said Nycteris, 'you must not go on this way. You must be a brave girl, and –'
> 'A girl!' shouted Photogen, and started to his feet in wrath. 'If you were a man, I should kill you.'
> 'A man?' repeated Nycteris, 'what is that? How could I be that? We are both girls – are we not?'
> 'No, I am not a girl,' he answered; ' – although,' he added, changing his tone, and casting himself on the ground at her feet, 'I have given you too good reason to call me one.'
> 'Oh, I see!' returned Nycteris. 'No, of course! – You can't be a girl: girls are not afraid – without reason. I understand now: it is because you are not a girl that you are so frightened.'
> Photogen twisted and writhed upon the grass.[17]

This delightful reversal is only one aspect of MacDonald's endeavor in this narrative to depict what he calls 'the arrogance of all male creatures until they have been taught by the other kind.'[18] In the course of events Nycteris and Photogen realize that they have a great deal to learn from each other, and this realization gives them the power to overcome the witch. Their relationship becomes a synthesis in which light can be found in darkness and darkness in light.

This fairy tale is perhaps MacDonald's most outspoken statement on child-rearing. Watho's castle, personality, and treatment of the children assume symbolical forms of school, rigid teacher, and arbitrary programming. Against this system MacDonald pits the painful but meaningful exploration of two human beings who gradually recognize that their essence and autonomy depend on the interdependence of all things. Photogen and Nycteris come to revere the totality of nature by developing a receptivity to what they fear most. The confrontation with fear, however, enables them to see anew, to rethink and refeel their surroundings so that they gain ultimate pleasure from their senses and begin building a world commensurate with their ideals. MacDonald shuns Victorian prudery, as he did in almost all his fairy tales, and projects the symbolical sexual play and intercourse which can prepare the way for a wholesome union of the sexes.

MacDonald believed firmly that individuals could be 'cilivized' in a natural way to attain a devout reverence for the nature and needs of all living creatures, but he also had grave doubts as to whether people as a whole, that is, society, could attain the level of 'civilization' which separate individuals could. Here his notion of civilization was in direct contradiction to the class-bound civilization process of England, and his two book-length fairy-tales, *The Princess and the Goblin* and *The Princess and Curdie*, demonstrate to what extent he went against the Victorian grain. In the first narrative the Princess Irene is plagued by goblins who want to kidnap her and destroy her father's kingdom. She is protected by her omniscient and mysterious grandmother, who endows her with the fortitude and sensitivity necessary to cope with her enemies. Furthermore, she is aided by a brave miner's son named Curdie, who literally undermines the sinister plans of the goblins and puts an end to their kingdom. In the sequel, Curdie is in danger of becoming a 'beastly character' until summoned by the majestic grandmother. He then realizes that he was on the verge of becoming decrepit, and the grandmother sends him on a mission to help the father of Princess Irene because he is being poisoned by corrupt officials. On his way to the city of Gwyntystorm, Curdie organizes a squadron of forty-nine strange creatures and misfits, who ironically return order and justice to the community. Curdie marries Princess Irene, but they have no children. When they die, the people choose a new king who is interested mainly in mining for gold, and the people become corrupt and dissolute once again. Their self-destructive tendencies lead to the destruction and disappearance of the city.

Not a very happy end for a fairy tale, and one must ask why MacDonald wrote such a book in 1883, his very last one for children. Had he become pessimistic? Or, was this a warning to children? Was this MacDonald's way to keep the utopian impulse alive in his readers by pointing to the dangers of slumbering – not keeping one's creative sensitivities active in a religious way? There are indications that the two narratives taken as a whole expressed MacDonald's sober optimism: humanity must raise itself from a beastly state to form the utopian society and must constantly exercise creative and moral powers to pursue the ideal society. Otherwise, there will be a return to barbarianism.

MacDonald appears to have been greatly influenced by Novalis' and E.T.A. Hoffmann's notions of love and Atlantis in *Heinrich von Ofterdingen* and *The Golden Pot*. Both the German romantics have a woman incarnate a mystical concept of eros, and she becomes the mediator between the profane and the sacred. In pursuit of her love the protagonist discovers his own powers and identity, and only then is he able to create a compassionate relationship with all forms of life. Utopia becomes attainable, but only momentarily. Novalis has his Atlantis disappear in one tale, and Hoffmann sends his hero Anselmus to Atlantis, which is beyond the reach of the narrator and his readers. Implicit was critique of a mundane society too immersed in pettiness and routine to appreciate the divine nature of life and art.

It is obvious that this was MacDonald's perspective, too. Writing about late nineteenth-century England, he deplored the materialistic behaviour of the majority of people and the corruption of government. The relationship between Curdie and the princess is intended to be exemplary and provocative for young readers. In fact, MacDonald depicts the experiences and growth of the two protagonsits to mirror all that was wrong in English society. Princess Irene's communion with the other world – her mystical and creative powers – is distrusted by her governess and everyone around her. To a large extent, her behavior and views are the opposite of how children in Victorian England were socialized to behave. Even Curdie is suspicious of her and expresses doubts about her sanity and character until the very end of the first book. These doubts continue in the sequel, and because of them it seems that Curdie might become an ordinary, crass miner, insensitive to other people and the world around him. However, his love and admiration for the tiny princess is such that a spark of his great potential is still alive, and, through his imagination, he comes to symbolize all that *should be* but *could not be* – the coal miner/King's efforts in behalf of humanity are lost on a society in quest of power and wealth.

MacDonald himself never ceased deploring the evils of social influences which interfered with the natural and sublime endeavors of human beings to become perfect. Early in his life he grasped the importance of the German romantics' aesthetic critique of philistine society, and he drew out the mystical religious essence while still defending the powers of the imagination and creative artist. At the point where he entered the fairy-tale discourse for children in England, he could not help but be influenced by social reform movements and the ideas of Dickens and Ruskin. From 1864 to 1882 he made a major effort to expand the discourse of fairy tales and to shift the perspective from the legitimatory voice to one critical of the civilizing process. His works were just the beginning: 'classical' fairy tales were about to acquire a new quality of conscious social protest.

III

Though no two men could be more dissimilar in personality and conviction than George MacDonald and Oscar Wilde, there are striking similarities in their lives which account for a common endeavor to reformulate the terms of the civilizing process through the fairy tale in Victorian England. Both were born outside established English society, MacDonald in Scotland, Wilde in Ireland, two countries noted for their indigenous, quaint folklore and anti-English politics. Both were influenced by the social reform movement of their times and directly by artistic innovators with a political conscience such as John Ruskin and William Morris. Both hated hypocrisy and stodgy English upper-class conventions, and they sought to use their art to express religious views directly opposed to the Anglican Church. As we have seen, the form MacDonald's critique of society assumed in his fairy tales was influenced by his Christian mysticism; Wilde's was stamped by a unique commitment to Christian socialism which celebrated individualism and art. Ironically, Wilde the aesthete was more radical in what he preached through his compelling fairy tales than MacDonald the Christian reformer.

Wilde's fascinating life, art, and unfortunate end have been explored in depth by numerous scholars and critics – and the books pro and con Wilde keep coming.[19] Yet, very few have dwelt at length on the subject of his fairy tales, which are perhaps his best known works. Not only have they sold in the millions in different languages, but they have been adapted in various ways for stage, screen, radio and the record industry. Ironically, these unconventional tales have achieved classical status, and, since they are bound up with his rebellious life, it is important to consider certain aspects of his development as a writer to understand why he sought to transform the fairy-tale discourse and followed MacDonald's example, though he was never directly influenced by the Scotsman. If anything, both were moved by the same spirit – to change the anachronistic contents and style of fairy tales that did not pertain to the social and political realities of modern England.

As is well known, both Wilde's father William and his mother Jane Fracesca Elgee were social celebrities and writers, who led eccentric lives in Dublin. His father was noted for his discoveries in medicine and archeology and his exploits with women. His mother achieved fame as poetess, writer, and patriotic defender of the rights of the Irish. From the time he was two, Wilde participated at all meals with his parents and guests, and this participation is obviously the reason why he developed into such a skillful and polished raconteur. Yet, more important for his social and aesthetic views is the fact that Wilde was given the opportunity to witness how refined people played with social conventions to mock conformity, and he learned to explore alternatives to stifling forms of socialization at a very early age. As a consequence, he employed his extraordinary rhetorical and creative skills both to gain attention and to keep the world at a distance. In Dublin, where high society lived on smut and scandal, Wilde learned to assume poses and dedicate himself to his studies and art for the main purpose of survival.

After winning numerous awards at Trinity College, he went to Magdalen College at Oxford in 1874. There he came under the influence of Ruskin and Pater, who stimulated him in two directions which were not necessarily opposite as many critics like to believe. Ruskin drew Wilde's attention to social questions and the connections between art and concrete practical life while Pater demonstrated how private experience is essential for grasping the beautiful and profound nature of the external world. Ultimately, Wilde synthesized the notions of these two brilliant scholars to form his own social concept of aesthetics, and in some respects his own personality was symbolically most representative of this concept: Wilde was always bent on transforming himself into a work of art.

At Oxford, he became more daring and lavish in his dress, postures, conversation, writings, and deeds. Most of his contemporaries as well as critics who have written on his life have dismissed his dandyism as egocentric behavior and snobbism. Yet, there can be no doubt that he took his posturing and artful conversation seriously and came to perceive himself consciously and subconsciously as a type of artistic creation. As Philippe Jullian has remarked, Wilde was fond of saying that 'to get into society nowadays one has either to feed people or shock people – that is all.'[20] His years at Oxford were like an apprenticeship, except that he was his own teacher and learned to cultivate the bizarre and extraordinary. When he entered London society in 1878, Wilde began to make a fashion out of being preposterous while showing how society itself was even more preposterous in its ways. In a certain sense he became a late rendition of the court fool who was always pardoned for mirroring the foibles of aristocratic society despite his shocking truth. George Woodcock points out that 'in the course of two decades as a public figure in the London salons, he found out that the aristocrats did not even justify their wealth and privileges by displaying virtue or serving any social purpose, and he quickly came to despise the majority of them. In his plays they become the most grotesque figures, the Lady Bracknells and Lord Cavershams; upper-class stupidity is pilloried in his elderly parliamentarian aristocrats, and calculating vulgarity in his dowagers and duchesses.'[21]

At bottom Wilde's carefully calculated conversation and display were based on a contempt of the people whom he also admired. In this sense he was much different from another writer of fairy tales who loved and flirted with social prominence, the submissive Hans Christian Andersen. Like Andersen, Wilde felt himself more noble and worthy of respect than the nobility itself. Unlike Andersen, however, he refused to cow-tow to contemptible social conventions and authority, for he wanted to be accepted by society as unacceptable. That was his calling card, and the more he was accepted by society, the more he sought to break the norms and test the repressive tolerance of a cruel system of class justice.

From 1878 until the publication of *The Happy Prince and Other Tales* in 1888, Wilde was still in the process of learning his art, but this time his experiences were not contained within the halls of the university. He was exposed to social conditions in London, America, and the Continent and exchanged critical views on art and literature with the best writers of his day. His own poetry, criticism, lectures, and editorial work began to flower, and the appearence of his fairy tales signalled the advent of his great creative period: *The Soul of Man Under Socialism* (1891), *The House of Pomegranates* (1891), *The Picture of Dorian Gray* (1891), *Lady Windermere's Fan* (1892), *A Woman of No Importance* (1893), *The Ideal Husband* (1895), and *The Importance of Being Earnest* (1895). As Wilde became more innovative in his writing, he became more and more daring and intolerable in his personal and social life. Though he took pains to protect his family, he professed his homosexuality in the face of social recrimination and almost demanded that his art be idolized. Strangely, his art was both a means for establishing his individualism and maintaining distance from a demeaning society from which he expected great, if not excessive admiration.

It is most fitting that the volume *The Happy Prince and Other Tales* should be the work which was to launch his great creative period, for Wilde was highly disturbed by the way society conditioned and punished young people if they did not conform to the proper rules. Late in his life he wrote about the cruel treatment of juvenile delinquents that he witnessed in prison.[22] Yet, he had always been sensitive to the authoritarian schooling and church rigidity which most English children were expected to tolerate. His tales are imbued with a Christian socialist notion of humanism and contradict the civilizing process as it was practiced in England. To achieve the effect he desired, Wilde broke with the apologetics of classical fairy tales and the puerile Victorian stories in order to mirror social problems in Victorian England with a glimmer of hope – with a utopian impulse for change. As Isobel Murray points out,

> the gently Christian tone of 'The Happy Prince' – and of 'The Young King', written shortly after, and the quasi-biblical language do combine the fairy-tale mode with the shattering problems of Victorian poetry, privilege, and art, as Tennyson had most schematically outlined these in *The Palace of Art*. . . Themes that recur in Andersen certainly occur in Wilde. 'The Nightingale' is a parable about nature, art, and artifice which was bound to appeal to Wilde, and 'The Neighbouring Families' is similar in appeal. And Wilde probably learned from Andersen the witty, deflating touches which grace the stories, but never, even in 'The Selfish Giant', is he betrayed into such depths of sentimentality as Andersen. He takes witty talking animals and objects and uses them as frames for stories, as in 'The Devoted Friend', but he avoids Andersen's cloying moments, and generally transcends him.[23]

Perhaps a better word to describe Wilde's underlying purpose in writing his tales would be 'subversion' rather than 'transcension.' He clearly wanted to subvert the messages conveyed by Andersen's tales, but more important his poetical style recalled the rhythms and language of the Bible in order to counter the stringent Christian code. His interpretation of Christianity demonstrated the malpractice of the Church and questioned the compromising way Church leaders used Christianity to curb the pleasure instincts and to rationalize a socio-economic system of exploitation. Wilde's 'scriptural' tales were composed to enter into the discourse of the fairy-tale tradition and to shift its direction in a radical way. Key for understanding the socio-aesthetic tendency of the tales is his essay *The Soul of Man Under Socialism*, written in 1891.

Wilde had already conceived some of his central anarchistic ideas and notions of individualism in his significant essay *Chuang Tzu* on Taoism. *The Soul of Man Under Socialism* brings together his disparate views on socialism in response to a speech given by George Bernard Shaw on Fabian socialism, and its importance does not rest in its theoretcal contribution to the cause of socialism, but in the way it lends understanding to the unique socio-aesthetics of Wilde himself. One of his favorite sayings contended that it does not take much to make humans into socialists, but to make socialism human is a great task. This is the central idea of his essay which depends on Christ as its theoretical construct, and all his fairy tales evince the same sentiments. The major reason why Wilde argues for socialism is that it will lead to individualism in a humanitarian sense. At first he attacks private property and the philanthropy of the rich for preventing the rise of socialism. 'The true perfection of man lies not in what man has, but in what man is. Private property has crushed true Individualism, and set up an Individualism that is false. It has debarred one part of the community from being individual by putting them on the wrong road, and encumbering them. Indeed, so completely has man's personality been absorbed by his possessions that the English law has always treated offenses against his person, and property is still the test of complete citizenship.'[24] However, it is not only the elimination of private property which is necessary for socialism but the consequent development of an anti-authoritarian attitude, particularly among the poor. Christ is held up as the model of a person 'who is perfectly and absolutely himself,'[25] and, if people become Christlike, there will be no need for government. With socialism, the perfection of individualism, there will be no crime, and machines will free people to be creative. 'A map of the world that does not include Utopia, is not worth even glancing at, for it leaves out the one country at which Humanity is always landing. And when Humanity lands there, it looks out, and seeing a better country, sets sail. Progress is the realisation of Utopia.'[26] Wilde has a vested interest in speaking for socialism because its advent will further the cause of art, which 'is the most intense mode of Individualism that the world has known.'[27]

In the struggle for better living conditions, people have been conditioned too much to accept pain, and here Christ's suffering has in itself been regarded and misused as a goal in itself, 'for it is through joy that the Individualism of the future will develop itself. Christ made no attempt to reconstruct society, and consequently the Individualism that he preached to man could be realised only through pain or in solitude. The ideals we owe to Christ are the ideals of a man who resists society absolutely. But man is naturally social.'[28] What is significant here – and this is central for understanding the fairy tales – is that, on the one hand, Christ is upheld as a model of anti-authoritarianism and humanism, but that, on the other hand, he must be transcended through a common struggle of joy toward socialism. In contrast to Christ, 'the modern world has schemes. It proposes to do away with poverty and the suffering that it entails. It desires to get rid of pain, and the suffering that pain entails. It trusts to Socialism and Science as its methods. What it aims at is an Individualism expressing itself through joy.'[29] Paradoxically the individual struggle against society is not enough for the creation of individualism which entails a collective building of paradise on earth.

To a certain extent, Wilde was criticizing himself when he discussed the shortcomings of Christ with whom he obviously identified. The fact that he portrayed so many Christlike protagonists in his fairy tales did not mean that he wanted to propagate the Christian way as the path toward salvation. Nor did he feel obliged to indulge himself in Christian moralizing for the sake of children as some critics have mistakenly argued. Though Christlike behavior is laudable, it is not radical enough, nor is suffering acceptable as the recourse to a social system of domination which appears to be unchangeable. Actually, Wilde used the figure of Christ to show the need to subvert the traditional Christian message. *The Happy Prince* is a good example of how he placed the Christlike figure in a context aimed at altering classical fairy-tale discourse and at provoking readers to contemplate social change.

High above the city on a tall column sits the lead statue of the dead prince who appears magnificent because he is ornamented with sapphires, rubies, and gold. Everyone admires him, especially the town councillors, because he is so beautiful and appears to be the model of happiness which he once was. However, this happiness was based on ignorance, for he never realized how much his people suffered. The prince resolves to make up for his past negligence and egocentrism by bidding a devoted swallow to distribute the jewels to a poor seamstress, an artist, and a match-girl. Eventually the swallow dies because of exposure to the cold winter, and the statue is melted because it is no longer beautiful and useful to the mayor and councillors, who would like to have statues made of themselves.

It is obvious from this brief summary that the 'crucified' prince is Christlike and the swallow a kind of apostle. Their humane actions are exemplary. The prince overcomes an art for art sake's position and thereby reveals the social essence of all beauty. The swallow forgets about the fickle love he had for a reed and develops a compassion for the poor through his bond of love for the prince. The ideological perspective of the story contains both sympathy and critique of the prince, and thus Wilde is able to stress the great disparities in English society by ironically making the dead prince's pedestal so high that he can realize how miserable the common people are and how responsible he is for their misery, that is, as major representative of the ruling class. Yet – and this is the major point of Wilde's story – the individual actions of a Christlike person are not enough to put an end to poverty, injustice, and exploitation. Though the prince and bird may be blessed by God in the end, the mayor and town councillors remain in control of the city. These vain buffoons will certainly rule for their own benefit, and the philanthropic actions of the prince will go for naught.

The power of Wilde's story emanates from the unresolved tensions. The fabric of society is not changed. Nobody learns from the good deeds of the prince except perhaps the readers of the tale whom Wilde intended to provoke. In other words, the real beauty of the prince goes unnoticed because the town councillors and the people are too accustomed to identifying beauty with material wealth and splendor. Wilde suggests that the beauty of the prince cannot be appreciated in a capitalist society which favors greed and pomp. He does not preach the overthrow of these conditions. Rather his reverence for the prince is conveyed by rhythms and metaphors suggestive of a religious parable, and he makes his point by contrasting the prince with the town officials.

There is a discourse on manners and values in *The Happy Prince* which shows how deeply disturbed Wilde was by the hypocrisy of the English upper class and bourgeoisie. All his fairy tales were artistic endeavors to expose their wanton and cruel ways by juxtaposing Christlike figures to the norms reinforced by the civilizing process – and it should be stressed that Wilde took care to show that the Christ figure, too, had shortcomings. This figure was Wilde's aesthetic artefact, employed in his stories as a device to reveal social conflicts and contradictions. While the rejection of society along with compassion for the poor is upheld as humane and beautiful, Wilde wants us to become more aware of what constitutes the mechanisms of ugly action such as domination and exploitation. It is first by perceiving how the civilizing process contributes to degradation of human beings that one can begin to struggle against it.

For instance, in the initial tale of *The House of Pomengrates* Wilde continued to elaborate the theme presented in *The Happy Prince* by depicting the workings of society more clearly. Here, in *The Young*

King, a goatherd is jolted one day when he is told that he is the only heir (the illegitimate son of the king's daughter) of his royal grandfather, who is about to die. He is swept from nature to the city and must make preparations for his coronation after a period of mourning. However, he has visions which are very much like the epiphanies in MacDonald's tales, religious illuminations, which open the young king's eyes so that he can see that beauty in his society is based on the abuse of workers. Since he will have no part of this, he decides to ride to his coronation in his former garb as goatherd with a wild briar as his crown. Wilde reverses the notion of 'clothes make the people' and transforms the mock motif in Andersen's *The Emperor's Clothes* into a radical ideological statement.[30] The king as Christlike beggar opposes social conventions, the Church, and the nobility. When a priest tries to dissuade him from his actions, he asks: 'shall Joy wear what Grief has fashioned?'[31] The king epitomizes the individual who refuses to compromise until the people learn to see that society must change. His beggarly appearance is ennobled and becomes radiant in the eyes of his onlookers because he has found the social essence of beauty.

In contrast to the happy prince, who was ultimately crucified despite (or perhaps because of) his philanthropic measures, the young king points a way to utopia by setting a model of behavior which he hopes everyone will recognize and follow. Basically he demonstrates that the beautiful appearance of the civilized world merely serves to conceal barbaric working conditions. His rejection of robe, crown, and sceptre is a rejection of private property, ornamentation, and unjust power. By refusing to be parasitic, and by dressing in his original clothes, he becomes both an individual and equal among men. The beauty of his deed derives from a compassion for humankind and a realization that his own potential depends on whether people are truly free. Though the social antagonisms remain unresolved at the end, Wilde went beyond *The Happy Prince* by making his Christ figure into a symbol of joy intent on paving the way to utopia.

Actually most of Wilde's tales are not as optimistic as this one and follow more the pattern of *The Happy Prince* to compel readers to question why social relations do not give rise to a better world. *The Nightingale and the Rose*, *The Devoted Friend*, *The Remarkable Rocket*, *The Star Child*, and *The Fisherman and his Soul* generally depict how hypocritical social conventions and double standards serve to maintain unjust rule. The result is pain and suffering, and the plots of the tales deny a happy end because property relations and social character are not altered. The higest personal state one can achieve under such conditions is crucifixion. Wilde's style, the mode which he chose to present his views of religion, art, and civilization, involved a subtle reutilization of biblical language and traditional fairy-tale motifs. That is, he transformed the style and themes of the Bible and classical fairy tales and put them to new use to convey his notions of Christian socialism.

For instance, *The Star Child* is a reversal of Andersen's *The Ugly Duckling* and incorporates motifs of the birth of Christ.[32] Whereas Andersen sees beauty as connected to the duckling's outward grace as swan and subservience to the aristocracy of the swans, Wilde's ideological position implicitly mocked Andersen while presenting a more complex notion of beauty. For Wilde, beauty was based on a joyous recognition that misery can be overcome by opposing abusive power and private property. In *The Star Child* a beautiful boy who is proud, cruel, and selfish must learn that his fortunate appearance does not give him the right to maltreat less fortunate people. He is made ugly and placed in their position. After years of wandering and helping others, he regains his beauty which is more striking because it is spiritual, and he is recognized as a king who rules his people with justice and mercy. However, Wilde is not content to leave us with a notion that all's well that ends well for one person. The biblical tone which closes the story reads like a warning. 'Yet ruled he not long, so great had been his suffering, and so bitter the fire of his testing, for after the space of three years he died. And he who came after him ruled evilly.'[33] Unlike Andersen, Wilde constantly insisted upon the need to rid society of domination if the essence of beauty is to manifest itself.

In *The Fisherman and his Soul*, Wilde again reversed an Andersen story. This time it was *The Little Mermaid*, and instead of having a mermaid mutilate and mortify herself to acquire a soul, Wilde had a fisherman fall in love with a mermaid and discard his soul. However, his soul, representative of his super ego and social convention, is jealous and seeks revenge. It drives the fisherman to do evil deeds, but the fisherman's love for the mermaid is so strong that he succeeds in turning his back on church and society and becomes united with her at death. The fisherman's non-conformity is symbolically a refusal to comply with the interests of the priest and merchants. Love is a liberating experience and allows him to become one with himself without the interference of a 'soul.' Wilde ironically extols the life of a man who refuses a soul and thus considers him a saint. The reverential tone and religious imagery serve to denounce the hypocrisy of orthodox Christian practice which rationalized suffering in the name of the rich.

As we have seen, most of Wilde's tales end provocatively with Christ-like figures dying, and the reader is compelled to question why such remarkable protagonists could not fulfill themselves *within* society. The provocation emanates from Wilde's utopian impulse which was more positively developed in only two tales, *The Young King* and *The Selfish Giant*. The latter tale, one of Wilde's most popular, is perhaps his most consummate statement on capitalist property relations and the need to restructure society along socialist lines. There are three stages to the tale. The first involves the eviction of the children from the garden. The giant as landholder opposes the children as collective. The second stage is the epiphany. The selfish giant suffers because he cannot share his wealth. His heart melts when he realizes how his selfishness makes a young boy miserable. The final stage is the transformation of his garden into a paradise for the children. He shares his property with everyone and their joy as well. In this latter phase the giant searches for the little boy whom he had helped but does not find him until the moment before his death. It is then that he realizes the boy is the incarnation of Christ, who leads the giant to paradise. This ending can be interpreted in various ways. Obviously it is related to Wilde's homosexuality, and he depicted the love for the boy as a form of liberation. On another level, this love is the type of humane compassion which Wilde felt was necessary for the building of socialism. Finally, the giant's pursuit and union with Christ is the pursuit of Christ within us, and, as we know from his essay on *The Soul of Man Under Socialism*, this type of joyous individualism which can only flower in the progress made toward utopia.

Like MacDonald, Wilde was careful *not* to portray the contours of utopia because he was so familiar with the sordid conditions in Victorian England and realized that there would be a long struggle before we would even begin to catch a glimpse of real social utopia. Again, like MacDonald, this was the reason why he placed so much stress on reversing the process of socialization or civilization in his fairy-tale discourse. The building of a moral and aesthetic sensibility for social action was at the root of both writers' fairy tales. Whereas MacDonald wanted his protagonists mainly to rectify wrongs, Wilde insisted that his heroes try to grasp the roots of existence to change society. The patterns in most of their fairy tales are remarkably similar and reflect upon socialization in England. Generally speaking, a young ignorant and innocent protagonist experiences an awakening through a dream or vision. At this point the protagonist sees what ails society, and *his or her* actions tend to go against the *status quo* of society. The configurative action of the heroes implied a critique of the civilization process and a notion of utopia that reflected upon the actual social ossification in England. Given the social disparities and grim conditions in England at the end of the nineteenth century, it is no wonder that MacDonald and Wilde opted to stress the potential for human perfection rather than social perfection. If anyone was going to paint the possibilities for a modern utopia in fairy tales, it had to be done by a 'naive' American.

IV

It is to L. Frank Baum's credit that he spent nearly twenty years of his adult life portraying a fairy-tale utopia with strong socialist and matriarchal notions to express his disenchantment with America, if not with the course of western civilization in general. Baum was cut from the same mold as MacDonald and Wilde. Dreamer, idealist, reformer, a man who believed firmly in human perfection but who did not believe that perfect humanity could be attained through conformity to a society which allowed common people to be degraded. Like MacDonald and Wilde, he followed in the footsteps of Ruskin and Morris by instilling his art with social purpose. Between 1888 and 1901 there were over sixty utopian novels published in the United States, and Baum, an avid reader, was particularly fond of Edward Bellamy's *Looking Backward* (1888) and Morris' *News From Nowhere* (1891).[34] Yet, instead of using romance on which to base his conception of utopia, he chose the classical fairy tale. Most important is that he felt it incumbent upon himself to 'Americanize' this predominantly European literary genre, and in doing so he opened up new frontiers for the fairy-tale discourse on civilization and paved the way for later writers to experiment even more with the potential of *sequel* fairy tales to present radical alternatives to social reality.

There are very few book-length utopian fairy tales like *The Wonderful Wizard of Oz* that have managed to stay popular as a classic. This may, in fact, be due to the ingenuous manner in which it illuminates a way out of the *gray* world around us and awakens our creative energies, suggesting that we can become what we want to become without compromising our dreams. Right from its appearance in 1900, *The Wonderful Wizard of Oz* with those remarkable illustrations by W.W. Denslow captivated young American readers, and it was soon to charm adults as a musical play in 1902. Thereafter, the thirteen sequels along with the original book enchanted children and adults alike throughout the world. By 1939, it was made into a semi-animated musical film with memorable performances by Judy Garland, Bert Lahr, Ray Bolger, and Jack Haley, and the fairy tale's classicism was thus guaranteed film imortality by MGM.[35] The melody of 'somewhere over the rainbow way up high, there's a land that I dreamed of' continues to instill hope in millions of viewers who are led to believe that the experience of a trip to Oz may help them transform conditions at home. In this respect the film, though it changed many incidents, retained the utopian impulse of the book. Book and film celebrate the need for utopia. Yet, there is a tragic side to Baum's concept of Oz which the film and few critics have explored in depth: the book and its sequels emanate from the sensitivity of a naive writer who was disturbed by the Gilded Age, which glossed over the desperate economic plight of farmers and workers, especially in the Midwest. And the film, too, arose *against* the background of the great economic Depression of the 1930s.

Baum was not a philosopher and did not seek to expound great world-views in *The Wonderful Wizard of Oz*. If anything, he was astonishingly if not painfully ingenuous, good-hearted, and trusting. His writing reflects an unusual propensity for inventiveness and candor. He thrived on puns, the burlesque, and the preposterous. His style and message were direct and lucid: he hated violence and exploitation with a humane passion. There is very little subtlety in the plots of his books, and his characters, though unusual, rarely develop in a complex way. Such simplicity might make for boring reading (and does in some of the sequels), but there is a profound and scintillating vision of America conveyed through his charming fairy tales, and this critical insight endows them with extraordinary power. The frank, candid narratives are disarming and leave one's imagination dangerously open to subversive ideas. A trip to Oz is not escape because one is forced to become aware of what is absent in America and in the world at large. It is interesting that Baum initially felt that the gaps in Dorothy's gray dull life could be filled after one short trip to Oz. The more he became disappointed with the American way of life, however, the more he allowed Dorothy to spend time and enjoy herself in Oz. By Book Six, *The Emerald City* (1908), he had her turn her back on Kansas and 'home' for good. Home became Oz, self-imposed exile from America. A strange act. Was it the closing of the American frontier and the limitations of American society which drove Baum to compel Dorothy to remain in Oz? Just what was it that Baum saw in the American 'civilizing process' which forced him to make Oz invisible to the outside world for its own self-protection?

The course that Baum's own life took can help explain in part the nature of his discourse on civilization and utopia in the Oz books. His unique fall, downward social mobility, from the upper class, his experiences as actor, salesman, storekeeper, and journalist, his travels from East Coast to West Coast – all this provided him with an elementary basis for understanding and sympathizing with the plight of the common people in America during the Gilded Age – a period of massive economic expansion and crises. We must bear in mind that the self-pro-claimed 'non-political' Baum had an unusually perceptive political viewpoint which owed a great deal to utopian writings, American populism, and the sufragette movement. It is always intriguing to read the imaginative works of a writer who claims that he had very little to do with politics and yet made this the very core of his work. It is in such naiveté that one often finds the keenest political insights into the contradictions of the times.

Baum was born symbolically with a heart defect in 1856 in upstate New York.[36] His father Benjamin Ward Baum was a wealthy oil execu-tive and could afford to provide his son with the necessary care and protection which might allow him to lead a fairly normal life. Neverthe-less, Baum lived with the fear that he might have an attack and die at any moment, and this fear was the basis for his deep regard and zest for all forms of life and also for his avoidance of conflict and violence. Educated at home on a 15-acre estate outside Syracuse, Baum could explore the farm and the nearby woods to his heart's content. He took a particular delight in chickens which he bred and spent a great deal of time reading when not taking private lessons. It is interesting to note that he absorbed himself in the tales of Grimm and Andersen but dis-liked their violence, cruelty, and sadness. Baum was bent on seeing the brighter side of life, for he never knew how much more time he would have to appreciate the world around him.

Sent to the Peeksill Military Academy in 1868 because his parents wanted to bring their son the dreamer down to earth, he lasted less than two years because he hated the corporal punishment and discipline of the institution. Thereafter, he completed his education at home with private tutors, and Dickens became one of his favorite authors. By 1873 Baum was ready to try his hand at journalism and took a job as cub reporter for the *New York World*. Soon he became involved with other newspaper projects, and in 1875 he began managing a printing shop in Bradford, Pennsylvania, where he established the newspaper *The New Era*. Since his father owned some opera houses and theaters in New York and Pennsylvania, Baum began to manage them, and he became absorbed in the theater as writer and actor. His first real success was the Irish musical comedy *The Maid of Arran* (1881), and this play encour-aged him to make theater his career. Because of his naiveté, however he was bound for a rocky road. In many instances his father (almost like a 'fairy godfather') had already provided assistance and fortuitous connections or bailed him out when Baum's trust in people was abused.

This is not to say that Baum was the spoiled rich boy, who constantly needed a doting father. On the contrary, Baum was a tireless inventor, extremely gifted and versatile as musician, writer, manual worker.

There was no doubt that, in 1881, he was a young man on the rise, and, when he met Maud Gage that same year, it seemed that success was staring him in the eyes. Maud was the daughter of Matilda Gage, who collaborated with Susan B. Anthony and Elizabeth Cady Stanton to write the four-volume *History of Woman Suffrage*, and who was famous for her own work *Woman, Church and State*. Needless to say, Maud, who was educated at Cornell, came from a different social environment than Baum, and yet, they appeared to complement one another, she with her sober social ideas, and he with his boundless idealism and imagination. They were going to need both sobriety and idealism after their marriage in 1882 because a series of accidents and tragic events was about to send them on a course of downward social mobility.

In 1884 Baum lost his shares in an opera-house chain through bad management and fire. He then opened up a small company to sell crude oil products in conjunction with his father's business. However, his father's firm was failing because some employees were defrauding accounts. By the time Benjamin Baum died in 1887, the business had collapsed, and the oil fortune had all but vanished.

Like many Americans at this time Baum turned West toward new frontiers and moved to Aberdeen, South Dakota, with Maud and their first of three sons. He opened up a variety store called Baum's Bazaar, but since he continually gave credit to the poor customers, especially farmers, and spent a lot of time telling stories to youngsters who frequented the store, he was forced to close in 1890. This was at the height of a severe economic depression, and Baum was witness to the way in which farmers were exploited by bankers and businessman alike. Foreclosure and poverty were common conditions in South Dakota, and Baum wrote about them in *The Aberdeen Saturday Pioneer*, which he edited for one year. Then in 1891 he moved with his family (there were now three sons) to Chicago, where he had a series of jobs as reporter for the *Chicago Evening Post* and then worked as travelling salesman for a china and glassware firm. During the first six years in Chicago, he actually took part in a populist demonstration, and his sympathies were clearly with social reform groups which were highly active and radical at that time. However, his main worry was surviving and supporting his family. In 1897, fatigue and nasal hemorrhages which were signs of a stressed heart caused him to retire as a salesman, and he assumed the editorship of *The Show Window*, the first magazine in America to be published for window decorators. At the same time, encouraged by his mother-in-law Matilda Gage, who thought highly of his bedtime stories for his sons, he began producing children's books: *Mother Goose in Prose* (1897), *My Candalabara's Glare* (1898), and *Father Goose* (1899). All were successful, but it was the publication of *The Wonderful Wizard of Oz* in 1900 which enabled him to resign his position as editor of *The Show Window* and to dedicate himself to writing and the theater. Actually Baum never intended to write a series of Oz books. He followed *The Wonderful Wizard* with *Dot and Tot of Merryland* and Baum's *American Fairy Tales* in 1901, *The Life and Adventures of Santa Claus* in 1902 and *The Enchanted Island of Yew* in 1903. It was not until 1904 that he published a sequel, *The Marvelous Land of Oz*, and the reasons were mixed. First, there had been a large demand for a sequel to *The Wonderful Wizard* by readers of all ages, and the success of the musical adaptation in 1902 stimulated even more interest in Oz. Secondly, Baum had run into financial difficulty because of his theatrical ventures, and he knew that a sequel with dramatic possibilities would provide him with the funds he needed. Thus, he developed a curious relationship to the Oz books: it was his pot of luck to which he could turn when he needed money, and it was the means through which he had contact with hundreds if not thousands of readers who wrote and gave him suggestions for characters, incidents, and plots.

When Baum made a decision in 1909 to move to Hollywood permanently and try his hand at films – he was always ready for new experiments and fantastic projects and even thought of constructing an 'Ozland' on an island off the coast of California – he tried to bring an end to the Oz books with *The Emerald City of Oz* in 1910. However, his film company failed, and he declared personal bankruptcy in 1911. Soon thereafter, in 1913, he resumed publication of the Oz series with *The Patchwork Girl of Oz*. From then on, most of the works he wrote in California were concerned with utopian projections, and it appeared that they could only take on concrete form in Oz. This was only appropriate, for it was through the Oz books that he gained the feeling of bringing joy to innumerable readers who shared his utopian fantasy. And, as he became progressively ill due to his weak heart – he suffered laming facial attacks in 1914 and became bedridden in 1917 – he turned more and more to Oz as a source of comfort. All this was in his house 'Ozcot,' right near Hollywood where Walt Disney was to establish his studio years later. California was ideal for Baum's resting place, the final frontier. It was almost as if he had been driven from the East to West Coast in search of a better America knowing all the while, his dark secret, that it would never come. It was difficult to admit this, and perhaps this is why he endeavored until his death in 1919 to give hope to his readers that there may be another way of pursuing the American dream than the way it was being pursued in reality with vengeance.

There have been a number of fine and thorough studies of Baum's works, and there is even an international society and Baum journal dedicated to keeping his spirit alive. Yet, few of the essays written on Baum's Oz books have placed them in the historical context of a fairy-tale discourse, and very few have written about the tragic undertones of his writing. I should like to do both by emphasizing a distinction between *The Wonderful Wizard of Oz* and the five books which followed paying close attention to *The Emerald City of Oz*. As is well known, Baum wrote the Oz fairy tales in three phases, and the first two are highly significant because he initially wanted Dorothy to return home and face the 'gray' music of Kansas. In the second phase he kept shipping her back and forth between Oz and Kansas until he decided that Dorothy and her aunt and uncle would never be happy in America. The last phase – the eight sequels written in California – are interesting because they concern Baum's desire to complete the picture of utopia and to work through certain problems. In all his works the civilization of Oz is opposed to the American civilization, and it is most important to understand how and why his critique of American socialization and values became so severe that he placed Dorothy in permanent exile.

One of the most revealing studies of the original Oz fairy tale is Henry M. Littlefield's essay, 'The wizard of Oz: parable on populism,'[37] in which he convincingly demonstrates that the book reflects the immiserated state of farmers in South Dakota, the depression and strikes of the 1890s, the war with Spain, and Baum's democratic populism. His major thesis is that Baum 'delineated a Midwesterner's vibrant and ironic portrait of this country as it entered the twentieth century. . . throughout the story Baum poses a central thought: the American desire for symbols of fulfillment is illusory. Real needs lie elsewhere.'[38] The allegorical parallels which Littlefield draws are instructive. Led by naive innocence and protected by good will (Dorothy), the farmer (scarecrow), the laborer (tin woodsman), and the politician (lion) approach the mystic holder of national power (wizard) to ask for personal fulfillment only to learn that they must ultimately provide for it by themselves.

Littlefield's thesis must be qualified and expanded. To begin with Baum was by no means a Midwesterner, and his ideological perspective should be clarified if we are to grasp the essence of his discourse on American civilization through the fairy tale. By the time he began writing the Oz fairy tales, Baum had become 'declassed,' that is, he had fallen from the upper classes and had experienced the trauma of downward social mobility. Moreover, his political consciousness had been awakened through his mother-in-law's and wife's feminism, the farmers' struggles in the Midwest, and the populist movement. His portrait of America was that of an upper-class Easterner, whose social expectations had been betrayed, and who 'betrayed' his class by seeking to delude children of false illusions about America as a land of opportunity.

Such deep concern in American reality led Baum to transform and 'Americanize' the classical fairy-tale pattern and motifs found in the Grimm and Andersen narratives. Generally, the hero has three encounters of various kinds to reach a type of peripeteia and then another three encounters to achieve a goal. The encounters are most often with friends or qualities which the hero needs to overcome obstacles and evil. In *The Wonderful Wizard of Oz*, the gray landscape is immediately recognizable as American, and Dorothy is clearly as American as apple pie. What's more, she is an orphan who expresses great compassion for downtrodden eccentrics on her journey through Oz. The scarecrow, woodman, and lion are recognizable American types, and Baum employs traditional fairy-tale covention to synthesize their qualities through a *female* figure. His purpose is to bring loners and outcasts together to depict just how capable they are. Implicit is the notion that common people do not need managers or middlemen to run their affairs, that the latent creative potential in each simple person need only be awakened and encouraged to develop. Baum's major characters in *The Wonderful Wizard of Oz* are non-competitive and non-exploitative. They desire neither money nor success. They have little regard for formal schooling or silly social conventions. They respect differences among all creatures and seek the opportunity to fill a gap in their lives. In depicting their behavior, Baum develops a discourse on manners and norms which contradicts the standard discourse in the tales of Grimm and Andersen and questions the actual civilizing process in America.

Perhaps it was because he was petrified by what he witnessed in South Dakota and Chicago that Baum sought to subvert the American socialization process based on competition and achievement. There is no doubt but that he wanted to educate readers to the fact that individualism could be achieved in other ways – through tenderness, good will, and cooperation. To be smart, compassionate, and courageous are qualities which could be put to use to overcome alienation. The colors and ambience of Oz are part of an atmosphere which allows for creativity and harmony along with a sense of social responsibility.

Dorothy sees and feels this. She is 'wizened' by her trip through Oz, and Baum knows that she is stronger and can face the drabness of Kansas. This is why he closes the book in America: Dorothy has a utopian spark in her which should keep her alive in gray surroundings.

In his next four books, *The Marvelous Land of Oz* (1904), *Ozma of Oz* (1907), *Dorothy and the Wizard in Oz* (1908), and *The Road to Oz* (1909), Baum elaborated his concept of utopia and explored its social relations in contrast to America. In *The Marvelous Land of Oz*, Baum *seemingly* mocked the woman's suffragette movement, and yet, the 'hero' of his fairy tale turns out to be a 'heroine,' very much representative of feminine ideals. Many American librarians have yet to forgive Baum for a kind of 'transvestite' act – he turned the male Tip into a female so she could resume her proper form and become Ozma of Oz, the gracious and just ruler.[39] For whatever psychological reasons, whether it was because he had always desired to have a daughter, whether it was because he could never have a close relationship with his mother, whether it was because he sought the approval of his wife Maude, Baum extolled feminine qualities as prerequisites for the foundation of utopia. In *Ozma of Oz*, Dorothy and Ozma have their first encounter with the Nome King, who represents materialist greed and the lust for power for the sake of power. His defeat only brings out his sinister desire for revenge. In *Dorothy and the Wizard in Oz*, the ageless 6-year-old girl is reunited with the Wizard, and they are rescued by Ozma from underground creatures who have neither heart nor humane ideals. Here the wizard returns to Oz for good, the first of a series of moves from America to Oz. In *The Road to Oz* Dorothy meets the Shaggy Man, who possesses a love magnet, and he tells Dorothy that money makes people proud and haughty and that he doesn't want to be proud and haughty. All he wants is to have people love him, which they will do as long as he owns the Love Magnet. This may be necessary in America, land of strife and alienation, but once he lands in Oz, the Shaggy Man learns that he does not need possessions or magic to gain what he seeks. Ozma tells him that people in Oz are loved for themselves alone, and for their kindness to one another, and for their own good deeds. Thus, the Shaggy Man decides, like the wizard, to remain in Oz, where he is accepted and loved for what he is.

By the time Baum came to write *The Emerald City of Oz* in 1910, he had developed precise principles for his utopia, and he formulated them at the beginning of this book:

> Each man/woman, no matter what he or she produced for the good of the community, was supplied by the neighbors with goods and clothing and a house and furniture and ornaments and games. If by chance the

supply ever ran short, more was taken from the great storehouses of the Ruler, which were afterward filled up again when there was more of any article than the people needed.

Every one worked half the time and played half the time, and the people enjoyed the work as much as they did the play, because it is good to be occupied and have something to do.

There were no cruel overseers set to watch them, and no one to rebuke them or find fault with them. So each one was proud to do all he could for his friends and neighbors, and was glad when they would accept the things he produced.

Oz being a fairy country, the people were, of course, fairy people; but that does not mean that all of them were very unlike the people of our own world. There were all sorts of queer characters among them, but not a single one who was evil, or who possessed a selfish or violent nature. They were peaceful, kind-hearted, loving and merry, and every inhabitant adored the beautiful girl who ruled them, and delighted to obey her every command.[40]

Baum's 'socialist' utopia is a strange one since it is *governed* by a princess named Ozma, but there is no real hierarchy or ruling class in Oz. Ozma the hermaphrodite is a symbol of matriarchy and guarantees the development of socialist humanism in Oz by regulating magic, especially by banning black magic. Not only does she welcome the downtrodden Aunt Em and Uncle Henry, who had been maltreated by bankers and had become fully isolated in America, but she also protects Oz against the revengeful Nome king through a strategy of non-violence. *The Emerald City of Oz* is aesthetically the most innovative and thematically the most radical of Baum's fairy tales. The narrative is based on a twofold plot with dialectical scenes which infuse the action with dramatic suspense. While Dorothy endeavors to 're-civilize' Aunt Em and Uncle Henry by showing them the wonders of their new home, the Nome King amasses a large army and attempts to destroy Oz. Baum draws a parallel between the bankers, who are merciless and crush old farmers who can no longer be employed because of bad health, and the Nome King and his allies, the Whimsies, Growleywogs, and Phanfasms, who want to enslave people to attain wealth and power. Each step Aunt Em and Uncle Henry take to realize and appreciate the liberating principles and environment of Oz is matched by a step taken by the Nome King to undermine the utopian civilization. The narrative perspective leads the reader to identify with the cause of Oz, and Baum demonstrates insight and ingenuity in the way he has Ozma save Oz and guarantee its eternal existence. Since he was against violence of any kind, Baum invented a fountain with water of oblivion. One sip of the water makes one forget everything, especially one's evil intentions, and

Ozma's enemies are led to taste, forget, and return to their homes outside Oz. Baum did not preach a Christian turning of the cheek. Rather he was more aware that, if one uses the same methods as one's enemies, one can easily become like them. To become cut-throat and militant like the gnomes and bankers would have tarnished the spirit and principles of Oz, and so the endeavor to be different and humanitarian at the same time engenders a greater sense of creativity and humanity in Ozma and her friends. Yet, because of this conflict with enemies, Ozma decides to make Oz invisible and unapproachable by outsiders because they mean tragedy for utopia. From Baum's ideological viewpoint he grasped that technology in the hands of capitalist entrepreneurs would mean the doom of utopian developments like Oz. By making this land invisible, Baum was saying that the chances for the realization of utopia in America had been cancelled and forfeited. The American dream had no chance against the real American world of finance, which manipulated and exploited the dream for its own ends.

In one of the most incisive essays about the Oz books, Gore Vidal[41] agrees with Marius Bewley[42] that the tension between technology and pastoralism is one of the things that the Oz books are about, whether Baum was aware of it or not.

> In Oz he presents the pastoral dream of Jefferson (the slaves have been replaced by magic and good will); and into this Eden he introduces forbidden knowledge in the form of black magic (the machine) which good magic (the values of pastoral society) must overwhelm.
>
> It is Bewley's view that because 'the Ozites are much aware of the scientific nature of magic, Ozma wisely limited the practice of magic.' As a result, controlled magic enhances the society just as controlled industrialization could enhance (and perhaps even salvage) a society like ours. Unfortunately, the Nome King has governed the United States for more than a century; and he shows no sign of wanting to abdictate. Meanwhile, the life of the many is definitely nome-ish and the environment has been, perhaps, irreparably damaged. To the extent that Baum makes his readers aware that our country's 'practical' arrangements are inferior to those of Oz, he is a truly subversive writer.[43]

As I have endeavored to demonstrate, Baum was not alone in developing an 'art of subversion' through the fairy tale. With the rise of industrialization and the rationalized exploitation of the working classes came different social reform movements and improved methods of education which people used to expose the contradictions in the civilizing process of so-called advanced technological countries. Generally speaking, most writers of fairy tales in England and America of the nineteenth century continued to use the form to mollify and apologize for broken promises of a better life as working conditions and social relations became more stressful and alienating. However, as we have seen, there was a small but powerful oppositional group of fairy-tale writers like Dickens, Ruskin, MacDonald, Wilde, and Baum, to name but a few, who transformed the fairy-tale discourse on mores and manners through a political perspective which placed both the classical fairy tales and society in question. There was also a new and larger reading audience composed of young people from the working and *petit bourgeois* classes who were the targets of both traditional and oppositional fairy-tale writers. And, of course, upper-class children were consistently included as part of the intended general audience.

What is important for the reform-minded fairy-tale writers is that they saw the possibility of providing a new kind of political consciousness which might lend more social confirmation to the relatively 'new' readers of the lower classes and which might make the privileged readers aware of their true social responsibility. It is clear that there is a shift in the ideology of the narrative perspective away from that of Perrault, the Grimms, and Andersen in the late 1800s: another world is glimpsed through the ideological lens of writers who refused to legitimate the views of the upper classes in England and America, and who devised aesthetical configurations to convey socialist utopian impulses. In essence, the literary fairy tale was becoming more and more a political weapon used to challenge or capture the minds and sensibilities of the young. This had always been the case, more or less, but the genre in its classical form and substance had used magic and metaphor to repress the desires and needs of the readers. The new 'classical' fairy tales of MacDonald, Wilde, and Baum were part of a process of social liberation. Their art was a subversive symbolical act intended to illuminate conrete utopias waiting to be realized once the authoritarian rule of the Nome king could be overcome.

Notes

1 Cf. Jürgen Habermas, *Strukturwandel der Öffentlichkeit* (Berlin: Luchterhand, 1962).

2 In *Essays in the History of Publishing*, ed. by Asa Briggs (London: Longman, 1977), pp. 248–82. See also Roger Lancelyn Green, *Tellers of Tales* (London: Ward, 1965), pp. 23–73.

3 *Extraordinary Works of Fairy Tale and Fantasy* (New York: Stonehill, 1973).

4 *Ibid.*, p. xlvi.

5 'On fairy tales,' in *European Literary Theory and Practice*, ed. by Vernon W. Gras (New York: Delta, 1973), p. 352.

6 *Fantasy: the Literature of Subversion* (London: Methuen, 1981), p. 91.

7 *Ibid.*, p. 33.

8   *Ibid.*, p. 35.
9   *Ibid.*, p. 35.
10   For an extensive discussion of MacDonald's life, see Greville MacDonald, *George MacDonald and His Wife* (New York: Dial, 1924) and Richard H. Reis, *George MacDonald* (New York: Twayne, 1972).
11   *George MacDonald*, p. 45.
12   *Unspoken Sermons*, Second Series (London: Longmans, Green, 1885) p. 49
13   Quoted in Reis, *George MacDonald*, p. 43.
14   *The Complete Fairy Tales of George MacDonald*, intr. by Roger Lancelyn Green (New York: Schocken, 1977), p. 17.
15   *Ibid.*, p. 35.
16   For a thorough and stimulating psychoanalytic examination of the sexual implications in MacDonald's works, see Robert Lee Wolff, *The Golden Key: A Study of the Fiction of George MacDonald* (New Haven: Yale University Press, 1961)
17   *The Complete Fairy Tales of George MacDonald*, p. 267.
18   *Ibid.*, p. 271.
19   See E.H. Mikhail, *Oscar Wilde. An Annotated Bibliography of Criticism* (Totowa, New Jersey: Rowman and Littlefield, 1978) and also the useful bibliography in H. Montgomery Hyde, *Oscar Wilde* (London, Methuen, 1977), pp. 520-31.
20   *Oscar Wilde* (London: Paladin, 1971), p. 62.
21   *The Paradox of Oscar Wilde* (London: T.V. Boardman, 1949), p. 139.
22   Cf. Jullian, *Oscar Wilde*, pp. 283-97 and Hyde, *Oscar Wilde*, pp. 376-410.
23   *Introduction* to Oscar Wilde, *Complete Shorter Fiction* (Oxford: Oxford University Press, 1979), pp. 10-11.
24   *The Soul of Man under Socialism*, ed. by Robert Ross (London: Humphreys, 1912), p. 18.
25   *Ibid.*, p. 32.
26   *Ibid.*, p. 43.
27   *Ibid.*, p. 45.
28   *Ibid.*, p. 92.
29   *Ibid.*, p. 97.
30   See Volker Klotz's excellent short essay on the major ideological differences between Andersen and Wilde, 'Wie Wilde seine Märchen über Andersen hinwegerzählt,' in *Der zerstückte Traum: Für Erich Arendt zum 75. Geburtstag*, ed. by Gregor Laschen and Manfred Schlosser (Berlin: Agora, 1978), pp. 219-28.
31   *Complete Shorter Fiction*, p. 182.
32   See 'Wie Wilde seine Märchen über Andersen hinwegerzählt,' pp. 225-8.
33   *Complete Shorter Fiction*, p. 252.
34   See Frank Joslyn Baum and Russel P. MacFall, *To Please a Child. A Biography of L. Frank Baum* (Chicago: Reilly & Lee, 1961), which contains important biographical and historical material.
35   See Aljean Harmetz, *The Making of the Wizard of Oz* (New York: Knopf, 1978).
36   Aside from the biography by Frank Joslyn Baum and Russel P. MacFall, Raylyn Moore's *The Wonderful Wizard, Marvelous Land* (Bowling Green: Bowling Green University Press, 1974) has valuable insights for the study of Baum's life.
37   In *American Culture*, ed. by Hennig Cohen (New York: Houghton Mifflin, 1968), pp. 370-81. See also Fred Erisman, 'L. Frank Baum and the progressive dilemma,' *American Quarterly*, **20** (fall 1968), pp. 616-23.
38   *Ibid.*, pp. 373, 380.
39   Numerous critics have discussed the censorship exercised by American librarians against Baum. In particular, see Martin Gardner and Russel B. Nye, *The Wizard of Oz and Who He Was* (East Lansing: Michigan State University Press, 1957). This study was one of the first to re-establish Baum's significance for American culture.

40   *The Emerald City* (New York: Ballantine, 1979), p. 22. Reprint of the original 1910 edition.
41   See the two-part essay 'The wizard of the "wizard," ' *New York Review of Books*, **24** (29 September 1977), pp. 10–15 and 'On rereading the Oz books,' *New York Review of Books*, **24** (13 October 1977), pp. 38–42.
42   See 'The land of Oz: America's great good place,' in *Masks and Mirrors* (New York: Atheneum, 1970), pp. 255–67.
43   'On rereading the Oz books,' p. 42.

6 The Fight Over Fairy-Tale Discourse: Family, Friction, and Socialization in the Weimar Republic and Nazi Germany

Mildew

More than ever before, people are living with it. Children are not raised without it. They carry it with them or suffer until they themselves are like the father. Even the person who does not listen picks up the discussions of commonplace people. What remains is the sitting around the kitchen table, the gossip, the visit, the artificial laughter and the genuine poison which they spread among one another. Even the person who does not inhale is greeted by the confining stale air. It penetrates to the young man below and to the beautiful people above. Remains good and quiet here, good and mute there.

Ernst Bloch
Erbschaft dieser Zeit (1934)

Given the significant attempts in recent years to grasp the essential features of Weimar and Nazi culture and the crucial links between these two phases of German history, it is remarkable that very little attention has been paid to fairy tales.[1] I use the word 'remarkable' for good reasons. Unlike any country in the western world, with the possible exception of Great Britain, Germany has incorporated folk and fairy tales in its literary socialization process so that they play a most formative role in cultivating aesthetic taste and value systems. In fact, it is generally impossible to think about folk and fairy tales without first thinking about the Grimms and Germany. Though it is not wise to attribute too much influence to any one cultural product in the formation of national customs and consciousness, there is no doubt that folk and fairy tales participated heavily in the creation of beliefs and norms and symbolically reflected changes in the social orders of Germany. As we know, fairy tales in particular were used consciously and unconsciously during the rise of the bourgeoisie to indicate socially acceptable roles for children and to provide them with culture, the German version of *civilité*.

The very fact that the Nazis recognized the necessity to create a policy with regard to folk and fairy tales demonstrated a general awareness about their cultural impact on children and adults alike. Even before the Nazis arrived on the scene, there were debates among members of the educated class in Germany about negative and positive effects of folk and fairy tales, especially for children. These debates began during the eighteenth-century Enlightenment and have lasted until the present. As public disputes, they can be considered an extension of the fairy-tale discourse in the commensurate institution of criticism, and they deal with the effect that the tales have on the psyche of children and consequently on their social attitudes, behavior, and creativity. Since it is extremely difficult to measure such an effect, the different perspectives are significant mainly insofar as the *positions themselves* reveal ideological and social views about literature and child-rearing in a given historical epoch. In the case of Weimar and Nazi Germany, there is much that can be learned about the family, socialization, and cultural attitudes by studying the aesthetic production of fairy tales and their use in the public sphere. Since this topic is a vast one, I want to limit myself to the question of family behavioral patterns and the ideology of competition and domination.

The Weimar and Nazi periods are extremely important for grasping the general development of the fairy-tale genre in the western world at large. As we have seen, the discourse on civilization through the fairy tale for children was expanded, inverted, and subverted toward the end of the nineteenth century. This resulted in a fierce public struggle over the discourse at the beginning of the twentieth century, and nowhere was it so strikingly apparent as it was in Germany, that the fairy-tale discourse was bound up with the civilizing process. This was because of the tremendous social and political upheavals which polarized the society and compelled writers to assume clear-cut ideological positions in their symbolic acts. Parallels can be drawn to other countries at this time, and the analogies can help us perceive the broadly similar countours of the fairy tale for children in the West *as well as* the unevenness and particularity of cultural developments. As my chosen focal point in this chapter, the German literary fairy tales enable us to grasp the course that the civilizing process in the western world was taking, and, as a case study, it is interesting to see how they broke even more from the classical fairy-tale patterns to discuss domination and barbarism. The vital attempt to find an antidote to the mildew in Germany – Bloch's metaphor for those atavistic attitudes which the Nazis used to create their empire – reinvigorated the fairy-tale discourse in Weimar Germany and then succumbed to the poison of the 1930s. Since the concerns of the fairy tale for children and the fairy tale for adults were so close in Weimar and Nazi Germany, I shall try to show in this chapter how they formed a *pervasive* fight over fairy-tale discourse in which the future of civilization was often implied to be at stake. This battle was also being waged by fairy-tale writers in other western countries, and it is with an awareness of the *total* literary war, whose history is yet to be written, that Germany can help us grasp the points of historical gaps to be filled as critical text.

I

The significance of the classical fairy tale for children in Germany at the onset of the twentieth century can be measured to a large extent by the voluminous attention paid to the tale by scholars of different disciplines.[2] By 'classical' I am referring to the standard popular works of the Grimms, Andersen, and Bechstein, which were the major reference point in German debates and discussions and often regarded as folk tales. In the field of psychology, the most important works were written by Charlotte Bühler, *Das Märchen und die Phantasie des Kindes* (*The Fairy Tale and the Imagination of the Child*, 1919), Hans Hr. Busse, *Das literarische Verständnis der werktätigen Jugend zwischen 14 und 18* (*The Literary Comprehension of Working Youth between 14 and 18*, 1923), and Erwin Müller, *Psychologie des deutschen Volksmärchens* (*Psychology of the German Folk Tale*, 1928). Along with the interest of the Freudian and Jungian schools in dreams and their relationship to fairy tales, these studies pointed to the general importance of fairy tales in helping children develop full personalities, and they defended their positive virtues for role development and maturation within the socialization process. The sociological and pedagogical studies, Wilhelm Ledermann, *Das Märchen in Schule und Haus* (*The Fairy Tale in School and Home*, 1926) and Reinhard Nolte *Analyse der freien Märchenproduktion* (*Analysis of the Free Production of Fairy Tales*, 1931), documented the widespread popularity and use of the classical fairy tales and supported the findings of Bühler, Busse and others.[3] Walter A. Berendsohn endeavored to make clear-cut distinctions between the fairy tale and other short forms of narrative prose in *Grundformen volkstümlicher Erzählkunst in der Kinder- und Hausmärchen der Brüder Grimm* (*Basic Forms of the Popular Art of Narration in the Household Tales*, 1922). Researchers of a conservative folklore tradition sought to trace the symbolical figures of the classical fairy and folk tales to Nordic religions and myths. Here the work of Karl von Spiess, *Das deutsche Volksmärchen* (*The German Folk Tale*, 1925), Georg Schott, *Weissagung und Erfüllung im deutschen Volksmärchen* (*Prophecy and Fulfillment in the German Folk Tale*, 1925) and Werner von Bülow, *Märchendeutungen durch Runen. Geheimsprache der deutschen Märchen* (*The Meanings of Fairy Tales through Runes. The Secret Language of German Fairy Tales*, 1925) helped prepare the way for one-sided fascist studies and formative anthropological works in the field of folklore. Finally, Edwin Hoernle dealt at length with the reception and use of fairy tales from a Marxist point of view in *Die Arbeit in den Kommunistischen Kindergruppen* (*Work in the Communist Children's Groups*, 1923), which was developed in a more sophisticated way by Ernst Bloch[4] and Walter Benjamin[5] in the 1930s.

The heated discussion about the value and effects of the classical fairy tale during the Weimar Period must be seen within the context of a debate concerning the function of children's books in the socialization process unleashed earlier by Heinrich Wolgast's book *Das Elend unserer Jugendliteratur. Ein Beitrag zur künstlerischen Erziehung der Jugend* (*The Misery of our Literature for the Young. A Contribution to the Artistic Education of Youth*, 1896). Wolgast, a left-liberal, who sympathized with the Social Democratic Party,[6] helped found an organization called the *Jugendschriftenbewegung*, which sought to clean up books for children and young people and raise aesthetic standards. In the 1920s his position was best represented by Herman L. Köster, author of *Geschichte des deutschen Jugendliteratur in Monographien* (*History of the German Literature for Youth in Monographs*, written in 1906 and revised in 1927). As co-founder of the *Jugendschriftenbewegung*, Köster and others worked in the 1920s to keep the artistic standards of children's literature high and morally decent. Their basic ideological position, however, allowed more and more for chauvinistic and militaristic books and other illustrated volumes which implicitly reinforced the value system of the conservative wing of the bourgeoisie.

In opposition to this conservative trend in the *Jugendschriftenbewegung*, which was eventually taken over by the Nazis under the leadership of Severin Rüttgers, there was a strong movement led by communists, radicals, and progressives to politicize children's literature openly and thereby to raise the artistic and ideological quality of literature for young people. Since the classical fairy tale was used so prominently to help children adapt to expected roles in the bourgeois socialization process, it is not by chance that this genre was one of the first which socialists sought to revise and reutilize. In 1923, Edwin Hoernle argued that

> just in general we must learn again how to tell stories, those fantastic, artless stories as they were heard in pre-capitalist times in spinning rooms of the peasants and in homes of the artisans. The thoughts and emotions of the masses are mirrored here most simply and therefore are most clear. Capitalism with its destruction of the family and its mechanization of working human beings annihilated this old 'popular art' (*Volkskunst*) of telling tales. The proletariat will create the new fairy tales in which workers' struggles, their lives, and their ideas are reflected and correspond to the degree to which they demonstrate how they can become human time and again, and how they can build up new educational societies in place of the decrepid old ones. It makes no sense to complain that we do not have suitable fairy tales for our children. Professional writers will not create them. Fairy tales do not originate from the desk. The real fairy tale originates unconsciously, collectively in the course of longer time-spans, and the work of the writer consists mainly in refining and rounding out the material at hand. The new proletarian and industrial fairy tale will come as soon as the proletariat has created a place in which the fairy tales will be told, not read aloud, and will be composed orally, not repeated. Then machines, tools, boilers, trains, ships, telegraphs and telephones, mine shafts and chemical tubes will become alive and begin to speak just as previously the wolf or the water kettle in the folk tales of the peasantry and *petit bourgeois* spoke.[7]

As we know, this prediction by Hoernle has not become entirely true, but the production of progressive, socialistically oriented fairy tales did begin, and it began much sooner than he even realized. There were already clear socialist strains in literary fairy tales for children throughout Europe and America by the end of the nineteenth century. Still, it was not until the end of World War I that a barrage of demonstrable communist and socialist fairy tales for children presented itself. In Germany Hermynia Zur Mühlen began writing political fairy tales for children in 1921 with *Was Peterchens Freunde erzählen* (*What Little Peter's Friends Tell*), and she followed this with other collections, such as *Das Schloss der Wahrheit* (*The Castle of Truth*, 1924) and *Es war einmal . . . und es wird sein* (*Once Upon a Time . . . And It Will Come to Be, 1930*). In addition, Ernst Friedrich gathered some interesting political tales by Berta Lask, Carl Ewald, and Robert Grötzsch in *Proletarischer Kindergarten* (*Proletarian Kindergarten*, 1921) while Bruno Schönlank's *Grossstadt-Märchen* (*Big City Fairy Tales*, 1923), Walter Eschbach's *Märchen der Wirklichkeit* (*Fairy Tales of Reality*, 1923), Heinrich Schulz's *Von Menschlein, Tierlein und Dinglein* (*Little People, Animals and Things*, 1925), Cläre Meyer-Lugau's *Das geheimnisvolle Land* (*The Mysterious Country*, 1925), and Lisa Tetzner's *Hans Urian* (1931) demonstrated how fairy tales could be used to explain social contradictions to children in a highly illuminating way. However, the movement to radicalize fairy tales really never took root among children and adults in the Weimar Republic. The classical fairy tales of the Grimms, Andersen and Bechstein reigned supreme and were imitated by a host of mediocre writers who fostered a canon of condescending, morally didactic tales which were used basically to sweeten the lives of children like candy for consumption. Moreover, the classical fairy tale was now disseminated through radio and film, and this distribution made its impact even greater on children of all classes. The mildew was no longer spread just by everyday talk but also transmitted by the mass media. Modern technology in support of anachronistic ideology.

When the Nazis took power in 1933, there was a gradual change in the production of fairy tales for children. First, of course, the socialist experiments were banned. Secondly, writers were less and less encouraged to write fairy tales. The folk tales were considered to be holy or sacred Aryan relics. Therefore, the classical fairy tales of the Grimms, Andersen, and Bechstein were promoted as ideal on recommended reading lists for children along with those of Musäus, whereas the romantic fairy tales and other *Kunstmärchen* were to be avoided. What was now stressed and came to be part of a policy in regard to fairy tales was a cleansing policy to recover the pure Aryan tradition of the folk tale. As Christa Kamenetsky has pointed out:

> The National Socialist conception of folk, community, peasant, and folklore differed substantially from that which emerged from even the most nationalistic writings of Herder, the Brothers Grimm, Arndt, Goerres, or Jahn, as it combined some romantic notions with the ideological orientation of the Third Reich. The 'fighting folk community,' standing 'in a single column' behind the *Führer* in unity and unquestioning loyalty, had but little to do with the rural folk community of an idyllic village. The innocent folktale was transformed into an ideological weapon meant to serve the building of the Thousand Year Reich. Thus, Party official Alfred Eyd announced in 1935, 'the German folktale shall become a most valuable means for us in the racial and political education of the young.'[8]

This did not mean a new folk-tale or fairy-tale tradition was to be created (the way sought by socialists and communists). If one examines the folk-tale and fairy-tale collections and the production during the fascist period, it is actually remarkable how little was actually done to change the format of the books. One cannot speak of a folk tale in the strict sense of the word since most of the tales collected and published for children were the classical fairy tales of the Grimms, Andersen, and Bechstein. The illustrations were also drawn to a large extent from the nineteenth century (Rackham, Dulac, Doré) or imitated idyllic peasant scenes. In other words, there was no massive attempt to rewrite the tales stressing their Aryan features or to paint pictures with Nordic types. There was, however, an enormous effort made by educators, party functionaries, and literary critics to revamp the interpretation of the tales in accordance with Nazi ideology and to use these interpretations in socializing children. In addition, there were numerous articles and debates about fairy-tale films for children in the official party journal, *Film und Bild*.[9] Josef Prestel's remarks about the Nordic qualities of the classical fairy tale can give us an idea of the general tendencies of the fascist re-interpretation of the tales and how they were put to use:

> In heroic racist sense, new light is also shed on the role of the king's daughter in the fairy tale. She is the highest reward for the hero. Whoever risks his life will be rewarded in life. Whom does the king's daughter choose? The fearless one, the good-hearted, the loyal one, even if he is a herdsman or hunter. He brings with him the best qualities 'from the folk.' He enters the circle of the courtiers victoriously. The powerful qualities from the folk unite with the bearer of a noble race: the king's daughter as the reward of the hero is the symbol for the improvement of the species, of the high racist idea, of the perpetuation of the race, 'and so they are still living today.' . . The fairy tale provides in palpable images the reflection of the moral world radiated by the certainty of salvation associated with the child's optimism. Yes, it is made specifically to exhibit the virtues of the folk: loyalty, steadfastness, perseverance, fearless courage in the case of male heroes, a sense of sacrifice, humble dedication and sympathy in the case of female heroes.[10]

Aside from obvious anti-Semitic explications of such tales as *The Jew in the Thorn* or the association of thievery and cheating with Jews, most of the National Socialist interpretations stressed the struggle between two worlds, the pure Aryan versus the contaminated alien world. Thus, G. Grenz could interpret *Cinderella* in the following way:

> And so these worlds fight against each other, and it appears that deceit and falsehood triumph. But nature does not let itself be cheated and deceived. It opens itself up to the pure person and the devoted. It reveals its help to him! It fuses the suitable specimens of a species together, and in this way it perfects the natural laws with relentless logical consistency. And the prince finds the genuine, worthy bride because his unspoiled instinct leads him, because the voice of his blood tells him that she is the right one.[11]

If the classical fairy tale was used throughout the fascist period to give children a sense of their Nordic heritage and race and to provide them with notions of feudal community and heroic roles with which they were to identify, the tales also allowed children and young people to escape. That is, the books were not always read in the presence of Party teachers and functionaries, and, since many tales were not dressed with explicit political symbols or rewritten to preach the glories of the Third Reich, they could be used by children and adults alike to compensate for the political bombardment in their daily life. According to one historian of children's literature, the fairy tales became more and more popular toward the end of World War II because they were a kind of refuge from the bitter reality of the war and ideological warfare.[12] Still, the dominant social function of the classical fairy tale tended to further the illusion that the Nazis were recreating a folk community in keeping with the unfulfilled needs of the German people, who, under the leadership of Hitler, could now rise up, struggle, and reclaim their worthy position in the world.

As we have seen, there was hardly any change in the production of the classical fairy tales in the Weimar and Nazi periods, but there were definite changes in the strategic employment and interpretation of the tales in the public sphere. With regard to the literary fairy tale for adults, the changes during these two periods were much greater. The literary fairy tale as a variation of the folk tale had developed a long tradition of commenting and reflecting upon social reality in a critical fashion through the play upon and ingenious use of symbols, motifs, and plots. From the eighteenth century to the Weimar period, German fairy-tale writers had become famous if not notorious for their subversive skills. Depending on the particular author's political and philosophical viewpoint, the fairy tale was put to use as a socially symbolic act in a variety of ways. Therefore, it is perfectly logical when Hartmut Geerken in his collection of expressionist fairy tales *Die goldene Bombe*[13] set up the following categories to describe early twentieth-century experimentation with the tale: (i) God is dead – the human being in the cosmos; (ii) magic – black humor; (iii) knight's moves – satires – grotesque; (iv) astral aspects; (v) the Satanic in the double bed; (vi) social political; (vii) the old tale; (viii) Dada. His work brings together the tales of such different writers as Hans Arp, Hugo Ball, Bertolt Brecht, Theodor Däubler, Albert Ehrenstein, Hans von Flesch-Brunningen, Oskar Maria Graf, Victor Hadwiger, Franz Held, Georg Heym, Jacob von Hoddis, Franz Kafka, Klabund, Fritz Lamp, Kurd Lasswitz, Gustav Meyrink, Carlo Mierendorff, Alfred Mombert, Mynona, Oskar Panizza, Hans Reimann, Paul Scheebart, Hans

Schiebhelbuth, Kurt Schwitters, Reinhard Johannes Sorge, and Otto Stoessl. A good many of these names are practically unknown today; yet, these writers were well-known in their own day and represented an important avant-garde tradition in the arts that reflected great social changes at the beginning of the twentieth century. The collection of the tales dating from 1900 to 1930 reveals a continuity with the way the romantics used the fairy tales to project their dissatisfaction with the existing state of things in a highly complex symbolical mode. In commenting on the general tendency of the expressionist fairy tale, Christoph Eykmann has stated:

> The fairy tale in its veiled form often has the capacity to make what is meant more effective than the direct polemical assertion. One could almost expect that the typical expressionist could conceive his utopian ideal image of a more pure world better in the fairy tale than in any other literary form. But – just as in the non-fairy-tale literature of expressionism – the emphasis is placed almost exclusively on the aspect of criticism of the existing state of things and not on the anticipatory conception of the way things should be. To be sure, the goal in Scheebart's fairy tales is a better human world. However, it is thwarted by the forces of nature. In Hadwiger's tale, the representative of this better world, the giant, becomes the victim of a base reality. In Ehrenstein's tale The Guilt, humanity destroys itself. The way out of the stagnate social world succeeds only through death.[14]

As Eykmann himself admits, this overwhelming pessimism is not dominant in most of the fairy tales, but it is connected to the essential quality of the fairy tales written during the Weimar period. Unlike the romantics, who conceived new utopian worlds out of the breakdown of a social order reflected in their tales, fairy-tale writers for adults between 1919 and 1933 did not or could not posit utopian solutions. They developed another characteristic feature which evolved from the romantic fairy tale during the transition from feudalism to capitalism, namely the ambivalence of protagonists caught between changing social orders, desirous of creating new structures, but torn between the old and the new. If we consider some of the other disparate fairy-tale products of the Weimar period not collected by Geerken, then the open-endedness of the tales mirroring disturbed relations and ambivalence appears to be the central feature of the works. Hesse's Strange News from Another Planet, The Poet, and other fairy tales printed in 1919 project a longing for harmony and peace which was barely obtainable at that time in society, neither for his heroes nor for his readers. Thomas Mann's monumental Magic Mountain (1924), cast totally in the mold of the romantic fairy tale, depicts a floundering hero wallowing in mud at the end of his ironic narrative. Ödön von Horváth's *Sportmärchen* (*Sport Fairy Tales*, 1924) and his other tales written at' this time show the shallowness of *petit bourgeois* life and the uselessness of inherited traditions: his characters become caricatures of themselves, imprisoned by their own banal forms of speaking and thinking. Oskar Maria Graf sets the scenes of his fairy tales in *Licht und Schatten* (*Light and Shadow*, 1927) as though they were fragmented communities which must be pieced together again by people who have been ripped apart themselves. In two fairy tales composed in 1929, Bertolt Brecht touches upon the lack of communication in worlds turned topsy turvy. Even in the more conservative writings of Hermann Stehr and Hans Friedrich Blunck during the 1920s, there is an implicit quest for community, for the restoration of a world with virtue that will refurbish humanity on the verge of despair.

Though the artistic structures and contents of the fairy tales varied, there were two givens which were generally operative in Weimar writing: the old folk-tale and classical fairy-tale forms were useful only insofar as they provided models of anachronism which had to be superseded in configurations closely related to Weimar social reality; the configurations and protagonists had nothing to do with an idyllic folk community of the past but symbolized the breakdown of human relations in the capitalist world and thus revealed the negative trends of mechanization, automatization, and commodity fetishism. Given the fascist optimism and doctrinaire stress on a new world order, it is quite apparent why the new literary fairy tale of Weimar did not and could not thrive in Nazi Germany.

Most of the progressive fairy-tale writers fled Nazi Germany, and, if they continued to produce fairy tales at all, then they were not distributed and circulated in the fatherland. Whatever tales were allowed to circulate, such as those of Blunck, Stehr, Hesse, and Wilhelm Matthiessen, did not contradict the folk ideology of the National Socialists but could be used to further the Nazi orientation toward purity, loyalty, maternal sacrifice, and male courage. Thus, the critical tradition of the romantic fairy tale was deprived of a public and made to appear nefarious. Christa Kamenetsky points to a speech on 'The romantic fairy tale,' prepared by Dr Albert Krebs in the early 1930s, as an example of how the Nazis opposed the literary fairy tale.

> Krebs was the author of various school readers and anthologies, and his books were recommended by the editors of the educational journal *Die Volksschule*, issued by the National Socialist Teacher's Association. In line with recent trends, he called attention to the 'healthy and organic' world view of the folktale, contrasting it sharply with the 'artificial and

decadent view' of the literary fairy tale. The literary fairy tale, as an expression of the early Romantic writers, was the product of a baroque and distorted perception of reality, he said, and it should be kept off the children's book shelves.[15]

Not only were the romantic fairy tales to be banned from children, but they were re-evaluated for adults and declared inferior to the classical tales. As a result of the folk ideology and the disregard of the literary fairy tale, considered alien to folk culture, few fairy tales of any consequence were produced by pro-fascist writers, and few German writers at all dared to use the literary genre to express their dissatisfaction with the existing state of things. Gerhart Hauptmann wrote his highly esoteric *Das Märchen*, imitative of Goethe's tale, in 1939, which contained a political statement of discontent. Ernst Wiechert wrote fairy tales toward the end of the war with a gun under a nearby pillow. These tales, which had anti-fascist features, were published only after the Nazi world order had collapsed. Fortunately, this collapse allowed German writers gradually to resume their experimentation with the literary fairy tale, and, to a certain degree, Hoernle's hope for a flowering of radically new fairy tales with modern paraphernalia and socialist ideas has been given a second chance, but this development, too, is faced with a dominant fairy-tale discourse which looks at radical utopianism askance.

II

Given the fact that classical fairy tales were the most widespread stories known to children and adults in Weimar and Nazi Germany and used extensively in the socialization process, it is important that we consider the patterns and normative roles portrayed in these tales and analyze their possible ideological implications. The results may help us understand more about the social and cultural tendencies in these two periods of German history and their effect on the fairy-tale discourse in general. Since classical fairy tales were not written during this period but used in a particular political way to educate both children and adults, it is necessary to compare and contrast their function as exemplary cultural products with the literary fairy-tale experiments which were, if anything, provocative and disquieting. Here the new and innovative forms may reveal what changes in the civilizing process were under way and may still be under way in our time. As usual, we shall see that the issues of power and domination are crucial for the interpretation and reception of fairy tales as they pertain to the family and socialization.

In his essay 'Familie und Natur im Märchen,' Max Lüthi asserts that the family plays a predominant role in the magic folk tale (*Zaubermärchen*).[16] It is not the extended family (*Grossfamilie*), as is commonly believed, but the small or nuclear family (*Kleinfamilie*) which is central to the fairy tale. According to Lüthi, the concentration on the small family provides the simple and comprehensible framework of the tale. Within this structure it is not harmony which characterizes familial relations but rather tension, argument, and conflict. Lüthi makes the following major points:

(1) The child is often endangered by parents who want to give the child away or who are compelled to do this; by evil stepmothers, brothers, and sisters, who are jealous of the child; by a hunter or servant who is commanded to kill the child.

(2) Most fairy tales do not concern children but the young individual who generally breaks with the family and leaves home at the outset of the tale. The major theme concerns the maturation of the individual. This maturation is not fostered by the family and social milieu. The young person must rely on nature and his/her own gifts to discover happiness.

(3) Marriage is the goal of most fairy tales, but it is not the subject matter. Like the royal realm it is symbolic. Both male and female protagonists strive for this goal, and often the family itself causes difficulties.

(4) The antagonists in the fairy tale are more often humans and members of one's own family than animals.

In sum, the danger in the intimate circle and the safety in nature and the universe are special forms of interdependence and isolation in which the basic pattern of the fairy tale's image of humankind can be seen. And the intensification of familial tensions to the point of death is not to be interpreted merely from the psychological and anthropological side. Such intensification is characteristic of the entire style of the fairy tale which seeks to move to extremes all over, in the portrayal of beauty and reward as well as in the portrayal of crime and punishment. In addition, the readiness for sacrifice, the capacity to suffer and the perseverance of the sister who saves her brothers, and of the wife who seeks the husband are intensified and become unreal (and are at the same time transposed so that they become visible). Here, too, there are strong tensions and exertion, but of a positive kind. The power of love in familial relations is not completely concealed in the fairy tale. It also appears in great intensity. And, when reality is dark, possibility remains light, the royal marriage radiates as goal.[17]

Lüthi's hypotheses are helpful but also misleading if we are to comprehend the overall meaning of the depiction of the family in the classical fairy tale. Before I deal with Lüthi's findings in detail, it is necessary to take into consideration Eleasar Meletinsky's remarks about marriage in the classical fairy tale.

> One of the forms with a social function was the marital 'exchange,' and the result was the social consolidation of the tribes. It was with this that the exchange of all values began. In this way the 'marital exchange' originates in myth. In the fairy tale, where the matter no longer concerns the welfare of the tribe but rather individual happiness, the marital 'exchange' removes itself more and more from its 'communicative function' and assumes a new meaning. Indeed, for the individual it means a particular 'miraculous' escape from exposed social conflicts which are embodied by forms of daily relations in the fairy tale. (It must be noted that the family in the fairy tale is to a great degree an extended family (*Grossfamilie*), that is, it typifies the patriarchal community of the semi-gentile type.). . . The basic contradictions (the types of life-death, etc.) accede to lively social conflicts which are generally revealed in the family sphere. The mediation is expressed in the way the hero flees the conflict and moves to a higher social status. This change of social status originates as a result of marriage with the king's son, the merchant, or the king's daughter, depending on who the protagonist is. Thus, in the fairy tale the 'marriage' becomes the means of mediation for a person to emancipate him or herself from basic social relations.[18]

Meletinsky, who combines Claude Levi-Strauss' findings with his own research, contradicts Lüthi in regard to two significant points. First, he correctly associates the family in classical fairy tales with the patriarchal extended family. Secondly, he indicates how marriage is not simply the goal of most fairy tales but, as *mediation*, it informs the way all characters relate to one another and, as such, it determines the normative actions of the protagonists and plots. Moreover, Meletinsky's anthropological method points to a more substantial approach toward comprehending the significance of family and familial relations in fairy tales than Lüthi's literary descriptive method. The role of the family in the classical fairy tale cannot be evaluated merely by noting the characters, motifs, and ontological dilemmas. Rather we must analyze the configurations and constellations formed through the interaction of characters representing familial types who stress certain values and world views. In the specific case of the classical fairy tale, we must try to grasp the sociogenetic references of the family conflicts and patterns in relation to the ideology and social function maintained by the family in the tale.

Neither Lüthi nor Meletinsky are concerned with the reception of the classical fairy tale in a specific historical epoch, nor does either one operate with a clearly defined notion of family and socialization. Thus, their studies are limited in that they explain what occurs among family members without exploring the underlying socio-historical origins and implications of the tales. They also remain within the general discipline of folklore and regard the *Zaubermärchen* as a folk tale. In our present study we must go beyond their work if we are to learn how fairy tales with their images of family and ideology of competition and domination functioned in the socialization process of Weimar and Nazi Germany.

As we know, the *Zaubermärchen* studied by Lüthi and Meletinsky had already become classical literary fairy tales as a result of the work of the Grimms and their disciples in the nineteenth century. The original primitive and feudal components were re-worked and adapted to the bourgeois value system which was in ascendance at this time. In sum, the classical fairy tale as recorded by the Grimms and later by other researchers and also adapted by writers like Bechstein contained a mixture of elements from pre-Christian periods, feudalism, and early capitalism, but the terms of the language and normative patterns as selected, recorded, altered, and published were heavily influenced by the bourgeois civilizing process. What then does this mean when we talk about the family and socialization in classical fairy tales, particularly of the Grimms' vintage?

Here I want to operate with certain assumptions developed by Mark Poster in *Critical Theory of the Family*.[19] Poster's study is significant in that he endeavors to define the family *not* according to size but with regard to issues connected to emotional patterns. For him, the family has a function within the socialization process, but, as an institution, it is primarily the social location where psychic structure is most decisively prominant.

> The family is here conceptualized as an emotional structure, with relative autonomy, which constitutes hierarchies of age and sex in psychological forms. The family is conceived as a system of love objects. Child-rearing patterns are theorized as interactional processes, focusing on the first three stages of development (oral, anal and genital). In these interactions, a pattern of authority and love is instituted by the adults forming a background to the strategies for raising children. Finally, a pattern of identification can be discerned which cements the bonds between adults and children. When these categories are studied in detail, a concrete family structure becomes intelligible.[20]

Poster also adds that, 'while the family generates a psychological pattern of internalized age and sex hierarchies, it also participates in larger social institutions. The types of this participation must be made intelligible.[21]

If we bear in mind Poster's ideas, particularly those concerning emotional patterns and interactional processes, we get a more differentiated picture of the family in the classical fairy tale than the one suggested by Lüthi and Meletinsky. To demonstrate what this image or picture might signify, I want to take the fourteen most popular fairy tales for children in Germany listed by Charlotte Bühler in 1919[22] to examine interaction, familial relations, bonds, and their ideological meanings as they pertain to domination and competition. The tales in question are: *Little Red Riding Hood, The Wolf and the Seven Kids, Sleeping Beauty, Hansel and Gretel, Snow White, Mother Holle, Cinderella, Brother and Sister, The Goose Maid, The Frog Prince, The Master Thief, King Thrushbeard, Jorinde and Joringel, The King of the Golden Mountain*. At times I shall refer to other Grimms' tales with the assumption that they were also widely known. Significant is that the basic type of the popular Grimms' fairy tale was the *Zaubermärchen* and not the *Schwankmärchen* (anecdotal tale), which tended to be more socially critical. In other words, social reception tended to be conservative.

The milieu of the fairy tales reflects feudal agrarian conditions, and the characters are either of the nobility, peasantry, or third estate (*burgher*). In other words three social types of families are depicted with distinctions made according to power, money, and sex. Though all family members are rarely present, each household gives indication that it is large. We must remember that servants and close relatives belonged to the extended family. Even the animals (such as the goat) have seven children or more, and most of the tales work with three, seven, or twelve children and suggest that it is a *sin* to be without children. In other words, fertility and large families are esteemed in the fairy tale. At the head of the extended family is an authoritarian male, who makes most of the decisions (*Sleeping Beauty, The Frog Prince, King Thrushbeard, King of the Golden Mountain*). If the mother, queen, or fairy godmother appears in a more active role than the male, she still acts in favor of a partriarchal society. Whether she be good or evil, her actions lead a young woman to seek salvation in marriage with a prince (*Cinderella, The Goose Maid, Snow White*). To prove her worth, the young girl must display through her actions such qualities as modesty, industriousness, humility, honesty, diligence, virginity. Moreover, she must be self-effacing and self-denying. The young man is generally more active and must demonstrate such characteristics as strength, courage, wisdom, loyalty, and, at times, a killing instinct (*King of the*

Golden Mountain). In all the social classes, the young male and female protagonists may have conflicts with their original family, but they do not reject the institution of the patriarchal family. They move away from their family, interact with outsiders to show their value, an exchange value, so that they can be considered worthy to contract a marriage or to be accepted in a new community and gain individual happiness. In the process, though one may move away from a conflict-ridden family and up in social class, the basic hierarchical order (father as supreme followed by mother, male and female children) of the patriarchical family is not altered but rather reaffirmed. The 'dream' of the lower-class character or oppressed person is fulfilled not through the creation of a new social order and family relations, but through living up to the expectations of defined roles and gaining recognition both inside and outside the original family.

To marry and become queen and king of a realm has many socio-psychological implications which would take too long to explore at this point. However, one thing is certain: the family is constituted through marriage by a strong male head, the decision-maker, whose absolute power and wisdom provide the framework within which one behaves and relates in the family and community. The male as savior is dominant and protects the virtues of the humble if not humiliated female (*King Thrushbeard*), and together they bring about the restoration of traditional family patterns, emotional bonding and interaction, in keeping with social values and patterns of identification which can be associated with those of the rising bourgeoisie. Though it is clear that the classical fairy tale is stamped by feudalism, the narrative perspective of the Grimms 'magic fairy tales' fuses a peasant world view with the democratic–humanitarianism of the rising-bourgeoisie. Thus, the treatment of family members is often differentiated by class, money, and power, but the overriding emotional pattern which emerges from the various depictions of family interaction centers on principles of moral restriction, sexual repression, abstention set by male figures, who reward the accumulation of the proper bourgeois values with a good solid marriage or place in a secure social order. The bourgeois values are often mixed with the aristocratic ideology of might makes right, but, for the most part, justice is based on the judicious use of power by paternal leaders who know what is best for the wives and children. In some tales, especially those concerned with royalty, the notion of the family implies a kingdom as institution. Here the family takes second place to the realm, which designates what is to be valued and to assume priority in the civilizing process. It is important to have a strong leader of the realm who sets a model for the rest of society. The image of the family is closely related to the social order as reflected in the behavior of the king and queen. Here we see again a blend of feudal absolutism and bourgeois qualities which were accepted and cultivated by the Grimms in their reworking of the folk tale into the classical fairy tale. There is a pervasive sense of enlightened aristocracy in most fairy tales forging familial roles and patterns of behavior among the peasantry, bourgeoisie and nobility which reveal that the magic and enchantment of the tales have a limited utopian function: they transform the situation of the protagonists into an improved situation so they can become parents and masters of institutions which are essentially *not* of their own making. The emotional patterns, the roles, relations, attitudes, and goals of the exemplary family in the magic fairy tale of the Grimms resembled those which actually came to be upheld by the dominant bourgeois family type in the Weimar Republic and Third Reich. Thus, the grounds for the reception of the classical fairy tales for children were favorable in both epochs, even though different aspects and ideological components may have been stressed.

In dealing with the reception of the tales in these two epochs, there is a danger in assuming that they were always used in an ideological manner to persuade children to conform to the dominant standards in the particular socialization process, or that they had a definite socio-psychological effect (or can have) on children. There is no doubt that they were and still are highly instrumental in the socialization process in Germany. Yet, the fact is that it is virtually impossible to determine the specific individual meaning a fairy tale may have for a child and extremely difficult to gauge the overall meaning in a given epoch. Only by studying the general discourse on fairy tales, the fairy-tale discourse itself, and the mode by which fairy tales were put to use by adults can we draw some valid conclusions about their possible effect on manners, taste, and social views. In the case of the Weimar Republic we know that there were various types of families (peasant, proletarian, *petit bourgeois*, bourgeois, and aristocratic) and that the reception varied from class to class. Generally speaking, the actual use through picture books, radios, schools, advertisements, coupon stamps in cereal boxes and cigarette packages, plays, films and instruction in schools stressed *Kindertümlichkeit* (childishness), the moral illusion of a *heile Welt* (harmonious world), nationalism, and such values as diligence, industry, obedience, thrift, and purity. Since the tendency had become greater in the dominant bourgeois practice of child-rearing to give more care to the child and to stress orderliness and propriety, it was felt that the tales provided normative patterns for a healthy maturation of the mind and imagination, and that they reinforced belief in solid

Germanic qualities. Certainly, the roles of the female and male patterns of interaction in the tales which allowed for authoritarianism corresponded to forms of behavior which children were expected to accept in the family and society. That is, the paradigmatic structure of familial relations in the classical fairy tales did not contradict the standard bourgeois family model or policies of upbringing which were current in the Weimar Republic.

In the Nazi epoch these fairy tales assumed an even greater importance, especially those of the Grimms which were included as part of the Nordic cultural heritage. Depending on the element to be stressed, the feudal world picture could be and was used to substantiate Nazi ideology. In regard to the family, the elements of fertility, the assertive courageous prince, the virtuous self-sacrificing mother, and industrious children could be viewed as the qualities which went into the making of an ideal Germanic family. Actually, if we look closely at the Nazi interpretations and use, we can see that they fit a policy which actually undermined solidarity within the family. As Ingeborg Weber-Kellermann has pointed out,[23] the family was not to play a major role in the socialization process but was considered primarily functional for production and reproduction in an economic–biological sense. While the emotional patterns of interaction in the tales were accepted, the Nazi interpretations stressed elements which suited their policies, i.e. community and race over family, the king and realm over all. All heroic qualities and actions were associated with the necessity to purify the world and establish a new Reich, whereby leadership and authority were associated with the *Führer*. The submissive role of the woman, who must sacrifice herself for the good of the king or kingdom coincided with the shifting Nazi policy which encouraged women to remain at home, raise large families, and create a household which functioned harmoniously for the good of the Reich. When women were obliged to work in factories, plants, and offices later in the 1930s, the element of sacrifice in the fairy tale was appropriately slanted to rationalize new policies.[24]

One feature of the classical fairy tale which appealed to children and adults alike in Weimar and Nazi Germany was the restoration of fixed roles in a stable family blessed with good fortune. Despite the major differences in the ideology of these two periods, Weimar and Nazi leaders favored monogamy, large families, paternal domination, deference to authority figures, and family adherence to state policies. The classical fairy tale creates the illusion in its configuration that, despite conflicts among family members, the traditional family and its emotional patterns (the mildew) can be restored. The tale appears to move forward while clinging desperately to the past. That is, the traditional social order and family are viewed as goals once the friction has been resolved. The appeal and use of the fairy tale in both the Weimar and Nazi epochs had a great deal to do with Ernst Bloch's notion of *Ungleichzeitigkeit* (non-synchronism) and *Heimat* (home).[25] In both historical periods the classical fairy tale kept alive those unfulfilled wishes and needs of the lower strata of society and offered compensation to all classes of people who felt bypassed by swift technological progress and socio-economic changes which uprooted them psychologically so that they were actually unable to move with the times. Nor could they articulate their dissatisfaction and maladjustment concretely. They were swept off their feet and looked around for footing with anxiety. Thus, there was a longing for the good old times, for the stability and order of what was projected to be a more idyllic period. To this extent, the classical fairy tale with its traditional image of the family and marriage and its promise of *Heimat* was used as a stabilizing factor in the socialization process of both the Weimar and Nazi periods in Germany.

This general tendency is also the reason why the literary fairy-tale experiments for children and adults must be taken into consideration and compared with the classical fairy tale and its use in these periods. They represent symbolic attempts to intervene in the civilizing process perceived to be destructive, reflect artistically about competition and domination in the family and society, and project possible alternatives to the existing state of affairs. Let us look at some of the remarkable literary fairy tales first for children, then for adults, in both the Weimar and Nazi periods. The fact that they are barely known today is all the more reason why we should try to reconstruct their discourse.

III

In the Weimar period, the work of Hermynia Zur Mühlen, Bruno Schönlank, and Lisa Tetzner is significant.[26] Though there were differences among them, they all shared a common starting point: they wanted to depict actual social conditions as experienced by a working-class child largely in urban environments under the influence of modern technology, and they indicated that the poor conditions within the family could not be transformed unless major social changes were made. The narrative point of view is that of the oppressed. The magic and fairy-tale motifs are employed to expose (not disguise) the source of domination and real social contradictions.

Schönlank's fairy tales in *Grossstadt-Märchen* (1923) tend at times to be sentimental and idealistic. Nevertheless, he does manage to probe the underlying reasons for tension and friction in the family and society. In *Die geflickte Hose* (*The Patched Pants*) an old widow does housework for rich people and can barely feed and clothe four sons. The youngest son Franz wears only hand-me-downs from his older brothers. Since his clothes are always patched, the other children make fun of him. One day Franz and his brothers meet an old junk dealer with two parrots. They are invited into his store where all the used garments, articles, and junk tell the boys stories about their previous owners and how hard life is. The junk dealer himself reveals that he was once rich and had refused to help a poor man when he wanted to sell an old picture. Since the rich man called the picture junk, the poor man sentenced him to learn the real meaning of junk. This was how the rich man became transformed into the junk dealer and his two spoiled daughters into parrots. In the years that followed the junk dealer tells how he discovered that sorrow, love, and joy went into the making of junk and how he came to regard used items as more valuable than jewels. After hearing this story, Franz himself learns to value his patched pants as the product of love, and, when he is asked to give them up to the parrots, he hesitates but then does this out of sympathy for them. This act of consideration leads to their retransformation into two beautiful girls, and the father becomes strong once again. They all head for Franz's home where the junk dealer tells the mother that they want to live with her and make each other's burden lighter. In *Das Märchen vom Lokomotivenpfiff* (*The Fairy Tale about the Whistle of the Locomotive*) the same motif of solidarity is introduced by an organ grinder man who brings the people together and gives them the feeling that they can transform themselves and the city when they are united, work and play together. This is also true of *Die bunte Stadt* (*The Colorful City*), in which an entire city is pictured as gray and the people, gloomy, with the exception of a cheerful young man apprenticed to a painter. One day, after he helps a poor old woman, he is given a magic pot containing a female painter who enables him to paint anything and everything with a wide variety of colors. So he paints the city in a colorful way, and the people begin to change their demeanor. The young man marries the female painter, and the city continues to benefit from their work. In all of Schönlank's tales the interaction of family members among the poor is changed from domination to cooperation. Poverty and oppression are only overcome through collective action or by using one's talents and imagination for the benefit of the community. The roles of men and women are not set according to traditional patterns. The emphasis in all relations is placed on change and the possibility to effect emotional patterns so that they convey a sense of justice. The typical conservative happy ending gives way to an optimistic belief in the necessity and goodness of social change.

The theme of social transformation is also stressed in most of Zur Mühlen's innovative tales, which incidentally were translated into English as *Fairy Tales for Workers' Children* and published by the Daily Worker Publishing Company in 1925. In Der Spatz (*The Sparrow*), a young sparrow leaves his *petit bourgeois* home because he finds it too pretentious and stifling. His parents want him to admire the richer more noble birds and become like them. However – and here Zur Mühlen writes against Andersen and his *Ugly Duckling*) – the young sparrow wants to show his parents and other sparrows that even the smallest birds can fly to other countries like the larger ones and live and work under more favorable conditions. He leaves home, and, through his courage, determination, and intelligence, he manages to travel thousands of miles to the South. Along the way he learns how the world is divided into the poor and the rich, oppressed and oppressors, and he wants to return and impart his knowledge to his brothers and sisters so they can free themselves from their narrow confines. However, the sparrow dies under way, and his message must be carried by a young boy, who will apparently continue his struggle.

The death of an animal who dedicates his life to the emancipation of oppressed people is also central to *Der graue Hund* (*The Gray Dog*), in which a dog dies to save the life of a young black slave in America who escapes to the North. Zur Mühlen places the motif of sacrifice in a different context from the classical fairy tale where wives and children are generally portrayed as self-sacrificial so they can win the love of a male. Here the sacrifice is for a group of dominated people who want to do away with exploitation. Implicit is a change of traditional family relations of domination. Hence, the sparrow leaves the *petit bourgeois* home, and the slave and dog run away from the feudalistic plantation.

In other tales, such as *Die Brillen* (*The Glasses*), *Die Rote Fahne* (*The Red Flag*), and *Wie Said der Träumer zu Said dem Verräter wurde* (*How Said the Dreamer Became Said the Traitor*), Zur Mühlen was concerned with demonstrating how exploitation, domination, and injustice arise from the accumulation of property and wealth and how social conditions can be altered. Unlike the classical fairy tales, she did not portray marriage and the re-establishment of royal realms at the end of her stories. Rather she stressed permanent struggle and change. Illusions were avoided in her fairy tales to illuminate the hope for a better world. The virtues (often the same stressed by the bourgeoisie) were shaped to endorse qualitatively different emotional patterns and non-alienating social relations. Consequently, the function of the family itself underwent a change. Young people were depicted in her tales as moving out beyond the narrow confines of the enclosed private family and considering all people as members of one large family where collective support and struggle against oppression are regarded as the means to bring about more humane and satisfying living conditions.

The movement toward uniting in one family with all races and creatures of the world is depicted in the extraordinary fairy-tale novel *Hans Urian, The Story of a Trip Around the World* (1931) by Lisa Tetzner. Similar to the structure of Brecht's play *Man is Man*, in which Galy Gay goes out to buy some fish at a market and winds up learning how men are made into monsters, this fairy tale shows how Hans, a poor 9-year-old, goes out to earn bread for his starving family and then is compelled to take a trip around the world to learn under what oppressive conditions people must work to obtain bread. Once he learns from the baker that he cannot have bread without money, no matter how hungry his family is, he meets the rabbit Trillewipp, who is also looking for food to nourish his mother and family. They join forces, and, since they learn that there is money and bread to be had in America, they decide to fly there. (Trillewipp's long ears are like propellers, and he has the magic power of flying.) On the way they befriend the Eskimo Kagsgsuk, and, in the States, they meet Bill, whose rich father produces canons for war efforts. Everywhere they go in the States, the children learn that people want to take advantage of them and the rabbit, exploit them without giving them money for their labor. In Africa and later in China, the children are captured and treated like slaves as is Trillewipp. Finally, in order to save themselves, the children form a circus troupe, place Trillewipp in a cage, and pretend to be cruel to him like other human beings. After wandering through China and Mongolia, they make their way to Russia where, for the first time, they are treated humanely and placed in an orphanage with other children while Trillewipp is set free. The children learn to work with other young people and determine their needs and wants. After some time, Hans and Trillewipp fly home, and Trillewipp suggests that Hans become a rabbit and live with his family since rabbits treat each other in a more humane way then humans treat each other. However, Hans refuses arguing that he wants to improve conditions at home and help make humans more humane. Yet, he encounters difficulties when he arrives. The police and his teacher want to exclude him from the community and school while his mother and children from the neighborhood welcome him. After hearing his story, the children unite and insist that the school take him back since he had not broken any laws: he merely went on a long errand to bring some bread to his mother.

Written in 1928/29 and published in 1931, Tetzner's book has a curious history. It was banned by the Nazis in 1933, and, when republished in West Germany after World War II, it was banned again in 1948 by the American occupation forces because it defamed the United States. Viewed historically, it is clear that Tetzner used the Soviet Union as a model society in which children are respected, protected, and encouraged to work together so they can design their own destinies. At the time she wrote her fairy tale, such a model corresponded more to reality than today, though America has certainly not lost its symbolic value as a capitalist jungle. In general her symbolic act was geared to transforming Russia into a utopian construct for German children, and the configurations of the tale map out a strategy for the conception of utopia: the solidarity and trust developed between Hans the German, Kagsgsuk the Eskimo, Bill the American, and Trillewipp the rabbit from different classes and races represent emotional bonds of normative interaction upon which future familial and social relations could be based. Again, as in the tales of Schönlank and Zur Mühlen, the family is poor and suffers because social relations are based on money, power, and exploitation. The lower class family, as it is, must be changed and can only be changed if external social conditions are improved. The notion of family as the nucleus of society is extended in the narrative discourse along class lines of solidarity to include all oppressed people. Consequently, the value of an individual is not based on exchange value, dependent on the material wealth and power of the family, but on the use of talents to bring about equality and cooperation. The family remains to be defined, that is, redefined. The ending is open. One does not live happily ever after. The ending means struggle and insight into possible new relations.

The few examples we have of new literary fairy tales in Nazi Germany point in another direction. For instance, the volume *Geschichten aus der Murkelei* (1937) by Hans Fallada contains tales which stress themes that recall the cruel German classic *Struwwelpeter*. Almost all the stories deal with children who are naughty or veer from the moral and ethical standards of the times. They are either punished brutally or tormented until they learn how to conform. In the very first tale, *Geschichte von der kleinen Geschichte* (*Story about the Little Story*), a child who does not want to eat his meal is sent to bed and forbidden to listen to stories by his mother. Even worse is the story of *Nuschelpeter*, who is beaten up by a school comrade so that he learns to pronounce words correctly. Almost all the stories are intended to awake fear in children who might be different, pursue their own interests, or experiment with new forms of relations. In some tales like *Geschichte von Brüderchen* (*Story about the Little Brother*) and *Geschichte von Murkelei*, emphasis is placed on the biological function of the family as reproduction center and as place where children are socialized to respect laws out of fear. The emotional patterns elaborated in the plots center on fertility and obedience and are based on the domination of male authoritarian figures who exert their power through corporal punishment or withdrawal of love.

Whereas Fallada's tales were not explicit ideological stories and were more in keeping with the traditional bourgeois literature of *Kindertümlichkeit*, Hilde Stansch's *Das Kind im Berge* (*The Child in the Mountain*, 1944) fulfilled all the proper notions of an ideal fascist fairy tale for children. The setting is the idyllic countryside. Unna and her husband Helge have been married for some years and have always yearned for children, but their wishes have not been heard. Unna goes to the wise relative Erda, who reveals to her a way to have children. This involves searching for the holy mountain, and, after many adventures, she finds the holy child in the cradle. When she returns to her husband, she gives birth to twelve children in the coming years. The secret of fertility is passed on to her when Erda dies, and from Unna to her oldest daughter upon her death. The wisdom and secret remain in their blood. All the elements for a perfect Aryan fairy tale are here: the woman as mother earth, fertile, humble, wise. The man, strong and productive, portrayed in the fields. The chosen race endures and will endure unto eternity.

Not all the literary tales produced during the Nazi period were as conservative and regressive as those written by Fallada and Stansch. For instance, Paul Alverdes' *Das Männlein Mittentzwei* (*The Mannikin Mittentzwei*, 1937) has certain elements which constitute a critique of the negligent way children treat toys, objects, and other creatures. However, neither Alverdes' tale nor other fairy tales produced explicitly for children such as those by Blunck, Matthiessen and the writers for *Auerbachs Kinderkalender*, during the Nazi epoch introduced new notions of familial interaction or social behavior which suggested a break with racist prejudice, domination, authoritarianism, and false illusions about the hard realities of the Third Reich. If there were innovative experiments in the field of children's literature, then they tended to reinforce the dominant fascist ideology and emotional patterns of authoritarianism. This can be seen clearly in the primers, almanacs, and general fiction produced at that time. The literary fairy tale for children was deemed less suitable for such purposes. Besides, as we know, the classical fairy tale in its traditional format could be used to illustrate correct living in the family and community in accordance with Nazi ideology.

IV

If we now turn to the literary fairy tales produced for adults during the Weimar and Nazi periods, the picture of the family in regard to ideological roles, emotional patterns, and domination is slightly different. In the Weimar period, there was much more variety and open criticism of traditional familial conditions. In the Nazi epoch, literary fairy tales were virtually abolished, and, aside from the publication of works from the eighteenth, nineteenth, and early twentieth centuries, there was relatively little continuity of the work which had blossomed in the 1920s. A brief look at fairy-tale discourse of the 1920s and the familial interactional patterns incorporated in the tales will indicate why.

Hermann Hesse more or less set the tone for the Weimar period when he published his collection of *Märchen* in 1919. Not only did they reflect his pacifistic concerns about the war, but they were also influenced by his marital problems and ambivalent desire to break away from traditional bourgeois family life. In this regard Hesse harked back to the early romantics, and his work is indicative of how other German writers in the early twentieth century regarded themselves as working within the deep-rooted *Kunstmärchen* tradition. Thus, it would be misleading to argue that his tales initiated an avant-garde experiment with fairy tales in the Weimar Republic or that other German writers were breaking with conventional fairy-tale discourse. If anything, they were expanding and subverting the discourse: Hesse's fairy tales and all the rest produced in the Weimar period are significant because they use the fairy-tale discourse in a variety of startling imaginative ways to comment on social problems which were affecting the course of the civilizing process.

Hesse published seven fairy tales in 1919: *Augustus, The Poet, Strange News from Another Planet, The Difficult Path, A Dream Sequence, Faldrun*, and *Iris*, and, just as his novels all tend to repeat the same message and pattern, so, too, these tales. A gifted young man senses that he has a poetic mission and feels confined by his parents or family. He breaks away from home, generally goes through two phases of sensuality and asceticism before he comes into his own. That is, before he reaches peace with himself and is satisfied with his personal development. Significantly, with few exceptions, the hero of Hesse's fairy tales does not remain within his old family or community or build a new society. He remains somewhat of an outsider, though there may be some reconciliation with the family he has spurned.

In *Augustus*, the young man who never appreciated the sacrifices his mother made for him, returns home after leading a decadent life for many years. There he repents and is mystically reunited with his dead mother through the intercession of his strange but saintly godfather. Still, he is nothing more than a repentant wanderer at the end. In *The Poet*, Han Fook abandons his fiancée and family to lead the life of a poet. He returns home only to find everyone dead, and yet, he himself has supposedly realized something more vital by foresaking the traditional way of family life. In *Strange News from Another Planet*, Hesse has a young boy learn about the meaning of chaos and killing so that he can become dedicated to harmony and help his neighbors restore their community after an earthquake. This is Hesse's only fairy tale in which there is some sense about the necessity of social cooperation for reconstruction. Generally speaking, Hesse's tales are anti-social and especially anti-family in their description of a pattern of rebellion and self-transcendence. The family is depicted as static, the bastion of conservatism. This is not always done in a negative sense, but family forms are revealed to be outmoded, and, if a young man wants to develop, he must leave this confining environment. Though Hesse himself may have thought of this option as liberating, there is a strong element of self-deception in his tales, for his heroes *escape* into an inner world which owes its validity only to the repressive tolerance of a society which prefers non-intrusive individuals to rebels who will not abide by its conventions in any way and defy society through social action. Whereas Hesse's heroes reveal a pattern of behavior and action critical of authoritarian behavior and arbitrary male domination, they also make a compromise or peace with the existing state of affairs. The rejection of the traditional patriarchal family is not absolute, and only in the happy soul of the chosen hero is there a suggestion of a real alternative: the male role of guru embodies new mystical and pacifistic norms which might have an exemplary value in contrast to the western civilizing process.

The importance of Hesse's tales in 1919 is that they signal the twofold way that other writers would reflect upon the family in the 1920s and 1930s: either there was a complete rejection of the commonplace mildew of philistinism and the traditional male authoritarian family which were mocked, parodied, or seriously criticized, or there was an attempt to portray how the family could be restored with normative patterns designating strong medieval bonds with teutonic overtones and true Christian love. Both extremes of the fairy-tale discourse must be viewed in light of the powerful and disparate tendencies among

German youth since the beginning of the twentieth century. The *Wandervogel Movement* became splintered after World War I so that there were numerous youth organizations and groups which were mobilized *against* the older generation. Nature, purity, and independence became slogans of bourgeois youth groups while other organizations sought party allegiances with the communists, socialists, or national socialists to articulate their protest. This was the background of the fairy-tale discourse about civilization at that time, and the various voices often spoke about patricide and protest.

For instance, in Geerken's anthology of expressionist fairy tales *Die Goldene Bombe*, the general tendency is to belittle the dominant bourgeois family and its corresponding role patterns. Most of the tales expose either explicitly or implicitly the hypocrisy of 'home sweet home.' The relations between human beings are portrayed as shallow and objectified because people base their behavior on competition, money, and power. The illusion of a possible restoration of the family and society is smashed in such tales as Hans von Flesch-Brunningen's *Der metaphysische Kanarienvogel* (1917) and Salomo Friedlander's *Die vegetabilische Vaterschaft* (1919). The classical fairy-tale happy ending with a new realm was inverted, for the expressionist writers viewed the family as an institution that cannot function to protect children nor provide them with the fortitude and skills to realize their needs and dreams. In the fairy tales of other writers during the Weimar period, such as Ödön von Horváth and Oskar Maria Graf, the picture is just as bleak.

Horváth wrote a series of fairy tales entitled *Sportmärchen, Fräulein Pollinger und andere Märchen*, and *Zwei Märchen* during the 1920s, and they were closely related to his folk dramas which satirized the banality and lack of communication among lower-class people. In *Das Märchen in unserer Zeit (The Fairy Tale in Our Time)* a young girl leaves her family to look for the fairy tale. No one can help her until she comes to an old horse who is about to be slaughtered because he is old and no longer useful. The horse remarks that she herself is a fairy tale and that she should tell him a story. After a moment's hesitation she does. Then the horse is carted away. When the young girl returns home and refuses to eat the horsemeat that is set on the table, her mother and the rest of the family call her a spoiled princess. She goes without eating, thinks about the horse and is no longer hungry. The lack of understanding which this young girl encounters is heightened in *Das Märchen vom Fräulein Pollinger*. Here Horváth tells the story about an average woman with an average figure and an average face who works in the bookkeeping department of an automobile repair shop. In order to be accepted by the men in the shop and to ride on their motor bikes, she sleeps with them every now and then. After going with one man named Fritz for a year, she becomes pregnant and is abandoned by him to shift for herself. No prince. No marriage. No family. Horváth explodes notions of the idyllic happy family life. Instead the crude and exploitative relations which depend on the commodity value of a person transforms all people into expendable merchandise.

It is the brutal aspect of life and family relations which is also stressed in Graf's collection of fairy tales entitled *Licht und Schatten* (*Light and Shadow*, 1927). Like many socialist writers of this period, Graf was not interested in portraying the imminent victory of the communist movement, rather in showing the extent to which human beings had been made into animals and deprived of a social consciousness. All his tales – and they were directed at young people – depict how barren, savage, and destitute family and social life have become. Even the fatherland must experience this. In a bitter, ironic narrative, *Was das Vaterland einmal erlebte* (*What the Fatherland Experienced One Time*), Graf has the fatherland transform himself into a human being to see who loved him the most. To his chagrin – he visits all social types and classes – he is constantly maltreated, ignored, beaten, and driven to beg. The only person who treats him kindly and with sympathy is a beggar who tells the fatherland his life history and how he had been accepted in society as long as he could produce and give something. But once he had become old and sick, no one cared about him. Both cry softly before they fall asleep holding hands like brothers. The notion that Germany was one big happy family is totally undermined in this tale and even more so in *Das Märchen vom König*, in which we have a terrifying picture of a patriarch. Here the king of the realm delights in starting wars and driving people to murder. He becomes so unruly that no one wants to act as his minister and carry out his orders. All the people flee him, and only a cripple is left in the kingdom, and he turns out to be the embodiment of all the fear, need, and injustice that the king had caused. The cripple succeeds miraculously in punishing the tyrant, and peace reigns again in the devastated country.

The dissatisfaction with the brutal and exploitative way in which people appeared to treat each other inside and outside the family during the Weimar period was expressed somewhat differently by more conservative writers of fairy tales such as Hermann Stehr and Hans Friedrich Blunck, two of the more popular authors of this epoch. In 1929 three tales by Stehr were published under the title *Das Märchen vom deutschen Herzen* (*The Fairy Tale about the German Heart*), which posed an alternative to the more critical and sardonic fairy tales of radical and progressive writers. For instance, in his title story about the *German* heart, Stehr tells how God first distinguished human beings from animals by giving them the power of reason. However, this made them rich, content, and competitive. Millions of human beings die through avarice and war so that the human species is threatened with extinction. God becomes worried and decides to provide a balance for the human beings left on earth, namely to give them more heart. He is particularly drawn to one creature with ash blond hair. ' "You lovely German man," he spoke into the blue eyes filled with expectation, "I shall give you the double flame of heart so that you can serve everyone in the name of heaven and thereby in overcoming yourself you will overcome everyone." '27 God, who is continually referred to as the immortal housefather, watches his favorite, the blond German man, carry out his will. The racist implications of this Christian message are also imparted in the fairy tale *Wendelin Heinelt*, in which the Aryan family Heinelt is set up as exemplary unit of blessed people united in the manner by which they help poorer people. According to Stehr's fairy tales, which reek in piety, the earth lacks Christian charity, and certain groups of people are chosen to recover the path to God. Though Stehr speaks out against exploitation and maltreatment of human beings, there are obvious ideological references in the pronouncements he makes about western civilization, especially in the tale about the German heart. The male role of patriarch parallels that of God, and it is only in following the dictates of both that one will find the divine life. The pattern of hierarchical relations in the traditional family is not altered. Rather it is to be restored and reinforced against the decadent forces of modernism.

The restoration of familial relations and fixed roles that corresponded more to an agrarian feudal world than the German urban settings of the 1920s was one of the major themes in the fairy tales written by Hans Friedrich Blunck between 1923 and 1931.28 Almost all his tales, directed at *both* adults and children, deal with the positive side of marriage and fertility and hark back to the folk tradition with sentimental nostalgia. The central characters are kings, queens, peasants, merchants, townspeople, dwarfs, nymphs, nixens, or creatures of the woods. The major magical character is Mother Holle, who often assumes the role of enchantress of love.

Typical of Blunck's pervasive ideological attitude toward the family, socialization, and domination (even if it is somewhat extreme) is the tale *Frau Holle and the Schifferfrau*, which begins as follows: 'There was one time that our dear God and Mother Holle came to earth again. The beautiful woman wanted to show how successful she had been in making our country into a garden. And the Lord asked how human beings were getting along with one another and whether his commands had been fulfilled. In particular, he wanted to know whether women were staying at home and whether men were moving about in life, struggling and working for their families.'[29] God and Mother Holle encounter the wife of a seaman who is dissatisfied because her husband is always away from home. God transforms husband and wife into a rose garden so that they can enjoy each other under idyllic circumstances. However, when he visits her again, she is not satisfied because her children do not have the opportunity to see much of the world and achieve great things. So God again transforms the woman and her husband so that they can sail about the seas. After some years pass, God comes for a third time, and the woman complains that her children have left her and that the life they lead is too rough. Now God is convinced, as well as Mother Holle, that it would be best for all if He returned things to the way they were at the beginning. 'Since then this has been the way with all good people. The women wait at home with their daughters when the men take to the wild sea.'[30]

In another tale, *Frau Holle und die Lebenden*, a young poet searches for Mother Holle since all the people on earth have lost their sense of love, and evil times have descended upon the world. His fiancée waits patiently for him, and their own pious love and self-sacrifice bring Mother Holle back to earth where she restores harmony to all God's creatures. In *Feinsmütterchen*, Mother Holle helps a rich councillor's wife become fertile. The woman, however, is ungrateful and disobeys Mother Holle's orders. So the good Mother Holle must punish her until the woman repents. Her reward is her transformation into a flower dedicated to her sons.

Most of Blunck's tales continually stress outworn features of the folk tales: the woman is self-sacrificial; the man is courageous and hardworking. If one steers a straight and virtuous path, there is no need to fear the wrath of God or Mother Holle. This is exemplified in *Die Bräutigamseiche* (*The Oak of the Bridegroom*) where magical forces reward a woman's diligence and patience with marriage. Blunck's tales are by no means preachy or overly didactic. However, the light, witty, stale and nostalgic atmosphere of a pastoral idyll convey a false picture of the changing family relations and socialization in the 1920s both in the agrarian and urban areas of Germany. Indeed, it was exactly this false image of family life and the projection of fixed hierarchical roles for men and women which the Nazis exploited to undermine the real needs of the masses which might make them more secure and fulfilled. Sweet harmony, prescribed roles, the divine sanction of supernatural forces which determine the fate of virtuous, hard-working men and women – this image created by Blunck in his fairy tales came out of his own desire in the 1920s to overcome the reified social relations and chaos which threatened to lead Germany to the brink of ruin. Yet, like many other writers who sought to recall the solid German folk tradition to point to a solution of social conflict in the 1920s, he helped spread mildew which became more and more poisonous in the hands of the Nazis.

V

It is not by chance that the fairy-tale discourses of Stehr, Blunck, Matthiessen and other writers with similar viewpoints were published during the Nazi period. Nor is it a coincidence that Blunck became a high Nazi official of culture. In fact, even the tales of Hesse were printed, though they were not particularly promoted by the fascists. What is significant to note is that, in contrast, the lively experimentation with the literary fairy tale which raised critical questions about social problems and stimulated thinking about outmoded roles and norms of the socialization process was forced into exile or banned. It was there that Thomas Theodor Heine, former editor of *Simplicissimus*, published his sardonic collection of tales entitled *Die Märchen* in 1935. The philosopher Max Horkheimer included a couple of fairy tales in his important work *Die Dämmerung* (1935) for political purposes. Both Alfred Döblin and Joseph Roth experimented with the genre in the 1930s while Brecht and Horváth included fairy tale motifs in their dramas. However, nothing of major significance in the fairy-tale genre was produced in exile, nor was there anything of value produced within the fascist fatherland, although there are two symbolic endeavors by Gerhart Hauptmann and Ernst Wiechert worth mentioning.

In 1941 Hauptmann wrote and published *Das Märchen* in *Die Neue Rundschau*. As a conscious attempt to vary Goethe's *Das Märchen* for the purpose of commenting on fascism, his tale remains too obtuse to be considered effective. Theophrast, an old wandering pilgrim, crosses a river with two will-o-the-wisps and arrives in a country where the old continues to live in new forms. He thinks of a lion, and suddenly it is there. Nor can he wish it away, and it seems to him that the lion was always with him as part of an awesome love (*Angstliebe*). He also encounters a snake from the Garden of Eden. The pilgrim has no set goal and continues to wander with the beasts until he meets a barefoot man named Johann Operin with whom he has various esoteric, cryptic discussions and strange adventures. The will-o-the-wisps want to lead the pilgrim to a crematorium where stupidity is burned, but Theophrast refuses since he knows that stupidity has no corpse. It has an immortal life. Thereupon, Theophrast leaves this country marked by its crematorium as a high temple, and he returns safely to his original habitat.

It is almost impossible to analyze this tale since the aesthetic structure is uniquely coded to correspond to Hauptmann's life and times. Although he had welcomed the rise of National Socialism in the early 1930s, Hauptmann had become disenchanted with the Third Reich, and he tended to become morbid in his old age. As a dramatist who had continually used fairy-tale motifs in his early works of the twentieth century to comment on social and political conditions, it is obvious that this was his intent in *Das Märchen*, and that fear prevented him from enunciating his critique in easily comprehensible symbols. Yet, one aspect is clear in the movement of the pilgrim who rejects a world which obviously reflects some of the more brutal aspects of Nazism. In other words, an initiation into the secrets of Nazism is refused, and the hero remains an outsider questioning a world that depends on a logic of irrationalism to rationalize its destructive tendencies.

Wiechert is much more direct in stating why he wrote his fairy tales, especially since they were published after the demise of the Third Reich: 'This book was begun in the last winter of the war as hate and fire burned the earth and hearts. It was written for all the poor children of poor people and for my own heart so that I would not lose my belief in truth and justice, for the world, as it is constructed in the fairy tale, is not the world of miracles and magicians but rather one of great and lasting justice about which children and people of every epoch have dreamed.'[31] Actually, Wiechert's fairy tales were not written specifically for children but more for adults, when one considers the complexity in statement and structure. Six of them, his *Zeitmärchen*, *Die Königsmühle* (*The King's Mill*), *Der Vogel 'Niemalsmehr'* (*The Bird 'Nevermore'*), *Die Wölfe* (*The Wolves*), *Sieben Söhne* (*Seven Sons*), *Die Liebste auf der Welt* (*The Dearest in the World*), are of particular interest because they deal with the war, exploitation, violence, and tyranny on a symbolical level. Since the settings of the tales are generally in the distant medieval past, the parallels to fascism can only be drawn if one knows the background of Wiechert's writing. He was not a socialist or radical who sought to portray the possibility of new social relations in the family. His position was that of a Christian moralist, who opposed the crimes of the Nazi period. Thus, his fairy tales carry certain contradictions with them: while they speak out for justice, they also lay the groundwork for further exploitation.

For instance, in *Die Wölfe*, a brother and sister demonstrate through their courage that justice can be attained by opposing the tyranny of a king. The sister sacrifices herself to a wolf to save her people from destruction, and the wolf turns out to be an enchanted king, who is freed through her actions. He then leads an army against the tyrant and becomes the rightful ruler of the kingdom. The girl becomes his adopted daughter and will take his place once he dies. The people are to serve and honor her. Harmony and justice are restored in this medieval society, but the hierarchical pattern and social relations are not really altered so that there is an illusion of justice based simply on the moral quality of a single individual.

In *Sieben Söhne*, a widow tries to protect her seven sons from being exploited by the king in a senseless war. After six of the sons die, she goes to the king to try to keep the youngest at home. In a direct critique of Nazi policy,[32] she attacks the king for not honoring motherhood. Her bravery, however, does not help save the youngest son. He, too, staunchly goes to his death, and the mother must learn to bear the burden. Implicit throughout the story is a notion of a higher judge, namely God, who stands above all, and who will make all the final decisions. When one's time is up, one must face fate as bravely as one can. Again, though the mother is presented in a dignified way, Wiechert does not suggest that basic role patterns and family socialization be altered. Though his fairy-tale protagonists act from ethical principles and pursue humane goals of mercy and justice, it is actually conceivable that even these tales might have been accepted and published during the Nazi period since there is no transformation of the patterns of domination. Power is to be used more discriminatingly and in the name of the people, and, as we know, Hitler thought of himself as a wise king who wanted to wield power for his people and to prevent sinister forces from invading the fatherland.

Hitler as fairy-tale king. Germany as glorious realm. The aesthetics of politics in the service of mystification. This fascist perversion of the bourgeois public sphere and its dire consequences for the German people conditioned the literary fairy-tale discourse during the 1930s and 1940s. As a whole, the genre was restricted and became antithetical to experimentation. The mildew of classical fairy tales that had been challenged in the 1920s was revived as staple to legitimize racism, sexism, and authoritarianism clothed in the form of the teutonic heritage. The atavistic designs of German fascism, however, could not conceal and repress the signs and demands for democracy which had already become so urgent in the 1920s. The Third Reich was doomed to failure from the beginning, and so, too, its many cultural institutions which appear gruesomely absurd to us today. Once World War II came to a close, the debate over civilization within the literary fairy-tale discourse began to surface again. Writers recommenced experimentation, and they gradually endeavored to show that the classical fairy tale for children had outlived its social purpose. They sought to liberate the form for progressive purposes, and the expansion and subversion of the fairy-tale discourse became increasingly noticeable not only in Germany but throughout the western world during the 1960s. It is to this development of the literary genre cultivated for children that we shall now turn.

Notes

1 Within the past fifteen years there has been a veritable deluge of studies on Weimar and Nazi literature and culture, but none has investigated the significance of the fairy tale. Among the best works for reference and background material are George Mosse, *Nazi Culture: Intellectual and Social Life in the Third Reich* (London: W. H. Allen, 1966); Peter Gay, *Weimar Culture. The Outsider as Insider* (London: Secker & Warburg, 1969); Wolfgang Rothe (ed.), *Die deutsche Literatur in der Weimarer Republik* (Stuttgart: Reclam, 1974); Horst Denkler and Karl Prümm, *Die deutsche Literatur im Dritten Reich* (Stuttgart: Reclam, 1976); Jost Hermand and Frank Trommler, *Die Kultur der Weimarer Republik* (Munich: Nymphenburg, 1978); John Willett, *The New Sobriety, 1917-1933. Art and Politics in the Weimar Period* (London: Thames and Hudson, 1978); Ernst Alker, *Profile und Gestalten der deutschen Literatur nach 1914*, ed. Eugen Thurnher (Stuttgart: Kröner, 1979).

2 The most exhaustive treatment of the debates is to be found in Ulrike Bastian, *Die Kinder- und Hausmärchen der Brüder Grimm in der literaturpädagogischen Diskussion des 19. und 20. Jahrhunderts* (Giessen: Haag & Herchen, 1981). See also Bernd Dolle, 'Märchen und Erziehung. Versuch einer historischen Skizze zur didaktischen Verwendung Grimmscher Märchen,' in *Und wenn sie nicht gestorben sind . . . Perspektiven auf das Märchen*, ed. by Helmut Brackert (Frankfurt am Main: Suhrkamp, 1980), pp. 165-92.

3 For other significant studies, see Ernst Linde, *Die Bildungsaufgabe der deutschen Dichtung* (Leipzig: Brandstetter, 1927); Alois Jalkotzy, *Märchen und Gegenwart* (Vienna: Jungbrunnen, 1930); Alois Kunzfeld, *Vom Märchenerzähler und Märchenillustrieren* (Vienna: Deutscher Verlag fur Jugend und Volk, 1926); Max Troll, *Der Marchenunterricht* (Langensalza: Beyer, 1928); Walter Wenk, *Das Volksmärchen als Bildungsgut* (Langensalza: Beyer, 1929).

4 See 'Das Märchen geht selber in der Zeit' (1930) in *Die Kunst, Schiller zu sprechen und andere literarische Aufsätze* (Frankfurt am Main: Suhrkamp, 1969), pp. 10-14. For a translation and discussion of this essay, see Jack Zipes, 'The utopian function of fairy tales and fantasy: Ernst Bloch the Marxist and J.R.R. Tolkien the Catholic, in *Breaking the Magic Spell: Radical Theories of Folk and Fairy Tales* (London: Heinemann, 1979).

5 See 'Der Erzähler,' in *Gesammelte Schriften*, Vol. 2, ed. by Rolf Tiedemann and Hermann Schweppenhäuser (Frankfurt am Main: Suhrkamp, 1977), pp. 438-65. For a translation, see Walter Benjamin, 'The storyteller,' in *Illuminations*, trans. by Harry Zohn (New York: Harcourt, Brace, 1968).

6 See Helmut Mörchen, 'Notizen zu Wolgast,' in *Literatur für Kinder*, ed. by Maria Lypp (Göttingen: Vandenhoeck & Ruprecht, 1977), pp. 13-20.

7 'Die arbeit in den kommunistischen kindergruppen' (1923), in *Das politische Kinderbuch*, ed. by Dieter Richter (Darmstadt: Luchterhand, 1973), pp. 220-1.

8   'Folktale and ideology in the Third Reich', *Journal of American Folklore*, **90** (1977), p. 169. See also Christa Kamenetsky, 'Folklore as a political tool in Nazi Germany', *Journal of American Folklore*, **85** (1972), pp. 221–35.

9   For more information about the trends at this time, see Peter Aley, *Jugendliteratur im Dritten Reich* (Gütersloh: Bertelsmann, 1967) and Wolfgang Emmerich, *Germanistische Volkstumsideologie. Genese und Kritik der Volksforschung im Dritten Reich* (Reutlingen: Tübingen Vereinigung fur Volkskunde, 1968). For two of the many publications on the fairy tale and film, see Adolf Reichwein, 'Märchen und Film,' *Film und Bild*, **2** (10 April 1926), pp. 114–18 and Max Meurer, 'Das Märchen in Bild und Film, von der Schule aus gesehen,' *Film und Bild*, **5** (15 May 1939), pp. 121–4.

10   *Märchen als Lebensdichtung* (Munich: Hueber, 1938), p. 86.

11   Cited in *Jugendliteratur im Dritten Reich*, p. 102.

12   See Irene Dyhrenfurth, *Geschichte des deutschen Jugendbuches* (Zurich: Atlantis, 1967), p. 262.

13   Darmstadt: Agora, 1970. Reprinted as Fischer-Taschenbuch, (Frankfurt am Main: Fischer, 1979).

14   'Das Märchen im Expressionismus,' in *Denk- und Stilformen des Expressionismus* (Munich: Fink, 1974), p. 126.

15   'Folktale and ideology in the Third Reich', p. 177, op.cit.

16   'Familie und Natur in Märchen,' in *Volksliteratur und Hochliteratur* (Bern: Francke, 1970), pp. 63–78.

17   *Ibid.*, p. 77.

18   'Die Ehe im Zaubermärchen', *Acta Ethnographica Academiae Scientarum Hungaricae*, **19** (1970), p. 288.

19   London: Pluto, 1978.

20   *Ibid.*, p. 155.

21   *Ibid.*

22   *Das Märchen und die Phantasie des Kindes* (Berlin: Springer, 1977), pp. 27–9. Reprint of the 1919 edition with an essay by Josephine Belz.

23   *Die deutsche Familie* (Frankfurt am Main: Suhrkamp, 1974), pp. 176–92.

24   See Renate Bridenthal, 'Something old, something new: women in Nazi Germany' and Claudia Koonz, 'Mothers in the fatherland: women in Nazi Germany,' in *Becoming Visible: Women in European History*, ed. by Renate Bridenthal and Claudia Koonz (Boston: Houghton Mifflin, 1977), pp. 422–44, 445–71 and Jill McIntyre Stephenson, *Women in Nazi Society* (New York: Barnes and Noble, 1976).

25   See 'Non-synchronism and the obligation to its dialectics,' *New German Critique*, **11** (spring 1977), pp. 22–38. Also important is Anson Rabinbach's analysis of non-synchronism in the same issue of *New German Critique*, 'Ernst Bloch's heritage of our times and the theory of fascism,' pp. 5–21.

26   There were numerous attempts to radicalize fairy tales and to make them more socially relevant for children. The works of Zur Mühlen, Schönlank, and Tetzner are among the best examples of this movement. For other significant writers and their tales, see the stories by Berta Lask, karl Ewald, and Robert Grötzsch in Ernst Friedrich (ed.), *Proletarischer Kindergarten, Ein Märchen-und Lesebuch für Gross und Klein* (Berlin: Buchverlag der Arbeiter-Kunst-Austellung, 1921); Bela Balázs, *Das richtige Himmelblau* (Munich: Drei-Masken Verlag, 1925) and *Sieben Märchen* (Vienna: Rikola, 1921); Robert Grötzsch, *Der Zauberer Burufu* (Berlin: Dietz, 1922); Bela Illes, *Rote Märchen* (Leipzig: Freidenker-Verlag, 1925); Kurd Lasswitz, *Traumkristalle* (Berlin: Emil Felber, 1928); József Lengyel, *Sternekund und Reinekind* (Dresden: Verlags-Anstalt proletarischer Freidenker Deutschlands, 1923); Eugen Lewin-Dorsch, *Die Dollarmännchen* (Berlin: Malik, 1923); Irene Rona, *Was Paulchen werden will* (Berlin: Vereinigung Internationaler

Verlagsanstalten, 1926); Maria Szucisich, *Die Träume des Zauberbuches* (Dresden: Verlags-Anstalt proletarischer Freidenker Deutschlands, 1923) and *Silavus* (Berlin: Malik, 1924); Julius Zerfass, *Die Reise mit dem Lumpensack* (Berlin: Dietz, 1925).

27 *Das Märchen vom deutschen Herzen* (Berlin: Horen, 1929), p. 13.
28 See *Gesammelte Werke*, 10 vols. (Hamburg: Hanseatische Verlagsanstalt, 1937)
29 *Ibid.*, Vol. 8, p. 32.
30 *Ibid.*, Vol. 8, p. 34.
31 *Sämtliche Werke*, Vol. 8 (Vienna: Desch, 1957), p. 9.
32 *Ibid.*, pp. 212–13.

7 The Liberating Potential of the Fantastic in Contemporary Fairy Tales for Children

> The point is that we have not formed that ancient world – it has formed us. We ingested it as children whole, had its values and consciousness imprinted on our minds as cultural absolutes long before we were in fact men and women. We have taken the fairy tales of childhood with us into maturity, chewed but still lying in the stomach, as real identity. Between Snow-White and her heroic prince, our two great fictions, we never did have much of a chance. At some point, the Great Divide took place: they (the boys) dreamed of mounting the Greta Steed and buying Snow-White from the dwarfs; we (the girls) aspired to become that object of every necrophiliac's lust – the innocent, *victimized* Sleeping Beauty, beauteous lump of ultimate, sleeping good. Despite ourselves, sometimes knowing, unwilling, unable to do otherwise, we act out the roles we were taught.
>
> Andrea Dworkin
> *Woman Hating* (1974)

Our views of child-rearing, socialization, technology, and politics have changed to such a great extent since World War II that the classical folk and fairy tales appear too backward-looking to many progressive-minded critics and creative writers. Not only are the tales considered to be too sexist, racist, and authoritarian, but the general contents are said to reflect the concerns of semi-feudal, patriarchal societies.[1] What may have engendered hope for better living conditions centuries ago has become more inhibiting for today's children in the western world. The discourse of classical fairy tales, its end effect, cannot be considered enlightening and emancipatory in face of possible nuclear warfare, ecological destruction, growing governmental and industrial regimentation, and intense economic crises.

Of course, there are numerous classical folk and fairy tales which still speak to the needs of children and illuminate possibilities for attaining personal autonomy and social freedom, and it would be foolish to reject the entire classical cannon as socially useless or aesthetically outmoded. Moreover, as we know, the classical fairy tale as genre has not been static. Such nineteenth-century writers as Charles Dickens, George MacDonald, John Ruskin, George Sand, Oscar Wilde, Andrew Lang, L. Frank Baum, and others, designated now as 'classical,' opposed the authoritarian tendencies of the civilization process and expanded the horizons of the fairy-tale discourse for children. They prepared the way for utopian and subversive experiments which altered the fairy-tale discourse at the beginning of the twentieth century. Hope for liberating changes in social relations and political structures was conveyed through symbolic acts of writers who criticized abusive treatment of children and the repressive methods of sexual pedagogization.

Still, the innovative tales for children produced during the first three decades of the twentieth century did not successfully reutilize fantastic projections and configurations of the classical fairy tales to gain wide acceptance among children and adults. If anything, the fantastic was used to compensate for the growing rationalization of culture, work, and family life in western society, to defend the imagination of children. The fantastic was really on the defensive while appearing to be offensive. Something else was on the march in the name of progress and civilization. The Taylorization of factory and office life, the panoptic organization of schools, hospitals, and prisons, the technical synchronization of art to create formations such as chorus lines and choreography resembling conveyer belts, the celebration of uniform military power in parade and warfare – these were the real sociopolitical tendencies against which the progressive and experimental fairy tales for children reacted at the beginning of the twentieth century. These were the forces which confined and subdued the protest elements in the fairy-tale discourse during the 1930s, 1940s, and 1950s.

Since then, the fantastic in fairy tales for children has been forced to take the offensive, and this situation has not arisen because the fantastic is assuming a more liberating role but because it is in the throes of a last-ditch battle against what many writers have described as technologically instrumental and manipulative forces which operate largely for commercial interests and cast a 'totalitarian' loom over society by making people feel helpless and ineffectual in their attempts to reform and determine their own lives. '1984,' 'Brave New World,' 'One-Dimensional Society' – these have become key words in critiques of social development in both the West and the East. In commenting on the fairy tale in the post-war world, Marion Lochhead has asserted that the near victory of fascism was of utmost concern to such writers as C.S. Lewis and J.R.R. Tolkien. 'Myth-making continues. The renaissance of wonder has reached maturity. And we need it. The conflict between good and evil – absolute evil – in which the child heroes of fantasy are caught up and taxed to the limit of their endurance has become a common theme.'[2] Yet, it is not merely the survival of good which is reflected in contemporary fairy tales but the fantastic projection of possibilities for non-alienating living conditions. Hope for such a future follows upon the struggles of the 1960s which were marked by civil rights movements, anti-war protests, the rise of feminism, and demands for autonomy by minority groups and small deprived nations throughout the world.

Since it would be too difficult to cover the entire development of the literary fairy tale for children in response to these struggles since 1945 and to demonstrate how and why fairy-tale writers have sought to use fantastic projections in a liberating manner, I want to limit myself to a small number of representative writers in England, the United States, Italy, Germany, and France who have expressly tried to make their tales more emancipatory in light of restriction in advanced industrial countries. My concern is twofold: I want to depict the motifs, ideas, styles, and methods used by these writers to make the fantastic projections within the fairy tales more liberating. I want to question whether the intentions of a liberating fairy tale can actually have the effect desired by the writer in societies where socialization is concerned most with control, discipline, and rationalization.

But before I address these two points, it is crucial to discuss the 'power' of the literary fairy tales in general, the classical and the innovative, to clarify the meanings of such terms as progressive and regressive, liberating and inhibiting. In other words, the classical fairy tales have not retained their appeal among children and adults simply because they comply with the norms of the civilizing process. They have an extraordinary power, and Georges Jean locates this power on the conscious level in the way all good fairy tales aesthetically structure and use fantastic and miraculous elements to prepare us for our everyday life.[3] Magic is used paradoxically not to deceive us but to enlighten us. On an unconscious level, Jean believes that the best fairy tales bring together subjective and assimilatory impulses with objective intimations of a social setting that intrigue readers and allow for different interpretations according to one's ideology and belief.[4] Ultimately, Jean argues that the fantastic power of fairy tales consists in the uncanny way they provide a conduit into social reality. Yet, given the proscription of fairy-tale discourse within a historically prescribed civilizing process, a more careful distinction must be made between regressive and progressive aspects of the power of fairy tales in general to understand the liberating potential of contemporary tales for children. Here I want to discuss Sigmund Freud's concept of the 'uncanny' and Ernst Bloch's concept of 'home' as constitutive elements of the liberating impulse behind the fantastic projections in fairy tales, whether they be classical or experimental. Their ideas will be related to Jean Piaget's notions of how children view and adapt to the world so that we can grasp the regressive and progressive features of contemporary fairy tales as politically symbolic acts seeking to make their mark on history.

I

In his essay on the uncanny, Freud remarks that the word *heimlich* means that which is familiar and agreeable *and* also that which is concealed and kept out of sight, and he concludes that *heimlich* is a word the meaning of which develops in the direction of ambivalence, until it finally coincides with its opposite, *unheimlich* or uncanny.[5] Through a close study of E.T.A. Hoffmann's fairy tale *The Sandman*, Freud argues that the uncanny or unfamiliar (*unheimlich*) brings us in closer touch with the familiar (*heimlich*) because it touches on emotional disturbances and returns us to repressed phases in our evolution:

> If psychoanalytic theory is correct in maintaining that every effect belonging to an emotional impulse, whatever its kind, is transformed, if it is repressed, into anxiety, then among instances of frightening things there must be one class in which the frightening element can be shown to be something repressed which *recurs*. This class of frightening things would then constitute the uncanny; and it must be a matter of indifference whether what is uncanny was itself originally frightening or whether it carried some *other* affect. In the second place, if this is indeed the secret nature of the uncanny, we can understand why linguistic usage has extended das *Heimliche* ('homely') into its opposite, das *Unheimliche*; for this uncanny is in reality nothing new or alien but something which is familiar and old-established in the mind and which has become alienated from it only through the process of repression. This reference to the factor of repression enables us, furthermore, to understand Schelling's definition of the uncanny as something which ought to have remained hidden but has come to light.[6]

Freud insists that one must be extremely careful in using the category of the uncanny since not everything which recalls repressed desires and surmounted modes of thinking belongs to the prehistory of the individual and the race and can be considered uncanny. In particular, Freud mentions fairy tales as excluding the uncanny.

> In fairy tales, for instance, the world of reality is left behind from the very start, and the animistic system of beliefs is frankly adopted. Wish-fulfillments, secret powers, omnipotence of thoughts, animation of inanimate objects, all the elements so common in fairy stories, can exert no uncanny influence here; for, as we have learnt, that feeling cannot arise unless there is a conflict of judgment as to whether things which have been 'surmounted' and are regarded as incredible may not, after all, be possible; and this problem is eliminated from the outset by the postulates of the world of fairy tales.[7]

Although it is true that the uncanny becomes the familiar and the norm in the fairy tale because the narrative perspective accepts it so totally, there is still room for *another kind of uncanny experience* within the postulates and constructs of the fairy tale. That is, Freud's argument must be qualified regarding the machinations of the fairy tale. However, I do not want to concern myself with this point at the moment but would simply like to suggest that the uncanny plays a significant role in the act of reading or listening to a fairy tale. Using and modifying Freud's category of the uncanny, I want to argue that *the very act of reading a fairy tale is an uncanny experience in that it separates the reader from the restrictions of reality from the onset and makes the repressed unfamiliar familiar once again.* Bruno Bettelheim has mentioned that the fairy tale estranges the child from the real world and allows him or her to deal with deep-rooted psychological problems and anxiety-provoking incidents to achieve autonomy.[8] Whether this is true or not, that is, whether a fairy tale can actually provide the means for coping with ego disturbance, as Bettelheim argues,[9] remains to be seen. It is true, however, that once we begin listening to or reading a fairy tale, there is estrangement or separation from a familiar world inducing an uncanny feeling which is both *frightening and comforting.*

Actually the complete reversal of the real world has already taken place before we begin reading a fairy tale on the part of the writer, and the writer invites the reader to repeat this uncanny experience. The process of reading involves dislocating the reader from his/her familiar setting and then identifying with the dislocated protagonist so that a quest for the *Heimische* or real home can begin. The fairy tale ignites a double quest for home: one occurs in the reader's mind and is psychological and difficult to interpret, since the reception of an individual tale varies according to the background and experience of the reader. The second occurs within the tale itself and indicates a socialization process and acquisition of values for participation in a society where the protagonist has more power of determination. This second quest for home can be *regressive* or *progressive* depending on the narrator's stance *vis-à-vis* society. In both quests the notion of home or *Heimat*, which is closely related etymologically to *heimlich* and *unheimlich*, retains a powerful progressive attraction for readers of fairy tales. While the uncanny setting and motifs of the fairy tale already open us up to the recurrence of primal experiences, we can move forward at the same time because it opens us up to what Freud calls 'unfulfilled but possible futures to which we still like to cling in fantasy, all the strivings of the ego which adverse external circumstances have crushed, and all our suppressed acts of volition which nourish in us the illusion of Free Will.'[10]

Obviously, Freud would not condone clinging to our fantasies in reality. Yet, Ernst Bloch would argue that *some* are important to cultivate and defend since they represent our radical or revolutionary urge to restructure society so that we can finally achieve home. Dreaming which stands still bodes no good.

> But if it becomes a dreaming ahead, then its cause appears quite differently and excitingly alive. The dim and weakening features, which may be characteristic of mere yearning, disappear; and then yearning can show what it really is able to accomplish. It is the way of the world to counsel men to adjust to the world's pressures, and they have learned this lesson; only their wishes and dreams will not hearken to it. In this respect virtually all human beings are futuristic; they transcend their past life, and to the degree that they are satisfied, they think they deserve a better life (even though this may be pictured in a banal and egotistic way), and regard the inadequacy of their lot as a barrier, and not just as the way of the world.
>
> To this extent, the most private and ignorant wishful thinking is to be preferred to any mindless goose-stepping; for wishful thinking is capable of revolutionary awareness, and can enter the chariot of history without necessarily abandoning in the process the good content of dreams.[11]

What Bloch means by the good content of dreams is often the projected fantasy and action of fairy tales with a forward and liberating look: human beings in an upright posture who strive for an autonomous existence and non-alienating setting which allows for democratic cooperation and humane consideration. Real history which involves independent human self-determination cannot begin as long as there is exploitation and enslavement of humans by other humans. The active struggle against unjust and barbaric conditions in the world leads to home, or utopia, a place nobody has known but which represents humankind coming into its own:

> The true genesis is not at the beginning, but at the end, and it starts to begin only when society and existence become radical: that is, comprehend their own roots. But the root of history is the working, creating man, who rebuilds and transforms the given circumstances of the world. Once man has comprehended himself and has established his own domain in real democracy, without depersonalization and alienation, something arises in the world which all men have glimpsed in childhood: a place and a state in which no one has yet been. And the name of this something is home or homeland.[12]

Philosophically speaking, then, *the real return home or recurrence of the uncanny is a move forward to what has been repressed and never fulfilled.* The pattern in most fairy tales involves the reconstitution of home on a new plane, and this accounts for the power of its appeal to both children and adults.

In Bloch's two major essays on fairy tales, *Das Märchen geht selber in Zeit* (The Fairy Tale Moves on its Own in Time) and *Bessere Luftschlösser in Jahrmarkt und Zirkus, in Märchen und Kolportage* (Better Castles in the Air in Fair and Circus, in the Fairy Tale and Sensationalist Literature),[13] Bloch is concerned with the manner in which the hero and the aesthetic constructs of the tale illuminate the way to overcome oppression. He focuses on the way the underdog, the small person, uses his or her wits not only to survive but to live a better life. Bloch insists that there is good reason for the timelessness of traditional fairy tales. 'Not only does the fairy tale remain as fresh as longing and love, but the demonically evil, which is abundant in the fairy tale, is still seen at work here in the present, and the happiness of "once upon a time," which is even more abundant, still affects our visions of the future.'[14]

It is not only the timeless aspect of traditional fairy tales which interests Bloch, but also the way they are modernized and appeal to all classes and age groups in society. Instead of demeaning popular culture and common appeal, Bloch endeavors to explore the adventure novels, modern romances, comics, circuses, country fairs, and the like. He refuses to make simplistic qualitative judgements of high and low art forms, rather he seeks to grasp the driving utopian impulse in the production and reception of art-works for mass audiences. Time and again he focuses on fairy tales as indications of paths to be taken in reality.

What is significant about such kinds of 'modern fairy tales' is that it is reason itself which leads to the wish projections of the old fairy tale and serves them. Again what proves itself is a harmony with courage and cunning, as that earliest kind of enlightenment which already characterizes *Hansel and Gretel*: consider yourself as born free and entitled to be totally happy, dare to make use of your power of reasoning, look upon the outcome of things as friendly. These are the genuine maxims of fairy tales, and fortunately for us they not only appear in the past but in the now.[15]

If Bloch and Freud set the general parameters for helping us understand how our longing for home, which is discomforting *and* comforting, draws us to folk and fairy tales, we must now become more specific and focus on the interest of children in fairy tales. In fact, we already know from sociological and psychological studies which originated after World War I[16] that children between the ages of five and ten are the first prime audience of fairy tales of all kinds. Given this common knowledge and research, which have been variously interpreted, we must ask whether the interest of children in fairy tales can be related to their *desire* for an ideal home, i.e., a world or state in which they come into their own.

In *Child and Tale: The Origins of Interest*, André Favat explores the usefulness of Jean Piaget's theories to explain why children are drawn to fairy tales.[17] By concentrating on the age group between 6 and 8, Favat demonstrates that the content and form of the 'classical' fairy tales (Perrault, Grimm, and Andersen) correspond to the way a child of this age conceives the world according to Piaget. During this particular phase of development, children believe in the magical relationship between thought and things, regard inanimate objects as animate, respect authority in the form of retributive justice and expiatory punishment, see causality as paratactic, do not distinguish the self from the external world, and believe that objects can be moved in continual response to their desires. Favat maintains that such a child's conception of the world is generally affirmed by the fairy tale, even though the tale may not have been created precisely to meet the needs of children.

Between the ages of 6 and 8 the child perceives his/her world tested more and more by outside forces, and it is for this reason that Favat makes careful differentiations when he talks about the response of children and their need for stability. Following Piaget, Favat also stresses that the relative development of children and their conception of the world have to be qualified by specific cultural socialization undergone by the children. Thus as the animism and egocentrism of children give way to socialization and greater conscious interaction in society, there is a general rejection of the fairy tale by age ten. About this time children have become more acclimated to the real world and view the fairy tale as an impediment to further adjustment. Only later, after adolescence is completed, do young people and adults return to fairy tales and fantasy literature, quite often to recapture the child in themselves.

To recapture the child is not a frivolous project but a serious undertaking for self-gratification and self-realization. Such earnestness can be seen in the initial attraction of children to fairy tales. As Favat maintains:

> Children's turning to the tale is no casual recreation or pleasant diversion; instead, it is an insistent search for an ordered world more satisfying than the real one, a sober striving to deal with the crisis of experience they are undergoing. In such a view, it is even possible, regardless of one's attitude toward bibliotherapy, to see the child's turning to the tale as a salutary utilization of an implicit device of the culture. It would appear, moreover, that after reading a fairy tale, the reader invests the real world with the constructs of the tale.[18]

If we synthesize Freud, Bloch, and Favat's notions of Piaget in regard to home as liberation, we can now grasp the liberating potential of the fantastic in fairy tales. On a psychological level, through the use of unfamiliar (*unheimlich*) symbols the fairy tale liberates readers of different age groups to return to repressed ego-disturbances, that is, to return to familiar (*heimlich*) primal moments in their lives, but the fairy tale cannot be liberating ultimately unless it projects on a conscious, literary, and philosophical level the objectification of home as real democracy under non-alienating conditions. This does not mean that the liberating fairy tale must have a moral, doctrinaire resolution, but that, to be liberating, it must reflect *a process of struggle* against all types of suppression and authoritarianism and posit various possibilities for the concrete realization of utopia. Otherwise, the words liberating and emancipatory have no aesthetical categorical substance.

Piaget notes that, from age 6 to age 12, children's sense of morality and justice change from a belief in retributive justice through expiatory punishment to distributive justice with equality. Corresponding to the early phase of development, the traditional folk tales and classical fairy tales tend to reinforce a regressive notion of home by centering on arbitrary authority (generally in the form of monarchs or monarchs in the making) as the last instance of justice. Raw power is used to right wrongs or uphold a mixture of feudal and bourgeois patriarchal norms constituting a 'happy end,' which is not to be confused with utopia. It is exactly this configuration in the classical tales – and there are many exceptions[19] – which caused numerous authors in the course of the last two centuries to experiment with the fairy-tale discourse. And, as our own conception of what constitutes the substance of liberation in western culture has changed, the revised literary fairy tales for children have steadily evinced a more radical and sophisticated tendency. The question we must now ask is how some contemporary writers, whom I shall designate as 'counter-cultural,' endeavor to make their tales more liberating and conducive to the progressive pursuit of home in contrast to the regressive pursuits in the tales of yesteryear.

II

In examining the unique narrative modes developed by 'counter-cultural' fairy-tale writers, it will become apparent that their experimentation is connected to their endeavors to transform the civilizing process. They interject themselves into the fairy-tale discourse on civilization first by distancing themselves from conventional regressive forms of writing, thinking, and illustration: the familiar is made unfamiliar only to regain a sense of what authenticity might be on a psycho- and sociogenetic level. Or, to put it another way, by seeking what 'unadulterated' home might mean under non-alienating conditions, the fairy-tale writers transfigure classical narratives and distinguish their final constellations of home by provoking the reader to reflect critically upon the conditions and limits of socialization. The counter-cultural intention is made manifest through alienating techniques which no longer rely on seductive, charming illusions of a happy end as legitimation of the present civilizing process, but make use of jarring symbols that demand an end to superimposed illusions. The aim is to make readers perceive the actual limits and possibilities of their deep personal wishes in a social context.

The narrative voice probes and tries to uncover the disturbing repressed socio-psychological conflicts so that the young reader might imagine more clearly what forces operate in reality to curtail freedom of action. Uncomfortable questions about arbitrary authoritarianism, sexual domination, and social oppression are raised to show situations which call for change and can be changed. In contrast to the classical fairy tales of the civilizing process, the fantastic projections of the liberating tales are not used for rationalistic purposes to instrumentalize the imagination of readers, but rather to subvert the controls of rationalization so that readers can reflect more freely upon ego disturbances and perhaps draw parallels to the social situation of others which will enable them to conceive of work and play in a collective sense.

Needless to say, there are a multitude of ways one can write a liberating tale. Here I want to concentrate on just two major types of experimentation which have direct bearing on cultural patterns in the West. One type can be called the transfiguration of the classical fairy tale. Generally the author assumes that the young reader is already familiar with the classical tale and depicts the familiar in an estranging fashion. Consequently, the reader is compelled to consider the negative aspects of anachronistic forms and perhaps transcend them. The tendency is to break, shift, debunk, or rearrange the traditional motifs to liberate the reader from the contrived and programmed mode of literary reception. Transfiguration does not obliterate the recognizable features or values of the classical fairy tale but cancels their negativity by showing how a different aesthetic and social setting relativizes all values. To this extent the act of creative transfiguration by the author and the final artistic product as transfiguration are geared to make readers aware that civilization and life itself are processes which can be shaped to fulfill basic needs of the readers. Though the liberating and classical fairy tales may contain some of the same features and values, the emphasis placed on transfiguration as process, both as narrative form and substance, makes for a qualitative difference.

The second type of experimentation similar to transfiguration can be called the fusion of traditional configurations with contemporary references within settings and plotlines unfamiliar to readers yet designed to arouse their curiosity and interest. Fantastic projections are used here to demonstrate the changeability of contemporary social relations, and the fusion brings together all possible means for illuminating a concrete utopia. In effect, both the narrative techniques of fusion and transfiguration are aimed at disturbing and jarring readers so that they lose their complacent attitude toward the status quo of society and envision ways to realize their individuality within collective and democratic contexts. However, what distinguishes the contemporary writers of liberating tales is their strident, anti-sexist,. and anti-authoritarian perspective.

For instance Harriet Herman's *The Forest Princess* varies the traditional *Rapunzel* fairy tale to question male domination and sexual stereotypes. Her story concerns 'a princess who lived alone in a tall tower deep in the woods. An invisible spirit had brought her there when she was just a little girl. The spirit watched over her bringing her food and clothing and giving her special gifts on her birthday.'[20] One day after a storm she saves a prince who had been shipwrecked. At first she thinks that, she, too, is a prince since she looks very much like him and does not know that there àre differences in sex. They begin living together and teaching each other their respective skills. But the prince misses his home, and the princess agrees to go to the golden castle if he will teach her the secrets of that place. However, the princess is compelled to change at the golden castle – to wear fancy clothes and make-up and to restrict her activities to the company of other girls. Against the orders of the king she teaches them how to read, and, since the prince does not want to go riding with her, she practices riding by herself. On the prince's fourteenth birthday she exhibits her astonishing riding skills to the entire court. The king decides to reward her with one wish, and she replies: 'Your majesty, what I have done today could have been done by any of the boys and girls in your land. As my reward I would like the boys and girls to ride horses together, to read books together and to play together.'[21] But, the king refuses to grant this wish, saying that the boys and girls are happy the way they are – despite their protests. The princess realizes that she must leave the golden castle, and nobody knows where she is today. However, we are told by the narrator that after her departure her wish came to be fulfilled because fairy tales *must* end happily.

The irony of the ending suggests a contrast: though fairy tales must end happily, life itself must not, and thus the reader is compelled to consider the reasons for a lack of happiness or home in reality.[22] Moreover, the possibility for a comparison with the traditional *Rapunzel* is given so that the authoritarian quality of the older tale becomes visible.

Similar to Herman's work, four women of the Merseyside Women's Liberation Movement in Liverpool, England, began publishing fairy tales to counter the values which had been carried by the traditional fairy tales – acquisitive aggression in men and dutiful nurturing of this aggression by women. They argued that 'fairy tales are political. They help to form children's values and teach them to accept our society and their roles in it. Central to this society is the assumption that domination and submission are the natural basis of all our relationships.'[23] In response they rewrote such well-known classics as *The Prince and the Swineherd, Rapunzel, Little Red Riding Hood*, and *Snow White*. In *The Prince and the Swineherd* a gluttonous prince is made into the laughing stock of the people by Samia the swineherd. In *Red Riding Hood* the setting is a timbermill town in the North, and the shy little girl Nadia learns to overcome her fear of the woods to save her great-grandmother from the wolf, whom she kills. His fur is used as the lining for Red Riding Hood's cloak, and the great-grandmother tells her:

'This cloak now has special powers. Whenever you meet another child who is shy and timid, lend that child the cloak to wear as you play together in the forest, and then, like you, they will grow brave.'[24] From then on Red Riding Hood explores and goes deeper and deeper into the forest.

In both these tales the small, oppressed protagonists learn to use their powers to free themselves from parasitical creatures. Life is depicted as an ongoing struggle and process so that the 'happy' end is not an illusion, i.e. not depicted as an end in itself but the actual beginning of a development. The emancipatory element comes about when the fantasy (imagination) of the protagonists themselves is projected within the tale as a means by which they can come into their own and help others in similar situations.

Like the Merseyside Group, Tomi Ungerer has been drawn to rewriting *Little Red Riding Hood*, which he entitled 'a reruminated tale.' Though his perspective is emancipatory, it is much different from that of the Merseyside group. As in his revision of Andersen's *The Little Match Girl*, which he entitled *Alumette*, he is irreverent, sly, and anarchistic. His wolf, dressed like a classy baron, is much different from the devious wolf of the traditional tale, and his Red Riding Hood is 'the real no-nonsense one,' which means that she is not gullible or afraid to voice her opinion. We learn that her grandmother is mean and cranky and even beats her sometimes. So she stops to pick berries to delay her visit. When the wolf appears, he states candidly: 'I know of your grandmother and all I can say is that her reputation is worse than mine.'[25] He offers to take her to his castle and treat her like a princess in a fairy tale. Red Riding Hood is suspicious. She begins to ask questions about the wolf's jowls and tongue, and he insists that she stop asking foolish questions. He overcomes her objections and tells her that her parents and grandmother will be able to care for themselves. So the wolf and Red Riding Hood marry, have children, and live happily, and the nasty grandmother shrinks in size and remains mean as ever.

Ungerer's tale uses irony and clever reversals to break the sexual taboos of the traditional tale. The 'uncanny' wolf becomes identified with familiar sexual longings of childhood pleasure instincts, and the transformations in the tale are calculated liberating effects, measured against the super-ego function of the parents and grandmother. The wolf allows Red Riding Hood to grow and enter into a mature sexual relationship. What becomes 'home' in this fairy tale is less social in implications than in other liberating tales, but it does make a claim for the autonomy of the young girl and wolf, who demonstrate that 'reputations' spread through rumors of old tales no longer hold true and should not be taken at surface value today.

For the most part, the post-1945 tales of *Little Red Riding Hood* transfigure and criticize the traditional transgression perpetuated against the girl as a helpless, naive, and sweet thing and against the wolf as evil predator and troublesome male rapist. In *Little Polly Riding Hood*,[26] Catherine Storr depicted a clever and independent girl, whom a bumbling wolf would like to eat. Time and again she outwits the comical wolf, who uses the old *Red Riding Hood* tale as a manual on how one should behave. Naturally his announced expectations are never fulfilled. In a more serious vein, Max von der Grün rewrote the tale to comment on prejudice and conformity.[27] His Red Riding Hood is ostracized by the community because of her red cap, which is strongly suggestive of the anti-Semitic and anti-Communist feelings which existed in Germany at one time. There have also been tales written in defense of the wolf, such as Iring Fetscher's *Little Redhead and the Wolf* and Philippe Dumas and Boris Moissard's *Little Acqua Riding Hood*.[28] Fetscher gives a wry, mock-psychological interpretation which depicts the father killing the wolf because the beast had befriended Red Riding Hood's brother, whom the neurotic father disliked. In the story by Dumas and Moissard there is another ironic portrayal; this time it is Red Riding Hood's granddaughter who frees the grandnephew of the wolf from the zoo in the Jardin des Plantes because she wants to relive the classical story and become a star in Parisian society. However, the wolf is wise, for he has learned a lesson from the tragedies which have occurred in his family. He flees to Siberia and warns young wolves about the dangers of 'civilization' in France.

The reversal of the classical fairy tales is at the center of the other stories in Dumas and Moissard's book *Conte à l'envers*, and it is the basis of such other collections as Jay Williams' *The Practical Princess and other Liberating Tales*,[29] Jane Yolen's *Dream Weaver*,[30] and Hans-Joachim Gelberg's *Neues vom Rumpelstilzchen*.[31] The traditional stories are transfigured so that their repressive substance is subverted. The reversal of form, characters, and motifs is intended to expand the possibilities to question the fairy-tale discourse within the civilizing process.

Aside from the transfiguration of fairy tales, the second most common manner in which writers of fairy tales have endeavored to suggest options to dominant cultural patterns is through the fusion of actual references to disturbing social occurrences in contemporary society. Here I want to focus on four remarkable fairy-tale experiments in Italy, Germany, France, and England. The *international* quest for liberation and a new sense of home manifested in different fairy tales is clearly a reaction against *international* trends of domination, standardization, and exploitation.

In Italy there is a consistent protest for freedom in the creative work of Adela Turin, Francesca Cantarellis, Nella Bosnia, Margherita Soccaro, and Sylvie Selig. Seven of their books have been translated and distributed by the Writers and Readers Publishing Cooperative in London.[32] Significant here is the tale entitled *Of Cannons and Caterpillars*. The very first paragraph sets the dramatic predicament of modern society:

> No one in the palace of King Valour any longer remembered the first war. Not the ministers or the privy councillors, or the secretaries, observers, or the directors, or the reporters, the strategists or the diplomats; not even the generals, the colonels, the sergeants, the majors or the lieutenants. Not even Terence Wild, the very oldest soldier alive, stitched and re-stitched, with one glass eye, one wooden leg, and a hook in place of a hand. Because after the first war, there had been a second war, then a third, a fourth, a fifth, and then a twentieth and a twenty-first too, which was still going on. And no one in the palace of King Valour could remember anything about peaches or sparrows, or tortoise-shell cats, or bilberry marmalade, or radishes, or bed-sheets spread out to dry on green meadows. Besides, King Valour had become enthusiastic about his plans for a twenty-second war: 'Not a single tree will be left standing, not a blade of grass will survive; no, not one solitary shamrock or grasshopper,' so he predicted, 'because we have the ultimate weapon, diabolical defoliants, death-rays, paralysing gas and cannons of perfect accuracy.'[33]

Grotesque and comically exaggerated as King Valour may seem, his manner of thinking is not unlike that of some of our contemporary statesmen. His menace and madness are sadly recognized by his own wife Queen Delphina, who is sentenced to live in the modern skyscraper castle behind bullet-proof windows with her daughter Princess Philippina and 174 widows and war orphans, both boys and girls. Confronted with a synthetic, suffocating technological life, Delphina endeavors to teach her daughter about nature, including caterpillars, flowers, animals, vegetables, etc., by writing illustrated stories for her. As her storybook expands, Philippina and all the widows and orphans of the skyscraper become less sad. Then one 'evening King Valour returned in excellent humour: a new war had just been declared, and it promised to be the longest most homicidal ever. . . So he decided that the Queen, the Princess, widows, and orphans were to leave on a Saturday morning for the Castle of King Copious, which stood further away from the battlefields.'[34]

This decision turns out to be fortunate for the queen and her entourage. Along the way they stop at an abandoned castle ruined by wars, and because it is so beautifully situated in the country, they decide to renovate the buildings and cultivate the land. So they unpack the big Book, and all the dreams which had been pictured in the Book they now endeavor to realize in their surroundings. Many years pass, and we learn that King Valour and his wars are all but forgotten. However, the transformed castle flourishes in the middle of a busy, densely populated village, and everyone knows the name of Delphina, the legendary writer of the beautifully illustrated Book.

This extraordinary anti-war fairy tale is uniquely illustrated with pictures projecting a critique of authoritarianism and the possibility for collective democratic life: the entire concept of the fairy tale encourages the creative realization of peaceful coexistence. Moreover, it is a fairy tale in praise of the utopian power of fairy tales. Delphina manages to retain the principle of hope and humanism in the prison–castle of her husband by writing the illustrated Book for her compatriots. Given the opportunity to escape a sick situation, they become joyful and creative. Their sterile existence is exchanged for a life without fear and oppression. Thus finally they can come into touch with their own skills and harness technology to serve their collective needs in peace.

The dangerous potential of technology and bureaucracy to create means for enslaving humankind is portrayed with even greater insight and originality in Michael Ende's 270-page fairy-tale novel *Momo*.[35] This work was published in 1973, won the German Youth Book Prize, and has been translated into seventeen different languages. It recalls the struggles of a little Italian orphan, a wiry, ingenuous girl named Momo, somewhere between the ages of 8 and 12, who makes her home in the ruins of an ancient Roman amphitheater. Since she has the amazing gift of listening to people's problems in such a way that they are provided with the power to come to their own solutions, she is regarded as somewhat saintlike and is protected by everyone in the neighborhood. Surrounded by all sorts of children who play in the amphitheater and her two special friends, Beppo the street cleaner and Gigi the young con-artist, she lacks nothing and prospers through her wit and creativity. In general all the people in the district are poor, but they try to share and enjoy what they have with one another and struggle to improve the quality of their lives at their own pace and time. Unknown to them, however, their manner of living and playing is being threatened by the time-savers, men dressed in gray whose ash colored faces match their suits. They wear stiff round hats, smoke gray cigars, and carry blue-gray briefcases. Nobody knows who these men are, and everyone forgets them once they enter and influence their lives to conduct themselves according to such principles as 'time is money,' 'time is costly,' or 'saved time is double time.' So great is their clandestine impact that the city gradually begins to transform itself into a smooth-functioning machine. Buildings and streets are torn down to make way for modern technology and automatization. Everyone rushes around seeking ways to save time and make more money. The total architecture of the city informs the psyche of people's minds which are now geared to work for work's sake. The gray men gain control over everyone and succeed in isolating Momo. Only after she finds her way to the 'nowhere house' of Master Secundius Minitus Hora is she safe from the threat of the gray men, for it is Master Hora, a wizened and humane guardian of time, who can explain the essence of time to Momo – that it resides in the heart of each individual and can become as beautiful as the individual decides. Given this realization, Momo seeks to struggle against the gray men, and, with Master Hora's help and that of a magic turtle, she eventually undermines the nefarious plans of the gray men: time is liberated so that human beings can determine their destiny.

Ende's colorful fairy-tale novel is told in such a fashion that the events could seemingly take place in the past, present, or future. In unusual symbolical form he incorporates a critique of instrumental rationalization so that it becomes comprehensible for readers between the ages of 8 and 15. As is the case in most contemporary fairy tales with liberating potential, Ende has a female protagonist bring about or point a way to change. While Momo comes into her own as an individual, social relations appear to be reconstituted in a manner that will allow time to blossom for everyone. Nevertheless, there are problems with the ending of *Momo*, which is deceptively emancipatory. That is, Ende employs the fantastic to celebrate individualistic action or the privatization of the imagination. Such individualism is supposed to be the answer to the growing rationalization of everyday life, and it is celebrated in Ende's second best-seller, *Die unendliche Geschichte (The Endless Story*, 1979),[36] in which a fat, fearful boy named Bastian discovers that he can use his imagination to invent a never-ending story which helps him adjust to reality. Ende has Bastian steal a book, and, as the boy reads it in a secluded place, he feels summoned by the troubled realm of Phantásien, where he has numerous adventures. Aided by his devoted friend Atréju and magical animals, he prevents Phantásien from being destroyed. Upon returning to reality, he has a reconciliation with his father and feels strong and courageous enough to take on the world. In contrast to *Momo, The Endless Story* depicts a pursuit of home as a form of regression and compromise. Moreover, there are too many traditional clichés and stereotypes in Ende's endeavor to endorse the student revolt slogan 'all power to the imagination,' so that, in the final analysis, his story actually deludes readers and prevents them from seeing their potential and problems against the background of social forces manipulating and exploiting both consciousness and imagination.

Such delusion is not the case in Jean-Pierre Andrevon's remarkable fairy-tale novel *La Fée et le Géometre* (*The Fairy and the Land Surveyor*, 1981).[37] Andrevon describes an idyllic verdant country filled with fairies, dwarfs, gnomes, witches, magicians, elves, dragons, and sylphs, who live in harmony with one another without rules, money, or rationalized relations of production. Nor is nature threatened with gross exploitation. All creatures benefit from their interchange and exchange with one another, and sexual discrimination does not exist. Each individual works and plays according to his or her own need, that is, until Arthur Livingschwartz, an explorer, who works for an international conglomerate, discovers this paradise. From this point on, Andrevon portrays the gradual colonization of the verdant country. Technicians, scientists, soldiers, architects, and businessmen arrive and transform the small virgin land into a tourist resort with a tiny industrial capacity. Roads, towns, and factories are built. Nature is devastated and polluted. The gnomes, dwarfs, fairies, and elves are compelled to work for money and to regulate their time and lives according to the demands of outsiders, who now control the production of the country. There are intermarriages between humans and the fairy creatures, and some, like the fairy Sibialle and the land surveyor Loïc, try to oppose the onslaught of colonization and industialization. However, it is not until their daughter and other children from mixed marriages grow up and experience human exploitation and ecological destruction in the name of progress that a strong organized protest movement develops. There are struggles over the construction of nuclear reactors, the encroachment of nature by industry and highways – all without violence. These struggles commence as Andrevon concludes his narration:

> The country of the fairies will never be as it was before. The country of the fairies will not regress. To live does not mean to move backward but to move forward. It means to be like the shark and to advance unceasingly. And the shark is not a malicious creature. He must live like all of us. That's all.
> The best thing that can happen to the country of the fairies is not a

return to the past, nor should it seek to model itself after the human world. It can become *different*, mixing the qualities of fairies and humans alike.[38]

Whether this can happen, whether the struggle of the people in the verdant country to change their lives can succeed remains an open question at the end of this fairy tale. Yet, Andrevon manages to raise most of the significant social and political questions for today's youth in a discourse that provides an inkling of home. He does not paint rosy illusions by offering an individualistic solution to the instrumentalization of magic, fantasy, and natural needs the way Ende does in *The Endless Story*. In fact, he sees the collective opposition to possible ecological and social destruction arising out of the contradictions created by capitalist colonization itself. In this sense he views modern technology and industrialization as revolutionary, as transformative forces which can be beneficial to living creatures and nature, only if they are *not* employed for profit and exploitation. Unlike some romantic anti-capitalist writers of fairy tales like J.R.R. Tolkien and C.S. Lewis, who look back conservatively to the past for salvation, Andrevon knows that technology and industry are not evil *per se*. He assumes the viewpoint of the socialist ecologist and points toward the struggle for a qualitatively new type of 'homeland' with optimism.

Not all progressive fairy-tale writers are as optimistic as Andrevon is. For instance, Michael de Larrabeiti writes from the perspective of the urban lower class, and he draws different conclusions than Andrevon in his endeavor to subvert and satirize Tolkien's *Lord of the Rings* and Richard Adams' *Watership Down*. In his first fairy-tale novel *The Borribles* (1978)[39] he created fictional characters from his own childhood in Battersea, who are notable for their social defiance. Borribles are outcasts or runaways who value their independence more than anything else because they take a deep delight in being what they are. They avoid adults and especially policemen who represent arbitrary authority. Their ears grow long and pointed, a sign of their non-conformism, and, if they are caught by the law, their ears are clipped and their will is broken. Borribles exist everywhere in the world, but de Larrabeiti writes mainly about the Borribles who inhabit London.

In his first novel he wrote about the Borribles' great struggle with the high and mighty Rumbles, representative of middle-class snobs, and the loss of a vast treasure in the River Wendle. In the sequel, *The Borribles Go for Broke* (1981),[40] he depicted the further adventures of a small group of Borribles, who are manipulated by Spiff, the irrascible Borrible chief, to search for the lost treasure in the underground territory of the treacherous Wendles. Actually, the group of Borribles (consisting of the two tough girls Chalotte and Sidney, a Bangladeshi named Twilight, Stonks from Peckham and Vulge from Stepney) primarily wants to rescue the horse Sam, who had been of immense service to them on their Great Rumble Hunt. The police, however, have created a Special Borrible Group (SBG) under the command of the fanatic inspector Sussworth, and the Borribles are pursued with vengeance. In fact, at one point they are even captured by the SBG but then rescued by an extraordinary tramp named Ben, who is a grown-up Borrible in his own way. Though the Borribles and Ben have no difficulty in making fools of the police, it is a different story with the Wendles in the sewers of London. Spiff has instigated everything so that the Borribles must help him search for the lost treasure and eliminate the tyrannical chieftain Flinthead, who turns out to be Spiff's brother. Ultimately, Spiff and Flinthead are both killed, the Borribles escape, and Sam is rescued. However, the Borribles are not happy in the end unless they can continue bickering and arguing among themselves about their next step in opposition to the normal routine of an oppressive society.

It is difficult to do justice to the style and manner in which de Larrabeiti makes the unbelievable believable. His starting point is obviously the young *lumpenproletariat*, the down and out of the London lower classes. In this novel he begins by focusing on the interaction between Chalotte as hard-nosed courageous girl and Twilight as sensitive and sensible Bangladeshi. His immediate concern is to establish the integrity and skills of these two characters, generally representative of females and minority groups. Thereafter, he expands the scope of his attention by depicting the relations between Ben as adult dropout and the Borribles as defiant young outsiders. At first the Borribles distrust Ben, but they learn quickly that his principles are similar to theirs: he lives from day to day contented with the waste and abundance of a wasteful society, abhors the deadliness of routine, shuns profit-making, and minds his own business. All this is proclaimed in his special song:

> Let the world roll round an' round
> Wiv its hard-worked folk in fetters:
> All'oo think themselves yer betters,
> Money-mad and dooty bound.
>
> Make yer choice, there ain't so many,
> No ambition's worth a fart;
> Freedom is a work of art—
> Take yer stand with uncle Benny![41]

Together Ben and the Borribles reveal how creative and adroit one must be to gain and protect one's independence. Not only are they surrounded by powerful social forces demanding law and order just for the sake of law and order, but they must contend with each other's disrespectful and suspicious natures. De Larrabeiti's fantasy projection shows lower-class life more like it is than many so-called 'realistic' novels for young readers. He does not mince his words nor pull punches. His character portrayals and command of colloquial speech, especially Cockney, are remarkable. At times his plot lines are too contrived, and he lets his imagination carry him away. (Yes, even in fantasy literature this is possible.) Still he manages to employ the fairy-tale discourse to deal with themes pertaining to racial, sexual and political struggles of the present in such a way that young readers can comprehend the importance and urgency of protest by outsiders. There is no such thing as 'home' in this fairy-tale novel. It is the refusal of the Borribles to go home, to make a regular home, which demonstrates the false promises of the classical fairy tales that celebrate regressive notions of home in their so-called 'happy endings.'

III

Most of the tales discussed up to this point – and there are many more one could discuss[42] – provide a social and political basis for the fantastic projection so that it is instilled with a liberating potential. The configurations of the experimental fairy-tale discourse shift the perspective and meaning of socialization through reading. The active, aggressive behavior of male types in the classical fairy tales gives way to a combined activism on the part of both males and females who uncover those wishes, dreams, and needs which have been denied by social structures and institutions. The fantastic projections carried by the plots, characters, and motifs of the tales reflect the possibility for a transformation of constraining social conditions through major changes in social relations. The fairy-tale discourse in general is confronted with a demand to transform itself and become more emancipatory and innovative. The question, however, remains as to whether the experimental tales are truly liberating and can achieve their object. That is: can they have the desired effect on young readers?

Several critics have pointed to the difficulties in predicting the effect which emancipatory literature can have on children.[43] For the most part, particularly in regard to the classical fairy tales, children resist change. If they have been reared with the old tales, they do not want them altered. If their social expectations have been determined by a conservative socialization process, they find changes in fairy tales comical but often unjust and disturbing even though the tales purport to be in their interests and seek their emancipation.

Yet, it is exactly this *disturbance* which the liberating fairy tales seek on both a conscious and unconscious level. They interfere with the civilizing process in hope of creating change and a new awareness of social conditions. This provocation is why it is more important for critics to recognize the *upsetting* effect of emancipatory tales and to study their uncanny insinuations for old and young readers. The quality of emancipatory fairy tales cannot be judged by the manner in which they are accepted by readers but by the unique ways they bring undesirable social relations into question and force readers to question themselves. In this regard the liberating potential of the fantastic in experimental fairy tales will always be discomforting, even when concrete utopias are illuminated through the narrative perspective.

With some exceptions, the emancipatory tales are skillfully written and employ humor and artwork in original, stimulating ways to accomplish their paradoxical kind of discomforting comfort. The major difficulty facing the emancipatory fairy tales, it seems to me, lies in the system of distribution, circulation, and use of the tales, and all this is dependent on the educational views of teachers, librarians, parents, and those adults who work with children in community centers. The more regressive tales of Perrault, the Grimm Brothers, Andersen, and other conservative writers are used in schools, libraries, and homes without a blink of the eye, but the unusual, forward-looking, fantastic projections of the liberating fairy tales have not found general approval among the publishers and adults who circulate the tales.

This is not to say that there has been no headway made by the experimental fairy tales and by adults who experiment with fairy tales. Throughout the western world storytellers, writers, publishers, and educators have developed new methods and techniques to question and expand the classical fairy-tale discourse. In Italy, Gianni Rodari,[44] a well-known writer for children, has created a series of games intended to deconstruct classical fairy tales in the hope of stimulating children to create their own modern versions. By introducing unusual elements into the fairy tale, for instance, by making Cinderella disobedient and rebellious, or having Snow White meet giants instead of dwarfs and organizing a band of robbers, the child is compelled to shatter a certain uniform reception of fairy tales, to re-examine the elements of the classical tales, and to reconsider their function and meaning and whether it might not be better to alter them. In France, Georges Jean[45] has described various pedagogical means which he has used in schools to enable children to become more creative in their use of fairy tales. He describes certain card games in which children are called upon to change characters or situations of the classical fairy tales so that they relate more directly to their own lives. Jean considers the reinvention of fairy tales as a means for children to become aware of traditional discourse and the necessity to modernize it.

The works of Rodari, Jean, and others make it quite clear that until progressive social ideas are set into practice among adults, the liberating fairy tales will remain restricted in their use and effect among children. In other words, until there is a more progressive shift within the civilizing process itself, the liberating potential of these tales will be confined to those social groups seeking that end. One thing, however, is certain: the writers themselves have experienced some sense of liberation in projecting their fantasies through the magic of the fairy tales. Home for them is achieved through the creative production of these tales which allow them to regain a sense of their familiar longings through the uncanny. It is this sensory experience that they want to share with us symbolically, for their sense of liberation can only be confirmed when others, especially children, read and benefit from the subversive power of their art.

Notes

1   See Claire R. Farrer (ed.), *Women and Folklore* (Austin: University of Texas Press, 1975); Madonna Kolbenschlag, *Kiss Sleeping Beauty Good-bye: Breaking the Spell of Feminine Myths and Models* (New York: Doubleday, 1979); Marcia Lieberman, ' "Some day my prince will come": female acculturation through the fairy tale,' *College English*, **34** (1972), pp. 383–95; Allison Lurie, 'Fairy tale liberation,' *The New York Review of Books*, **42** (17 December 1970); Heather Lyons, 'Some second thoughts on sexism in fairy tales,' in *Literature and Learning*, ed. by Elizabeth Grugeon and Peter Walden (London: Ward Lock Educational, 1978), pp. 42–58; Robert Moore, 'From rags to witches: stereotypes, distortions and anti-humanism in fairy tales,' *Interracial Books for Children*, **6** (1975), pp. 1–3; Jane Yolen, 'America's Cinderella,' *Children's Literature in Education*, **8** (1977), pp. 21–9; Heide Göttner-Abendroth, *Die Göttin und ihr Heros* (Munich: Frauenoffensive, 1981).

2   *The Renaissance of Wonder in Children's Literature* (Edinburgh: Canongate, 1977), p. 154.

3   *Le Pouvoir des Contes* (Paris: Casterman, 1981), pp. 153–4.

4   *Ibid.*, pp. 206–9.

5   Reprinted in *New Literary History*, **7** (spring, 1976), pp. 619–45. See also Helene Cixous, 'Fiction and its phantoms: a reading of Freud's *Das Unheimliche*,' in this same issue, pp. 525–48.

6   *Ibid.*, p. 634.

7   *Ibid.*, p. 640.

8   See *The Uses of Enchantment: The Meaning and Importance of Fairy Tales* (New York: Knopf, 1976).

9 See my critique of Bettelheim's book, 'On the use and abuse of folk and fairy tales with children: Bruno Bettelheim's moralistic magic wand,' in *Breaking the Magic Spell: Radical Theories of Folk and Fairy Tales* (London: Heinemann, 1979), pp. 160–82.

10 Freud, 'The uncanny,' *New Literary History*, p. 630.

11 'Karl Marx and humanity: the material of hope,' in *On Karl Marx* (New York: Seabury, 1971), pp. 30–1.

12 *Ibid.*, pp. 44–5.

13 For a detailed discussion of Bloch's essays, see my chapter 'The utopian function of fairy tales and fantasy: Ernst Bloch the Marxist and J.R.R. Tolkien the Catholic,' in *Breaking the Magic Spell*, pp. 129–59.

14 *Ibid.*, p. 133.

15 *Ibid.*, p. 135.

16 See Charlotte Bühler, *Das Märchen und die Phantasie des Kindes* (Berlin: Springer, 1977), based on original 1918 edition; Alois Jalkotzy, *Märchen und Gegenwart* (Vienna: Jungbrunnen und Verlagsbuchhandlung, 1930); Alois Kunzfeld, *Vom Märchenerzähler und Marchenillustrieren* (Vienna: Deutscher Verlag fur Jugend und Volk, 1926); Wilhelm Ledermann, *Das Märchen in Schule und Haus* (Langensalza: Schulbuchhandlung von F.G.L. Gressler, 1921); Erwin Müller, *Psychologie des deutschen Volksmärchens* (Munich: Kösel and Pustet, 1928); Reinhard Nolte, *Analyse der freien Märchen produktion* (Langensalza: Beyer, 1931).

17 Urbana: National Council of Teachers of English, 1977.

18 *Ibid.*, p. 54.

19 There is a tendency to think that the patterns of folk tales and classical fairy tales do not vary much. However, this widespread belief, based on Vladimir Propp's *Morphology of the Folk Tale*, 2nd rev. edn. (Austin: University of Texas Press, 1968) fails to consider the effects of cultural differences on the contents and configurations of the tales. For a more differentiated viewpoint, see August Nitzschke, *Soziale Ordnungen im Spiegel der Märchen*, 2 vols. (Stuttgart: Frommann-Holzborg, 1976–7).

20 Berkeley: Rainbow Press, 1975, pp. 1–2.

21 *Ibid.*, p. 38.

22 Herman wrote a sequel to this story, *Return of the Forest Princess* (Berkeley: Rainbow Press, 1975), which is, however, not as stimulating and open-ended as her first tale.

23 *Red Riding Hood* (Liverpool: Fairy Story Collective, 1972), p. 6.

24 *Ibid.*, p. 5.

25 *A Storybook* (New York: Watts, 1974), p. 88.

26 *Clever Polly and the Stupid Wolf* (Harmondsworth: Puffin Books, 1967), pp. 17–23.

27 'Rotkäppchen,' in *Bilderbogengeschichten. Märchen, Sagen, Abenteuer*, ed. by Jochen Jung (Munich: dtv, 1976), pp. 95–100.

28 See Iring Fetscher, *Wer hat Dornröschen wachgeküßt?* (Frankfurt am Main: Fischer, 1974), pp. 28–32, and Philippe Dumas and Boris Moissard, *Contes à l'envers* (Paris: l'école des loisirs, 1977), pp. 15–26.

29 London: Chatto & Windus, 1979.

30 Cleveland: Collins, 1979.

31 Weinheim: Beltz & Gelberg, 1976.

32 See Adela Turin and Margherita Saccaro, *The Breadtime Story*; Adela Turin, Francesca Cantarelli, and Nella Bosnia, *The Five Wives of Silverbeard*; Adela Turin and Sylvie Selig, *Of Cannons and Caterpillars*; Adela Turin and Nella Bosnia, *Arthur and Clementine, A Fortunate Catastrophe, The Real Story of the Bonobos Who Wore Spectacles*, and *Sugarpink Rose*. All were published by the Writers and

Readers Publishing Cooperative between 1975 and 1977. There have also been translations in German and French.

33 *Of Cannons and Caterpillars*, p. 1.
34 *Ibid.*, p. 17.
35 Stuttgart: Thienemann, 1973.
36 Stuttgart: Thienemann, 1979.
37 Paris: Casterman, 1981.
38 *Ibid.*, p. 264.
39 London: Bodley Head, 1978.
40 London: Bodley Head, 1981.
41 *Ibid.*, p. 80.
42 For example, see Christine Nöstlinger, *Wir pfeifen auf den Gurkenkönig* (*We Don't Give a Hoot for the Pickle King*, Weinheim: Beltz & Gelberg, 1972); Ursula LeGuin, *The Wizard of Earthsea* (1968) and *Orsinian Tales* (1976); John Gardner, *Dragon, Dragon and Other Tales* (1975), *Gudgekin the Thistle Girl and Other Tales* (1976), and *The King of the Hummingbirds and Other Tales* (1977); Robin McKinley, *Beauty* (1980).
43 Cf. Nicholas Tucker, 'How children respond to fiction,' in *Writers, Critics, and Children* (New York: Agathon, 1976), pp. 177-8, and Maximilian Nutz, 'Die Macht des Faktischen und die Utopie. Zur Rezeption emanzipatorischen Märchen,' *Diskussion Deutsch*, **48** (1979), pp. 397-410.
44 See *Grammaire de l'imagination* (Paris: Francais Réunis, 1978).
45 *Le Pouvoir des Contes*, pp. 203-32.

Bibliography

Aley, Peter. *Jugendliteratur im Dritten Reich.* Gütersloh: Bertelsmann, 1967.

Alderson, Brian. 'Tracts, rewards and fairies: the Victorian contribution to children's literature.' In *Essays in the History of Publishing.* Ed. by Asa Briggs. London: Longman, 1977, pp. 248–82.

Alker, Ernst. *Profile und Gestalten der deutschen Literatur nach 1914.* Ed. by Eugen Thurnher. Stuttgart: Kröner, 1979.

Apel, Friedmar. *Die Zaubergärten der Phantasie. Zur Theorie und Geschichte des Kunstmärchens.* Heidelberg: Winter, 1978.

Ariès, Philippe. *Centuries of Childhood. A Social History of Family Life.* New York: Knopf, 1962.

———. 'At the point of origin.' *Yale French Studies,* **43** (1969), pp. 15–23.

Avery, Gillian. *Childhood's Pattern. A Study of Heroes and Heroines of Children's Fiction 1770–1950.* London: Hodder and Stoughton, 1975.

Barchilon, Jacques and Henry Petit. *The Authentic Mother Goose Fairy Tales and Nursery Rhymes.* Denver: Swallow, 1960.

Barchilon, Jacques. *Le Conte merveilleux francais de 1690 à 1790.* Paris: Champion, 1975.

Barchilon, Jacques and Peter Flinders. *Charles Perrault.* Boston: Twayne, 1981.

Barthes, Roland. *Writing Degree Zero.* Trans. by Annette Lavers and Colin Smith. New York: Hill and Wang, 1968.

———. *Elements of Semiology.* Trans. by Annette Lavers and Colin Smith. New York: Hill and Wang, 1968.

Bastian, Ulrike. *Die Kinder und Hausmärchen der Brüder Grimm in der literaturpädagogischen Diskussion des 19. und 20. Jahrhunderts.* Giessen: Haag & Herchen, 1981.

Baum, Frank Joslyn and Russel P. MacFall. *To Please a Child. A Biography of L. Frank Baum.* Chicago: Reilly & Lee, 1961.

Beckwith, Osmond. 'The oddness of Oz.' *Children's Literature,* **5** (1976), pp. 74–91.

Benjamin, Walter. *Illuminations.* Trans. by Harry Zohn. New York: Harcourt, Brace & World, 1968.

———. *Gesammelte Schriften.* Ed. by Rolf Tiedemann and Hermann Schweppenhäuser. 6 vols. Frankfurt am Main: Suhrkamp, 1977.

Berendsohn, Walter A. *Grundformen volkstümlicher Erzählkunst in den Kinder- und Hausmärchen der Brüder Grimm.* 2nd rev. edn. Wiesbaden: Sändig, 1968.

——. *Phantasie und Wirklichkeit in den Märchen und Geschichten Hans Christian Andersen.* Wiesbaden: Sändig, 1973.

Bettelheim, Bruno. *The Uses of Enchantment. The Meaning and Importance of Fairy Tales.* New York: Knopf, 1976.

Belmont, Nicole. *Mythes et croyances dans l'ancienne France.* Paris: Flammarion, 1973.

Bewley, Marius. 'The land of Oz: America's great good place.' In *Masks and Mirrors.* New York: Atheneum, 1970, pp. 255–67.

Bisseret, Noëlle. *Education, Class Language and Ideology.* London: Routledge & Kegan Paul, 1979.

Bloch, Ernst. *Das Prinzip Hoffnung.* Frankfurt am Main: Suhrkamp, 1959.

——. 'Das Märchen geht selber in der Zeit.' In *Die Kunst, Schiller zu sprechen und andere literarische Aufsätze.* Frankfurt am Main: Suhrkamp, 1969, pp. 10–14.

——. *Erbschaft dieser Zeit.* Frankfurt am Main: Suhrkamp, 1973.

——. *Ästhetik des Vor-Scheins.* Ed. by Gert Ueding. 2 vols. Frankfurt am Main: Suhrkamp, 1974.

Blount, Margaret. *Animal Land: The Creatures of Children's Fiction.* New York: Avon, 1974.

Blum, Jeffrey M. *Pseudoscience and Mental Ability.* New York: Monthly Review Press, 1978.

Book, Fredrik. *Hans Christian Andersen. A Biography.* Trans. by George C. Schoolfield. Norman: University of Oklahoma Press, 1962.

Brackert, Helmut (ed.). *Und wenn sie nicht gestorben sind . . . Perspektiven auf das Märchen.* Frankfurt am Main: Suhrkamp, 1980.

Bredsdorff, Elias. *Hans Christian Andersen.* London: Phaidon, 1975.

Brémond, Claude. 'Les bons récompensés et les méchants punis. Morphologie du conte merveilleux français.' In *Sémiotique narrative et textuelle.* Ed. by Claude Chabrol. Paris: Larousse, 1973, pp. 96–121.

——. 'Le méccano du conte.' *Magazine littéraire*, **150** (July-August 1979), pp. 13–15.

Bridenthal, Renate and Claudia Koonz (eds.). *Becoming Visible: Women in European History.* Boston: Houghton Mifflin, 1977.

Briggs, K.M. *The Fairies in Tradition and Literature.* London: Routledge & Kegan Paul, 1967.

Bühler, Charlotte and Josefine Belz. *Das Märchen und die Phantasie des Kindes.* Berlin: Springer, 1977.

Bülow, Werner von. *Märchendeutungen durch Runen. Die Geheimsprache der deutschen Märchen.* Hellerau bei Dresden: Hakenkreuz-Verlag, 1925.

Bürger, Christa. 'Die soziale Funktion volkstümlicher Erzählformen – Sage und Märchen.' In *Projekt Deutschunterricht l.* Ed. by Heinz Ide. Stuttgart: Metzler, 1971, pp. 26–56.

Butor, Michel. 'On fairy tales.' In *European Literary Theory and Practice.* Ed.

by Vernon W. Gras. New York: Delta, 1973, pp. 351-6.

Chorover, Stephan. *From Genesis to Genocide. The Meaning of Human Nature and the Power of Behavior Control.* Cambridge: MIT Press, 1979.

Coffin, Tristram Potter. *The Female Hero in Folklore and Legend.* New York: Seabury, 1975.

Cook, Elizabeth. *The Ordinary and the Fabulous.* Cambridge: Cambridge University Press, 1969.

Cott, Jonathan (ed.). *Beyond the Looking Glass. Extraordinary Works of Fairy Tale and Fantasy.* New York: Stonehill, 1973.

Corten, Irina H. 'Evgenii Shvarts as an adapter of Hans Christian Andersen and Charles Perrault.' *The Russian Review,* **37** (1978), pp. 51-67.

Coveney, Peter. *The Image of Childhood.* London: Penguin, 1967.

Cox, Marian Roalfe. *Cinderella. Three hundred and forty-five Variants.* London: Publications of the Folklore Society, 1892.

Dahl, Svend and H.G. Topsoe-Jensen (eds.). *A Book on the Danish Writer Hans Christian Andersen: His Life and Work.* Copenhagen: Det Berlingske Bogtrykkeri, 1955.

Dal, Erik. 'Hans Christian Andersen's Tales and America.' *Scandinavian Studies,* **40** (1968), pp. 1-25.

Darton, F.J. *Children's Books in England.* Cambridge: Cambridge University Press, 1960.

Dégh, Linda. *Folktales and Society.* Bloomington: Indiana University Press, 1969.

―― (ed.). *Folklore Today.* Bloomington: Indiana University Research Center for Language and Semiotic Studies, 1976.

――. 'Grimm's household tales and its place in the household: the social relevance of a controversial classic.' *Western Folklore,* **38** (1979), pp. 83-103.

Denkler, Horst and Karl Prümm (eds.). *Die deutsche Literatur im Dritten Reich.* Stuttgart: Reclam, 1976.

Di Scanno, Teresa. *Les Contes de fées à l'époque classique (1680-1715).* Naples: Liguori, 1975.

Dixon, Bob. *Catching Them Young: Vol. 1, Sex Race and Class in Children's Fiction; Vol. 2, Political Ideas in Children's Fiction.* London: Pluto, 1977.

Doderer, Klaus (ed.). *Klassische Kinder und Jugendbücher.* Weinheim: Beltz, 1969.

Dolle, Bernd. 'Märchen und Erziehung. Versuch einer historischen Skizze zur didaktischen Verwendung Grimmscher Märchen.' In *Und wenn sie nicht gestorben sind . . . Perspektiven auf das Märchen.* Ed. by Helmut Brackert. Frankfurt am Main: Suhrkamp, 1980, pp. 165-192.

Dorson, Richard M. *Folklore and Fakelore.* Cambridge: Harvard University Press, 1976.

Drews, Jörg (ed.). *Zum Kinderbuch.* Frankfurt am Main: Insel, 1975.

Duerr, Hans Peter. *Traumzeit. Über die Grenze zwischen Wildnis und Zivilisation.* Frankfurt am Main: Syndikat, 1978.

Duffy, Maureen. *The Erotic World of Faery.* London: Hodder and Stoughton, 1972.

Dundes, Alan (ed.). *The Study of Folklore.* Englewood Cliffs: Prentice-Hall, 1965.

Durand, Gilbert. *Les Structures anthropologiques de l'Imaginaire.* Paris: Bordas, 1969.

Dworkin, Andrea. *Woman Hating.* New York: Dutton, 1974.

Escarpit, Denise. *La littérature d'enfance et de jeunesse en Europe.* Paris: Presses Universitaires de France, 1981.

Elias, Norbert. *Über den Prozess der Zivilisation.* 2 vols. Frankfurt am Main: Suhrkamp, 1977.

——. *The Civilizing Process.* Trans. by Edmund Jephcott. Vol. 1. New York: Urizen, 1978.

Elschenbroich, Donata. *Kinder werden nicht geboren.* Bensheim: päd. extra, 1980.

Emmerich, Wolfgang. *Germanistische Volkstumsideologie. Genese und Kritik der Volksforschung im Dritten Reich.* Reutlingen: Tübingen Vereinigung für Volkskunde, 1968.

Erisman, Fred. 'L. Frank Baum and the Progressive Dilemma.' *American Quarterly*, **20** (1968), pp. 616–23.

Eschbach, Walter. *Märchen der Wirklichkeit.* Leipzig: Oldenburg, 1924.

Eykmann, Christoph. 'Das Märchen im Expressionismus.' In *Denk-und Stilformen des Expressionismus.* Munich: Fink, 1974, pp. 125–43.

Farrer, Claire R. (ed.). *Women and Folklore.* Austin: University of Texas Press, 1975.

Favat, André F. *Child and Tale: The Origins of Interest.* Urbana: National Council of Teachers of English, 1977.

Fehling, Detler. *Armor und Psyche: Die Schöpfung des Apuleius und ihre Einwirkung auf das Märchen.* Wiesbaden: Steiner, 1977.

Fend, Helmut, *Sozialisation durch Literatur.* Weinheim: Beltz, 1979.

Filstrup, Jane Merrill. 'Thirst for enchanted views in Ruskin's *The King of the Golden River.' Children's Literature*, **8** (1979), pp. 68–79.

Fink, Gonthier-Louis. *Naissance et apogée du conte merveilleux en Allemagne 1740–1800.* Paris: Les Belles Lettres, 1966.

Fischer, Maria. *Es war einmal – es ist noch. Das deutsche Märchen in seinen charakterlichen und sittlichen Werten.* Stuttgart: Union Deutsche Verlagsgesellschaft, 1944.

Foucault, Michel. *Discipline and Punish: The Birth of the Prison.* New York: Pantheon, 1978.

——. *The History of Sexuality.* New York: Pantheon, 1978.

Fox, Geoff, et al., Eds. *Writers, Critics, and Children.* New York: Agathon, 1976.

Fraser, James H. *Society and Children's Literature.* Boston: David Godine, 1978.

Gardner, Martin and Russel B. Nye. *The Wizard of Oz and Who He Was.* East Lansing: Michigan State University Press, 1957.

Gay, Peter. *Weimar Culture. The Outsider as Insider*. London: Secker and Warburg, 1969.

Gerstner, Hermann. *Brüder Grimm in Selbstzeugnissen und Bilddokumenten*. Hamburg: Rowohlt, 1973.

Göttner-Abendroth, Heide. *Die Göttin und ihr Heros*. Munich: Frauenoffensive, 1980.

——. 'Matriarchale Mythologie.' In *Weiblich-Männlich*. Ed. by Brigitte Wartmann. Berlin: Ästhetik & Kommunikation, 1980, pp. 202–40.

Green, Roger Lancelyn. *Tellers of Tales*. New York: Watts, 1965.

Greene, David L. 'The concept of Oz.' *Children's Literature*, 3 (1974), pp. 173–6.

Greene, David L. and Dick Martin. *The Oz Scrapbook*. New York: Random House, 1977.

Greimas, A.J. *Sémantique structurale*. Paris: Larousse, 1964.

Grenz, G. 'Vom Märchenerzählen.' *Die Neue Gemeinschaft*, (December 1943), pp. 123–6.

Griswold, Jerome J. 'Sacrifice and mercy in Wilde's "The Happy Prince," ' *Children's Literature*, 3 (1974), pp. 103–6.

Gronbech, Bo. *Hans Christian Andersen*. Boston: Twayne, 1980.

Grugeon, Elizabeth and Peter Walden (eds.). *Literature and Learning*. London: Open University Press, 1978.

Habermas, Jürgen. *Strukturwandel der bürgerlichen Öffentlichkeit*. Neuwied: Luchterhand, 1962.

——. *Legitimation Crisis*. Trans. by Thomas McCarthy. Boston: Beacon, 1975.

Harmetz, Haljean. *The Making of the Wizard of Oz*. New York: Knopf, 1978.

Hearn, Michael Patrick (ed.). *The Annotated Wizard of Oz*. New York: Potter, 1973.

Held, Jacqueline. *L'imaginaire au pouvoir*. Paris: Les Éditions Ouvrières, 1975.

Hermand, Jost and Frank Trommler. *Die Kultur der Weimarer Republik*. Munich: Nymphenburg, 1978.

Herrmann, Ulrich. 'Literatursoziologie und Lesergeschichte als Bildungsforschung. Historische Sozialisationsforschung im Medium der Kinder- und Jugendliteratur.' *Internationales Archiv für Sozialgeschichte der deutschen Literatur*, 2 (1977), pp. 187–98.

Heuscher, Julius E. *A Psychiatric Study of Fairy Tales*. Springfield, Illinois: Thomas, 1963.

Heyden, Franz. *Volksmärchen und Volksmärchenerzähler*. Hamburg: Hanseatische Verlagsanstalt, 1922.

Hoernle, Edwin. *Grundfragen proletarischer Erziehung*. Ed. by Lutz von Werder and Reinhart Wolff. Darmstadt: März, 1969.

Hoggart, Richard. *The Uses of Literacy*. London: Chatto & Windus, 1957.

Honegger, Claudia. *Die Hexen der Neuzeit. Studien zur Sozialgeschichte eines kulturellen Deutungsmusters*. Frankfurt am Main: Suhrkamp, 1978.

Hurrelmann, Bettina (ed.). *Kinderliteratur und Rezeption*. Baltmannsweiler: Burgbücherei Schneider, 1980.

Hyde, H. Montgomery. *Oscar Wilde*. London: Methuen, 1976.

Jackson, Rosemary. *Fantasy: The Literature of Subversion*. London: Methuen, 1981.

Jalkotzy, Alois. *Märchen und Gegenwart*. Vienna: Jungbrunnen, 1930.
Jameson, Fredric. *The Political Unconscious. Narrative as a Socially Symbolic Act*. Ithaca: Cornell University Press, 1981.
Jan, Isabelle. *On Children's Literature*. New York: Schocken, 1974.
——. *Andersen et ses contes*. Paris: Aubier, 1977.
Jean, Georges. *Le Pouvoir des Contes*. Paris: Casterman, 1981.
Jolles, André. *Einfache Formen*. Tubingen: Niemeyer, 1958.
Jones, W. Glyn. *Denmark*. New York: Praeger, 1970.
Jullian, Philippe. *Oscar Wilde*. London: Constable, 1969.
Kaiser, Erich. ' "Ent-Grimm-te" Märchen.' *Westermanns Pädagogische Beiträge*, **8** (1975), pp. 448–59.
Kamenetsky, Christa. 'Folklore as a political tool in Nazi Germany.' *Journal of American Folklore*, **85** (1972), pp. 221–35.
——. 'Folktale and ideology in the Third Reich.' *Journal of American Folklore*, **90** (1977), pp. 168–78.
Karlinger, Felix (ed.). *Wege der Märchenforschung*. Darmstadt: Wissenschaftliche Buchgesellschaft, 1973.
Klotz, Volker. 'Wie Wilde seine Märchen über Andersen hinwegerzählt.' In *Der zerstückte Traum: Für Erich Arendt zum 75. Geburtstag*. Eds. Gregor Laschen and Manfred Schlösser. Berlin: Agora, 1978, pp. 219–28.
Kolbenschlag, Madonna. *Kiss Sleeping Beauty Good-Bye: Breaking the Spell of Feminine Myths and Models*. New York: Doubleday, 1979.
Kuhn, Andrea. *Tugend und Arbeit. Zur Sozialisation durch Kinder- und Jugendliteratur im 18. Jahrhundert*. Berlin: Basis, 1975.
Kuhn, Andrea and Johannes Merkel. *Sentimentalität und Geschäft. Zur Sozialisation durch Kinder-und Jugendliteratur im 19. Jahrhundert*. Berlin: Basis, 1977.
Kunzfeld, Alois. *Vom Märchenerzahlen und Märchenillustrieren*. Vienna: Deutscher Verlag für Jugend und Volk, 1926.
Laiblin, Wilhelm, Ed. *Märchenforschung und Tiefenpsychologie*. Darmstadt: Wissenschaftliche Buchgesellschaft, 1969.
Lanes, Selma G. *Down the Rabbit Hole*. New York: Atheneum, 1971.
Laruccia, Victor. 'Little Red Riding Hood's metacommentary: paradoxical injunction, semiotics and behavior.' *Modern Language Notes*, **90** (1975), pp. 517–34.
Ledermann, Wilhelm. *Das Märchen in Schule und Haus*. Langensalza: Schulbuchhandlung, 1921.
Leyen, Friedrich von der. *Das Märchen*. Leipzig: Quelle & Meyer, 1917.
Lieberman, Marcia. ' "Some Day My Prince Will Come": Female Acculturation Through the Fairy Tale.' *College English*, **34** (1972), pp. 383–95.
——. 'The feminist in fairy tales – two books from the Jung Institute, Zurich.' *Children's Literature*, **2** (1973), pp. 217–18.
Linde, Ernst. *Die Bildungsaufgabe der deutschen Dichtung*. Leipzig: Brandstetter, 1927.
Littlefield, Henry M. 'The wizard of Oz: parable on populism.' In *American Culture*. Ed. by Hennig Cohen. New York: Houghton Mifflin, 1968, pp. 370–81.

Lochhead, Marion. *The Renaissance of Wonder in Children's Literature.* Edinburgh: Canongate, 1977.

Lüthi, Max. *Die Gabe im Märchen und in der Sage.* Bern: Francke, 1943.

———. *Das europäische Volksmärchen.* 2nd rev. edn. Bern: Francke, 1960.

———. *Volksmärchen und Volkssage.* 2nd rev. edn. Bern: Francke, 1966.

———. *Märchen.* 3rd rev. edn. Stuttgart: Metzler, 1968.

———. *Once Upon a Time. On the Nature of Fairy Tales.* New York: Ungar, 1970.

———. 'Familie und Natur im Märchen.' In *Volksliteratur und Hochliteratur.* Bern: Francke, 1970, pp. 63–78.

———. *Das Volksmärchen als Dichtung.* Cologne: Diederichs, 1975.

Lurie, Alison. 'Fairy tale liberation.' *The New York Review of Books,* (17 December 1970), **42.**

———. 'Witches and fairies: Fitzgerald to Updike.' *The New York Review of Books,* (2 December 1971), **6.**

———. 'Ford Madox Ford's fairy tales.' *Children's Literature,* **8** (1979), pp. 7–21.

Lyons, Heather. 'Some second thoughts on sexism in fairy tales.' In *Literature and Learning.* Ed. by Elizabeth Grugeon and Peter Walden. London: Open University Press, 1978, pp. 42–58.

Lypp, Maria (ed.). *Literatur für Kinder.* Göttingen: Vandenhoeck & Ruprecht, 1977.

Lystad, Mary. *From Dr Mather to Dr Seuss: 200 Years of American Books for Children.* Boston: G.K. Hall, 1980.

MacDonald, Greville. *George MacDonald and his Wife.* London: Allen & Unwin, 1924.

———. *Reminiscences of a Specialist.* London: Allen & Unwin, 1932.

Mandrou, Robert. *De la culture populaire aux XVIIe et XVIIIe siècles.* Paris: Stock, 1964.

Manlove, C.N. *Modern Fantasy.* London: Cambridge University Press, 1975.

Marin, Louis. *Puss-in-Boots*: power of signs – signs of power.' *Diacritics* (summer, 1977), pp. 54–63.

Martin, Robert K. 'Oscar Wilde and the fairy tale: "The Happy Prince" as self-dramatization.' *Studies in Short Fiction,* **16** (1979), pp. 74–7.

Mayer, Hans. 'Vergebliche Renaissance: Das "Märchen" bei Goethe und Gerhart Hauptmann.' In *Von Lessing bis Thomas Mann.* Pfullingen: Neske, 1959, pp. 357–82.

———. *Aussenseiter.* Frankfurt am Main: Suhrkamp, 1975.

Meletinsky, Eleasar. 'Die Ehe im Zaubermärchen.' *Acta Ethnographica Academiae Scientiarum Hungaricae,* **19** (1970), pp. 281–92.

Meyer, Rudolf. *Die Weisheit der deutschen Märchen.* Stuttgart: Verlag der Christengemeinschaft, 1935.

Michaelis-Jena, Ruth. *The Brothers Grimm.* London: Routledge & Kegan Paul, 1970.

Mieder, Wolfgang (ed.). *Grimms Märchen – modern.* Stuttgart: Reclam, 1979.

Mikhail, E.H. *Oscar Wilde. An Annotated Bibliography of Criticism.* Totowa, New Jersey: Rowman and Littlefield, 1978.

Mörchen, Helmut. 'Notizen zu Wolgast.' In *Literatur für Kinder.* Ed. by Maria Lypp. Göttingen: Vandenhoeck & Ruprecht, 1977, pp. 13–20.

Moore, Raylyn. *Wonderful Wizard, Marvelous Land.* Bowling Green: Bowling Green University Popular Press, 1974.

Moore, Robert. 'From rags to witches: stereotypes, distortions and anti-humanism in fairy tales.' *Interracial Books for Children*, 6 (1975), pp. 1–3.

Morazé, Charles. *The Triumph of the Middle Classes. A Political and Social History of Europe in the Nineteenth Century.* London: Weidenfeld and Nicolson, 1966.

Mosse, George. *Nazi Culture: Intellectual and Social Life in the Third Reich.* London: W.H. Allen, 1966.

Mourey, Lilyane. *Introduction aux contes de Grimm et de Perrault.* Paris: Minard, 1978.

Moynihan, Ruth B. 'Ideologies in children's literature.' *Children's Literature*, 2 (1973), pp. 166–72.

Müller, Erwin. *Psychologie des deutschen Volksmärchens.* Munich: Kösel & Pustet, 1928.

Müller, Konrad. *Die Werwolfsage.* Karlsruhe: Macklotsche, 1937.

Muir, Pery. *English Children's Books 1600–1900.* New York: Praeger, 1954.

Niedlich, Kurd. *Das Mythenbuch.* Leipzig: Dürr'sche Buchhandlung, 1927.

Nielsen, Erling. *Hans Christian Andersen in Selbstzeugnissen und Bilddokumenten.* Hamburg: Rowohlt, 1958.

Nisard, Charles. *Histoires des Livres Populaires ou de la Littérature du Colportage.* Paris: Maisonneuve & Larose, 1968.

Nitschke, August. *Soziale Ordnungen im Spiegel der Märchen.* 2 vols. Stuttgart: Frommann-Holzboog, 1976–7.

Nolte, Reinhard. *Analyse der freien Märchenproduktion.* Langensalza: Beyer, 1931.

Nye, Russel B. 'The Wizardress of Oz – And who she is.' *Children's Literature*, 2 (1973), pp. 119–22.

O'Dell, Felicity Ann. *Socialisation through Children's Literature.* Cambridge: Cambridge University Press, 1978.

O'Donnell Elliott. *Werwolves.* London: Methuen, 1912.

Opie, Iona and Peter. *The Classic Fairy Tales.* New York: Oxford University Press, 1974.

Peppard, Murray B. *Paths Through the Forest. A Biography of the Brothers Grimm.* New York: Holt, Rinehard and Winston, 1971.

Piaget, Jean. *The Language and Thought of the Child.* Cleveland: World Publishing, 1955.

——. *The Child's Conception of the World.* Totowa, New Jersey: Littlefield, Adams, 1967.

Pinchbeck, Ivy and Margaret Hewitt. *Children in English Society.* 2 vols. London: Routledge & Kegan Paul, 1969.

Poster, Mark. *Critical Theory of the Family.* London: Pluto, 1977.

Prestel, Josef. *Handbuch zur Jugendliteratur.* Freiburg i. Brsg.: Herder, 1933.

——. *Märchen als Lebensdichtung. Das Werk der Brüder Grimm.*

Propp, Vladimir. *Morphology of the Folktale.* Ed. by Louis Wagner and Alan Dundes. 2nd rev. edn. Austin: University of Texas Press, 1968.

——. 'Les transformations des contes fantastiques.' In *Théorie de la littérature.* Ed. by Tzvetan Todorov. Paris: Seuil, 1965, pp. 234–62.

Psaar, Werner and Manfred Klein, *Wer hat Angst vor der bösen Geiss? Zur*

Märchendidaktik und Märchenrezeption. Braunschweig: Westermann, 1976.

Quintus, J.A. 'The Moral Prerogative in Oscar Wilde: A Look at the Tales.' *Virginia Quarterly Review*, **53** (1977), pp. 708–17.

Reis, Richard H. *George MacDonald.* New York: Twayne, 1972.

Richardson, Selma K., Ed. *Research About Nineteenth-Century Children and Books.* Champaign: University of Illinois Graduate School of Library Science, 1980.

Richter, Dieter. 'Kinderbuch und politische Erziehung. Zum Verständnis der neuen linken Kinderliteratur.' *Ästhetik und Kommunikation*, **4** (1971), pp. 5–12; 5/6 (1972), pp. 23–32.

——. (ed.). *Das politische Kinderbuch.* Darmstadt: Luchterhand, 1973.

——. 'Schöne Kindheit.' *päd. extra*, **1** (1979), pp. 20–3.

Richter, Dieter and Johannes Merkel. *Märchen, Phantasie und soziales Lernen.* Berlin: Basis, 1974.

lichter, Dieter and Jochen Vogt (eds.). *Die heimlichen Erzieher. Kinderbücher und politisches Lernen.* Reinbek: Rowohlt, 1974.

Robert, Marthe. *Sur le papier.* Paris: Grasset, 1967.

Roche-Mazon, Jeanne. *Autour des Contes des Fées.* Paris: Didier, 1968.

Rodari, Gianni. *Grammaire de l'imagination.* Paris: Français Réunis, 1978.

Röhrich, Lutz. 'Zwölfmal rotkäppchen.' In *Gebärden – Metapher – Parodie.* Dusseldorf: Schwann, 1967, pp. 130–52.

——. *Märchen und Wirklichkeit.* Wiesbaden: Steiner, 1974.

Rölleke, Heinz, Ed. *Die älteste Märchensammlung der Brüder Grimm.* Cologny-Geneva: Fondation Martin Bodmer, 1975.

Rothe, Wolfgang, Ed. *Die deutsche Literatur in der Weimarer Republik.* Stuttgart: Reclam, 1974.

Rüttgers, Severin. *Die Dichtung in der Volksschule.* Leipzig: R. Voigtländers Verlag: Leipzig, 1914.

——. *Erweckung des Volkes durch seine Dichtung.* Leipzig: Verlag der Dürr'schen Buchhandlung, 1933.

Saintyves, P. *Les Contes de Perrault et les récits parallèles.* Paris: Nourry, 1923.

Sale, Roger. *Fairy Tales and After: From Snow White to E.B. White.* Cambridge: Harvard University Press, 1978.

Schenda, Rudolf. *Volk ohne Buch.* Frankfurt am Main: Klostermann, 1970.

——. *Die Lesestoffe der Kleinen Leute.* Munich: Beck, 1976.

Scherf, Walter. 'Family conflicts and emancipation in fairy tales.' *Children's Literature*, **3** (1974), pp. 77–93.

Schmidt, Kurt. *Das Märchen.* Berlin: Matthiessen, 1940.

Schmitz, Victor August. *H.C. Andersens Märchendichtung.* Greifswald: L. Bamberg, 1925.

Schmölders, Claudia, Ed. *Die Kunst des Gesprächs.* Munich: Deutscher Taschenbuch Verlag, 1979.

Schoof, Wilhelm. *Zur Entstehungsgeschichte der Grimmschen Märchen.* Hamburg: Hauswedell, 1959.

Schott, Georg. *Weissagung und Erfüllung im Deutschen Volksmärchen.* Munich: Wiechmann, 1925.

——. *Das Volksbuch vom Hitler.* Munich: Eher, 1933.

Schwartz, Emanuel K. 'A psychoanalytic study of the fairy tale.' *American Journal of Psychotherapy*, **10** (1956), pp. 740–62.

Soriano, Marc. *Les Contes de Perrault. Culture savante et traditions populaires*. Paris: Gallimard, 1968.

——. 'Le petit chaperon rouge.' *Nouvelle Revue Française*, **16** (1968), pp. 429–43.

——. 'From tales of warning to formulettes. The oral tradition in French children's literature.' *Yale French Studies*, **43** (1969), pp. 24–43.

——. *Le Dossier Charles Perrault*. Paris: Hachette, 1972.

——. *Guide de littérature pour la jeunesse*. Paris: Flammarion, 1975.

Spiess, Karl von. *Das deutsche Volksmärchen*. Leipzig: Teubner, 1917.

——. 'Was ist ein Volksmärchen?' *Jugendschriftenwarte*, **7** (1938), pp. 143–50.

Spiess, Karl von and Edmund Mudrak. *Deutsche Märchen – Deutsche Welt*. 2nd edn. Berlin: Stubenrauch, 1939.

Spink, Reginald. *Hans Christian Andersen and his World*. London: Thames & Hudson, 1972.

Stephenson, Jill McIntyre. *Women in Nazi Society*. New York: Barnes and Noble, 1976.

Stirling, Monica. *The Wild Swan: The Life and Times of Hans Christian Andersen*. London: Collins, 1965.

Stone, Kay. 'Things Walt Disney never told us.' In *Women and Folklore*. Ed. by Claire R. Farrer. Austin: University of Texas Press, 1975, pp. 42–50.

Storer, Mary Elizabeth. *La Mode des contes de fées*. Paris: Champion, 1928.

——. *Contes de Fées du Grand Siècle*. New York: Publications of the Institute of French Studies, Columbia University, 1934.

Summers, Montague. *The Werewolf*. Hyde Park: University Books, 1966.

Tenèze, Marie-Louise, Ed. *Approches de nos traditions orales*. Paris: Maisonneuve et Larose, 1970.

Thompson, Stith. *The Folktale*. New York: Holt, Rinehart & Winston, 1946.

Tilley, Arthur. *The Decline of the Age of Louis XIV*. Cambridge: Cambridge University Press, 1929.

Tismar, Jens. *Kunstmärchen*. Stuttgart, 1977.

——. *Das deutsche Kunstmärchen des zwanzigsten Jahrhunderts*. Stuttgart: Metzler, 1981.

Traxler, Hans. *Die Wahrheit über Hänsel und Gretel*. Frankfurt am Main: Zweitausendeins, 1978.

Trevor-Roper, H.R. *Religion, the Reformation and Social Change*. London: Macmillan, 1967.

Trigon, Jean de. *Histoire de la littérature enfantine*. Paris: Hachette, 1950.

Troll, Max. *Der Märchenunterricht*. 2nd edn. Langensalza: Beyer, 1928.

Ussel, Jos van. *Sexualunterdrückung. Geschichte der Sexualfeindschaft*. Giessen: Focus, 1977.

Velten, Harry. 'The influence of Charles Perrault's contes de ma Mère L'Oie on German Folklore.' *Germanic Review*, **5** (1930), pp. 14–18.

Verdier, Yvonne. 'Grands-mères, sie vous saviez: le Petit Chaperon Rouge dans la tradition orale.' *Cahiers de Littérature Orale*, **4** (1978), pp. 17–55.

Vidal, Gore. 'The Wizard of the "Wizard." ' *The New York Review of Books*, **24** (29 September 1977), pp. 10–15; 'On Rereading the Oz Books.' *The New York Review of Books*, **24** (13 October 1977), pp. 38–42.

Viergutz, Rudolf F. *Von der Weisheit unserer Märchen*. Berlin: Widukind-Verlag, 1942.

Weber, Eugen. 'Fairies and hard facts: the reality of folktales.' *Journal of the History of Ideas*, **XLII** (1981), pp. 93–113.

Weber-Kellermann, Ingeborg. *Die deutsche Familie*. Frankfurt am Main: Suhrkamp, 1974.

——. *Die Kindheit*. Frankfurt am Main: Insel, 1979.

Wenk, Walter. *Das Volksmärchen als Bildungsgut*. Langensalza: Beyer, 1929.

Wilde, Oscar. *The Soul of Man under Socialism*. Ed. Robert Ross. London: Humphreys, 1912.

——. *Complete Shorter Fiction*. Ed. by Isobel Murray. Oxford: Oxford University Press, 1979.

Wisser, Wilhelm. *Das Märchen im Volksmund*. Hamburg: Im Quick-born Verlag, 1927.

Woeller, Waltraut. *Der soziale Gehalt und die soziale Funktion der deutschen Volksmärchen*. Habilitations-Schrift der Humboldt-Universität zu Berlin, 1955.

Wolff, Robert Lee. *The Golden Key: A Study of the Major Fiction of George MacDonald*. New Haven: Yale University Press, 1961.

Wolgast, Heinrich. *Das Elend unserer Jugendliteratur*. 7th edn. Worms: Wunderlich, 1950.

Wollenweber, Bernd. 'Märchen und Sprichwort.' In *Projektunterricht 6*. Ed. by Heinz Ide. Stuttgart: Metzler, 1974, pp. 12–92.

Woodcock, George. *The Paradox of Oscar Wilde*. London: Boardman, 1950.

Yearsley, Macleod. *The Folklore of Fairy-tale*. London: Watts, 1924.

Yolen, Jane. 'America's Cinderella.' *Children's Literature in Education*, **8** (1977), pp. 21–9.

Ziegler, Matthes. *Die Frau im Märchen*. Leipzig: Koehler & Amelang, 1937.

Zimmer, Christian. *Cinéma et politique*. Paris: Seghers, 1974.

Zipes, Jack. 'Down with Heidi, down with Struwwelpeter, three cheers for the revolution: towards a new socialist children's literature in West Germany.' *Children's Literature*, **5** (1976), pp. 162–79.

——. *Breaking the Magic Spell: Radical Theories of Folk and Fairy Tales*. London: Heinemann, 1979.

——. *The Trials and Tribulations of Little Red Riding Hood: Versions of the Tale in Socio-Cultural Context*. London: Heinemann, 1982.

Zur Lippe, Rudolf. *Naturbeherrschung am Menschen*. 2 vols. Frankfurt am Main: Suhrkamp, 1974.

Index

About the Author

Jack Zipes is Professor of German at the University of Florida, Gainesville. Among his books are *Breaking the Magic Spell, Don't Bet on the Prince, Victorian Fairy Tales,* and most recently, *The Brothers Grimm: From Enchanted Forests to the Modern World.* He also published a new translation of the complete fairy tales of the Brothers Grimm.